To Lynn and Sheila,
Best wishes,
  Peggy Stanton

# THE
# DANIEL
# DILEMMA

PEGGY
STANTON

# THE
# DANIEL
# DILEMMA

*THE MORAL MAN IN*
*THE PUBLIC ARENA*

**WORD BOOKS**
PUBLISHER
4800 WEST WACO DRIVE
WACO, TEXAS
76703

THE DANIEL DILEMMA:
THE MORAL MAN IN THE PUBLIC ARENA

ISBN 0-8499-0087-5
Library of Congress Catalog
Card Number: 78-59428
Printed in the United States of America

Illustrations by Peggy Stanton.

*To a very special Friend, whose
guidance and kindness were extraordinar
And to Bill, who should be the
tenth chapter in this book*

# CONTENTS

Introduction ................ 9

1. Andrew Young .............. 13

2. John McCormack ............ 39

3. Don Shula ................. 65

4. Gerald Ford ............... 87

5. Arthur Taylor ............. 113

6. Harold Hughes ............. 133

7. Ray Scherer .............. 155

8. Mark Hatfield ............ 179

9. James Buckley ............ 201

# ACKNOWLEDGMENTS

I am deeply grateful to Robert Hardgrove and my editor Anne Christian for their patience and wise counseling on the manuscript. I also owe a special debt to the people who cooperated with me on the book, in effect, providing me with an oral history of the subjects. They are too many to list here. But to all of them I wish to publicly express my appreciation.

# INTRODUCTION

The first remark occasioned by a glance at the title of this book is, "I don't get it. What is *The Daniel Dilemma?*" Very simply, it is the dilemma of the principled man in the public arena, the tension between personal morality and the possession of power.

In the Old Testament, the story of Daniel is the story of man's relationship to power and the Creator of power. The Bible describes Daniel as a man of great gifts; fair of face and form, keen of intellect, possessed of wisdom and understanding. His natural endowments keep him continually in the company of kings; all of whom consult him as to the meaning of their dreams. The dreams center on one basic message. The king's authority exists only by a grant from God. If the kings abuse their power, it will be taken away from them. As a result of Daniel's ability to translate the kings' visions, he is made the ruler of Babylon. But, unlike the kings, he never forgets the source of his power. When he is forced to make a choice between King Darius and God, he chooses God, knowing the choice will land him in the lion's den.

There are many morals in the saga of Daniel, but one is particularly obvious. Daniel's faithfulness to God did not remove pressure from his life. It sometimes increased it. Daniel was always engaged in the use of power. He was frequently challenged to abuse it in order to retain it. But never did Daniel defect to mere earthly authority. Never when his power was taken away, as in the lion's den, did he cease trusting God. As a result, he always survived the circumstance.

Today, swimming in an unending stream of scandalous headlines about public figures, we find ourselves wondering if Daniel was the last man to resolve his dilemma in favor of morality. For me, the question provoked a two-year examination of the problems of the moral man in the public arena. "Did you find *One?*" was a question frequently asked of me—an acute reflection of our disillusioned spirit. The answer is I found many, and I chose these nine to represent a far larger number. I was not seeking heroes. I was not seeking saints. I was seeking the relevance of faith to extraordinary lifestyles. Lifestyles laced with daily temptations and tremendous conflicts, where mere courage is not enough. The search led to extensive, taped interviews with each subject, their closest and oldest friends, their families, their colleagues. I delved at length into each man's past, probing the roots that shaped him, analyzing motivations for actions and reactions to the consequences of those actions. Whenever possible, I interviewed coparticipants in the subject's crucial decisions.

What emerged was a book of nine stories, amazingly varied but remarkably striking in some similarities to the biblical Daniel. Like Daniel, these are men of many gifts. All of them are possessed of a superior intellect. Some are classified as brilliant. All have achieved worldly success. Most have been recognized as leaders of their fellows. All of them believe in God.

None pretend to have all the reasons for that belief. Some are frank to admit they do not even seek them. Some feel a relationship to God the Father, some to His Son. Some speak of God as "It," a force they find hard to articulate. They do not know precisely what God is. But they know what He does. They come from different backgrounds, different religions, different upbringings. They are different in personality and different in philosophy. And yet, there is a distinct commonality.

All of these men have a strong sense of self. Some are even accused of being egotistical. And yet, they all have willingly humbled themselves to accept the gift of faith; to believe what they cannot understand, to admit to a Being greater than themselves.

Religion, atheists tell us, is the opiate of the masses. Sceptics call it a crutch for the insecure, the handicapped, the ignorant; the promise of Oz for the underprivileged. It is more difficult to dismiss God when He is important to the wise, the gifted, the wealthy and the powerful.

Perhaps the most interesting characteristic of these men is their strength, a kind of invulnerability to the exigencies of fate. Several have experienced, in the last years, swift and painful change in their lives. A President of the United States, having given all of his physical and mental prowess to retaining the most sought-after office in the world, lost it. A coach with one of the most outstanding records in football history suffered his first losing season. A former Senator faced a fate he had always prayed would not be his—the death of a daughter. A president of one of the most influential corporations in America was fired.

Every man admits to frustration, to pain, to humiliation. They all deny bitterness. Ultimately, each was able to see his crushing letdown as a disguised benefit, a refining, a shaping, a honing of themselves, an occurrence that was inevitable and necessary for their betterment. They did not stoke the fires of their disappointment. They reassessed, pondered, remeasured themselves. They went on to new goals.

Like Daniel, their power does not seem to lie in their possessions or their achievements, but in their reliance on a Supreme Being. Astonishingly, these men who have spent their lives chasing facts, figures, equations, seeking solutions to humanity's most pressing earthly problems, base their whole trust in God on simple, childlike faith. They can accept the fact that they cannot understand God, that an intelligence that created a universe, shaped clouds, sculpted mountains, dug oceans, planned the human family is a mind of such infinite depth that no finite mortal intelligence, no matter how brilliant, can ever fully comprehend it. They can accept the fact that, no matter the evidence, without supernatural aid from the Almighty, man struggles hopelessly with his existence.

In the end, it is the lives of believers, not their words, that speak to the reality or the absence of God. If we cannot see him or touch him, we *can* see if he makes a difference.

In these men he did.

PEGGY STANTON

K. Stinton

# 1 | ANDREW YOUNG

Andrew Young thought he heard a car backfiring. Then he looked up at the balcony where Martin Luther King had been standing. All he could see were the bottoms of his friend's shoes protruding over the edge of the balcony. Only seconds ago, King had been leaning on the railing, joshing with his staff in the courtyard, waiting for Ralph Abernathy to finish soothing his chin with shaving lotion.

Martin must be clowning again, Andy thought. It was a good sign. It meant King was emerging from the depression that had enveloped him for days because of the violence that had erupted during the Memphis garbage demonstrations. A short while ago, when Young returned from an all-day negotiating session in the federal courthouse, King had engaged him in a pillow fight—"Just started beatin' on me with a pillow." Young knew from past experience that being playful was Martin's way of reacting to pressure. The battle of the feathers had lasted for some time before King decided to go up to his room and dress for dinner.

Reverend Bernard Lee did not think Martin was clowning. He did not think the cracking sound he heard was a car backfiring. "I knew it was a shot." Reverend Lee raced up the steps leading to King's balcony, Jesse Jackson and Andy Young at his heels. Martin Luther King was lying in a bath of blood, his eyes open and staring, the right side of his face shorn to the skeleton. Andy Young could see that the bullet went "right through his throat and hit the spinal cord—I knew that was it!"

Within minutes, the Memphis police force, who earlier in the evening had announced to King that they had been removed from his "detail," were surrounding the Lorraine Motel. Where did the shot come from, they wanted to know. Young, Jackson, and Lee stood like an archery squad, their arms stretched in the direction of a rooming house opposite the balcony.

When the ambulance crew brought a stretcher up to the balcony, King's aides gently placed their leader on it, tersely commanding the police, "Don't touch him! You've done enough!"

Ralph Abernathy rode in the ambulance with King. Bernard Lee and Andrew Young followed behind in a limousine that had been put at King's disposal by a Memphis funeral director. Solomon

Jones, the driver, was sobbing. "Stay behind the ambulance," Reverend Lee shouted. "Drive man. Stay right behind the ambulance." But Solomon's tears were faster than his reflexes and Lee could see that footage was accumulating between the limousine and the ambulance. "Hey, man, stay right behind there. Don't slow down! Hey, Solomon, if you don't stop boo-hooin', we'll be in the damn ambulance, too." Andrew Young said nothing.

When they arrived at the hospital, Bernard Lee and Ralph Abernathy went into the emergency room with Martin King. Andrew Young went to a telephone. When Coretta King picked up the phone in Atlanta, Young told her she better come to Memphis right away. Then, he made another phone call to Atlanta. "Martin's been shot," he told his wife Jean. "He's been taken to the hospital. He's still alive." The information came through the receiver in curt, short sentences, without emotion, without excitement. And yet, there was an unfamiliar tone in her husband's voice, Jean thought, ". . . a tone of despair."

"We called Coretta," Andrew continued, "and she's on her way to Memphis."

Jean immediately took the cue. The children. "I'll get right on over to Martin's house," she promised her husband.

Inside the emergency room, Bernard Lee stood against the wall, watching the doctors massaging Martin King's heart. A nurse approached him, "I'm sorry, you'll have to leave."

"Your business is on that table there," Lee replied. "We're not going to leave until you take care of it."

The doctor asked Lee to remove King's watch. Lee walked over to the table, and took off the watch. He could see the pupils of Martin's eyes were dilated. After thirty minutes, the doctors ceased their efforts. At the age of thirty-nine, Martin Luther King was dead. Martin had prepared him for this, Lee thought. The day John Kennedy was killed, he had found King sitting on his bed watching the news on television. "I'll never reach forty," he had told Lee.

Andrew Young was outside the hospital, talking to the press, trying to control the large crowd that was accumulating. The atmosphere was ripe for violence, and it was Andrew Young's job to convince the throng of black people swelling in front of him that hatred and bitterness and violence would dishonor what Martin Luther King was about.

One of the doctors broke the news to the people and the press. Then Young, Abernathy, Lee—the staff of Martin Luther King's Southern Christian Leadership Conference—went back to the Lorraine Motel and gathered in their dead leader's room. Andrew Young led a discussion about how best to keep King's dream of nonviolence alive. "We had a theory in the movement," he says.

"You expected death. The only purpose of death was to try and stop the movement. And while you could not stop death, you could make sure that the movement didn't stop as a result of anybody's death." Martin's plan for bringing the poverty-stricken to the door of the Congress was already underway. King's staff decided that the Poor People's campaign would take place, and that Ralph Abernathy would be the new President of SCLC. When Andy Young finished all the chores he had to do, he wept. For the last eight years, Martin King was "probably the best friend I had."

As the days passed, Andrew Young's thoughts were consumed with Martin's family. Coretta had taken the news very calmly, and he was never to see her break down during the entire ordeal. He felt a responsibility to talk to King's four children, just to answer any questions they might have. But the children already had the answers: "Daddy wouldn't want us to hate the man who killed him, would he?" was the way eight-year-old Dexter King summed it up.

For the next several months, Andrew Young and the SCLC staff were so involved with bringing the Poor People's campaign to Washington, so intent on keeping their fallen leader's movement alive, that they did not see SCLC too was going to the grave.

According to Bernard Lee, who was King's personal aide and constant companion, Martin Luther King had had an unwritten will for SCLC, one he did not even tell his wife about, although learning of its alleged existence now "clears up a lot of mysteries for me," she says. Since Rev. King had always expected death, even joking frequently that the bullet meant for him was likely to be stopped by one of the fellows who were forever hovering around him to get their pictures taken, he had made plans for the line of succession in SCLC leadership. He wanted Ralph Abernathy, says Lee, to serve as an interim president, in a short while stepping aside and turning the leadership over to Andrew Young.

Lacking the charisma, personal force, and the prestige of Martin Luther King, Abernathy was unable to keep rein on such strong personalities as Jesse Jackson, James Bevel, and Hosea Williams. As it became clear that SCLC was unraveling under the weight of egos and individualities, Young made a last desperate effort to bring the conflicting parties back into a cohesive force. He asked a psychiatrist and a psychologist to a "tea" session, a kind of marathon group counseling for SCLC's top level staff to discuss, according to Bernard Lee, "where we all were individually and where we should be going." And it was in that meeting that Hosea sold a "wolf ticket" to Andy Young.

"Hosea was a perpetual wolf ticket seller," says Reverend Lee. "That means always talking about what you're going to do, being super-militant, super-aggressive. Having more spunk than anybody else. . . . He would always rib Andy about being middle class, coming from Long Island, from the National Council of Churches, and that he [Hosea] was a raw kind of street fella and that nobody else had any movement savvy but Hosea."

As the meeting tried to progress, Hosea began marketing his "wolf tickets" under Andy Young's nose. "You do that one more time," District of Columbia delegate Walter Fauntroy remembers Andy saying, "and we're going to test our commitment to nonviolence."

Hosea ignored the warning and to the amazement of the gathering, unflappable Andy Young came across the table after Hosea. "My understanding of nonviolence," Young recalls with some amusement, "was never pacifism. I was very small in school and sometimes people didn't respect you unless you made 'em." Instilling a little "respect" in Hosea was a large task since Hosea was about fifty pounds heavier than Andy Young, "and there was nothing I could do to hurt him. Well, his asthma got him and he started wheezin' and carryin' on and then he quit pickin' on me and we've been very good friends ever since."

But the "rumble," as Walter Fauntroy dubbed the altercation, served to break up the tea session. "That was the beginning of the end" in Bernard Lee's mind, of the Southern Christian Leadership Conference as a powerful national force, and the inauguration of a crucial decision period for Andy Young. He was the executive vice president of SCLC, in effect the chief of staff. Martin King had been the out-front man, the spokesman, the leader; Andy the man behind the scenes, the administrator, an idea generator.

"The thing that made it possible for Martin to lead," says Andy, "was that he was so far above everybody else in terms of national prestige that nobody could afford to compete with him. But even with him, they all tried. I mean there were such strong egos. . . . I could handle things administratively with him being the person out front, but there was almost nobody else for me to work with." Young was faced now with a decision as to where to take Martin Luther King's goals for the black people.

He was at the Rubicon again, just as he had been when he graduated from college, nominally educated but unprepared, he felt, for the world. "I began to realize that I was supposed to be a man and I really didn't know what life was all about. . . . I'd had such a good time and done so little studying. . . . I read what I wanted to read and didn't care what the teacher said to read. I didn't care about my grades as long as I did well enough not to get put out."

Mrs. Young thinks part of the reason that her son was "floundering" after graduation from Washington D. C.'s Howard University was that "he was only nineteen years old." She remembers Andrew as "real precocious. . . . We had a nursery school connected with my church. When I'd go to the market in the morning, I'd take him with me and when he passed the nursery and saw the children he would want to stay." So when his brother Walter was born and Andrew resented the new little stranger who was taking over his home, Dr. and Mrs. Young decided to let him try nursery school. After all, he had been asking his parents to read him the newspapers at the age of three. He was more than ready. Within a few months, the teachers were urging him into kindergarten. And it wasn't long before the kindergarten instructor was also anxious to move him out, according to Mrs. Young. "He took over. The other children didn't have a chance." And so, at the age of four, Andrew Young was in the first grade.

Dr. Andrew Young, Sr., had high hopes for Andrew, Jr. Both his sons, Andrew and Walter, grew up in his New Orleans dental office learning to work in the lab, and Dr. Young thought they both had aptitudes for his profession. "Everybody can't be a dentist. You have to know how to use your hands. Your mind is important too, but you can have the brightest kind of mind and if you can't use your hands, you're out of place. They both had good minds and good hands." It was also a career where a black man could have a reasonable amount of financial security. "But," Dr. Young adds, "Andrew was never interested in materialism."

"Even if I'm a doctor," Andy argued with his parents, "I'm not going to have any money. I would never refuse anybody. And I would never overcharge anybody like some doctors do."

Andy Young's distaste for the comfortable life was innocently encouraged by a doctor's daughter to whom he was engaged in college. "She was a typical black bourgeoise doctor's daughter. I used to get terribly upset in those days because whenever we went out, she'd go downtown on Connecticut Avenue to buy a new evening gown for two hundred dollars. And in the forties and fifties, two hundred dollars was something! She was an only child and she had a car. Materially, she had everything that she wanted, and that let me know I didn't really want that kind of life."

Following his junior year in college, Andy returned to New Orleans to find the United Church of Christ's new minister, Nicholas Hood, temporarily in residence, waiting for the parsonage to be readied for occupancy. "When he came home and found out a minister was living in his house," says Reverend Hood, "he was incensed. He didn't have much respect for clergymen."

Despite the fact that Daisy and Andrew Young were deeply religious people, their oldest son had rebelled against his devout upbringing. He remembers being outraged at an early age during a

Sunday School session "because somebody told me that a person went to heaven in a flaming chariot."

"How did they do that?", little Andy had wanted to know.

"You're not supposed to ask how," answered the teacher.

"Well, why not?"

"You're supposed to have faith."

Andy Young strode out of the class in disgust.

"And then in college, I only went to chapel when people like Eleanor Roosevelt or Indira Gandhi came to talk. It had to be pretty special for me to go by the chapel, and yet during that time I probably prayed pretty regularly." He still found himself getting down on his knees at night, as he had always seen his parents do. "I mean it was just something you were supposed to do." One night the devotion came to an unusual end. "I was down on my knees prayin' and one of the guys came in and hit me with a fraternity paddle. And I knelt there and I finished my prayin' and I got up and I knocked the hell out of him."

Despite the fact that Andrew Young initially greeted Reverend Hood with "cold indifference," he was forced by proximity, to observe the twenty-six-year-old minister's style of working, and almost in spite of himself, he was impressed. "Nick had just finished the Yale Divinity School and he completely broke the stereotypes on religion," Andy says. "He was young. He was very politically and socially minded. He was very dedicated to community service. He talked about voter registration as part of religious life. He was interested in developing housing for the poor and food programs for the children in the neighborhood."

"My motto has always been," explains Reverend Hood, who is now a pastor and a city councilman in Detroit, Michigan, "the soul cannot be saved apart from the society in which it grows. The idea being, you really can't do much about the inner life of man unless you do something about where he lives and works and plays."

It was Reverend Hood's work with the neighborhood children that got Andy involved initially with church projects, albeit reluctantly. "I didn't want to be associated with Nick particularly, but he was living in my house and I almost had no choice."

He was still "having a ball. . . . I was enjoying my life." Nicholas Hood was just a little too serious for happy-go-lucky Andy Young. Nevertheless, his final year at Howard found Andy reading the Greek classics, Plato, Socrates, the Marcus Aurelius meditations, instead of the books he was assigned by his professors. He began to ponder "ultimate questions." His soul was warming to the idea of a personalized religion, his mind questioning the purpose of existence. Driving home to New Orleans after graduation from

Howard University, he found an answer in a manner he least expected.

"We stopped in North Carolina. That was in the days of segregation, so we couldn't stay in motels. We went to this church camp to spend the night. There was an extra bed in a room with a young missionary who happened to be white and a classmate of Nick Hood's at Yale. And this fellow—I don't even remember his name; we never talked very much—had gone on to Cornell and gotten a master's degree in agriculture and now he was on his way to Rhodesia as a missionary. It really bugged me, because here was somebody who was going to really do something with his life, doing something for somebody else. And he was white, and they were black and why shouldn't I be doing something like that? He never talked to me about it. . . . It was just simply what he was."

The next morning, Andy and several friends decided to run to the top of nearby King's Mountain. Young, who was in the peak of physical condition, having just completed track season, quickly out-distanced his pals, reaching the top of King's Mountain long before the rest of them. "When I got there, I was physically exhausted. . . . I was wringing wet and I took off all my clothes and hung 'em on a rock to dry. And . . . I don't know . . . I just sat out there, looking from the top of this mountain at all of these green fields and valleys and other mountains and it occurred to me that everything works much too well about this universe and that somebody had to do all this and that the same Person who created this whole universe also created me and just like everything out there has a purpose, I must have a purpose, too."

It was, he admits, a powerful moment, but "I didn't say anything about it. I went out and got a New Testament." From then on, "it just seemed like my life wasn't in my control any more. . . . Things just began to happen." Like Nicholas Hood asking Andy to accompany him to Texas to attend an interracial church conference, the idea being that Reverend Hood would go to Texas for religion and Andy Young would go to Texas to see a former college roommate in San Antonio and party. "We were driving through these little country towns and we were afraid of being lynched because black folk didn't go out in that part of Texas much. . . . and interracial conferences weren't very popular. . . . I mean you could get killed for that." To add to their anxiety, the church conference was deep in the woods and very difficult to locate. "We were so relieved to finally find the place that I wasn't about to drive back through those woods to go on to San Antonio and Nick says 'You're not going to leave me here all alone.' "

So Andy stayed the night, and the next day the director of the conference approached him. "Look," he said, "there are about a hundred young white people here who have never met a Negro that they could converse with on their level. They have only known the stereotypes and they have only known people from a distance. It would really be a help to us if you would just stay around for a few days."

R & R in San Antonio was fast fading from view. "They sort of put the burden of race on me," Andy Young chuckles. "And I ended up staying and getting very involved in the conference."

Nicholas Hood was at first unaware that any changes were taking place in his companion. "I did notice that he was a little more interested than I expected him to be. He would sit in my Bible study group and it appeared to me that he was taking in a little bit more than the fun-loving guy that I had with me should be taking in. He didn't raise any questions, but he seemed to be hanging onto every word that he could hear. . . . The emphasis was upon the commitment of one's life to Jesus Christ and evidently the Spirit was moving in him and I didn't know it. . . . At one time, I thought a process was taking place and then I said, 'Oh no! It's impossible.' "

On the way back to New Orleans, Andy questioned Reverend Hood intensively. What had the commitment to the Church meant to him? Why did he turn his back on medical school the very summer he was accepted? "I told Andy that when I was a college student I had planned to go in a different direction, but I had had the experience of working with young people and seeing their joy at finding new meanings in the faith. . . . I told him of the joy and satisfaction I had known."

It wasn't until a totally preoccupied Andy Young drove straight through an intersection "and almost killed us" that Reverend Hood realized how deeply Andy was contemplating a change of avenues in his own life.

Instead of going back to graduate school at Howard University as planned. Andy volunteered to take a semester off and work with a National Council of Churches young people's program. The job afforded no pay—only room and board on the Hartford Theological Seminary campus.

Since he was on Seminary grounds, he thought he might as well take a theological course or two. Then one day he phoned Daisy Young. "Mother, I have decided . . . to go into the ministry. I feel that this is what I want to do."

It was a surprise, but then Daisy Young had always thought her children should pursue the station in life that would make them happiest.

And certainly, even as a boy, Andrew frequently had seemed happier looking out for the welfare of others. He would plead with his mother to visit the old people in their parish, because they were "so lonely." Often Mrs. Young had had several unexpected small visitors for dinner, because Andrew was afraid some of the children roaming the street in their block weren't going to be fed. When Mrs. Young had objected to his playing with a boy who had been in a detention home, Andrew had counseled her, "If we don't play with him, he's going to get involved with the bad boys and go right back in there again." And at Howard University, Mrs. Young had discovered that her son's weekly allowance "never did him" because he was financing friends' meals. "My roommate is hungry. I can't go to dinner and see my roommate hungry," he would explain. He was like the grandmother he adored, who was always feeding alcoholics and beggars in the Young's kitchen, much to the terror of her daughter.

But if Daisy Young could readily accept her son's decision to become a minister, Dr. Young swallowed the news with admitted "disappointment." And disappointing a father one respected as much as Andrew, Jr. respected Andrew, Sr. was not easy. "Daddy was always very rational and the most even-tempered person," says Andy Young. Dr. Young continually counseled his sons, "Don't get mad. Get smart." When Andy was only three, his father had begun teaching him the futility of anger. "He would box with me. . . . tease me all the time, slap me in my face—gently—but hard enough so I knew I was being hit, and the harder I'd rush in to try and get to him, the more he'd slap me around and he'd say, 'If you rush in on somebody all emotional like that, all you're going to do is get beat up. You have to wait and take your time and pick your punches.' "

It was all right to cry, Dr. Young had said, but not out of weakness. Cry for joy. Cry when you're sad. Never cry from pain. "I cry all the time," Andy Young admits today, "but I don't ever cry when I'm hurtin'."

During the first months at Hartford Seminary, Young was housed, for lack of space, in the girls' dormitory. It was in this unlikely setting that he began contemplating a life of celibacy. Being surrounded by women is, Young chuckles, actually a great place to consider giving them up. (One suspects he saw too many rollered heads and faded bathrobes scampering down hallways.)

"I guess I had decided from all the girls that I knew, there weren't any that were willing to put up with what I was planning my life to be. I mean going to Angola as a missionary was not something you talked about with the average young black woman."

During the summer, the United Church of Christ sent Young to help pastor a small parish in Marion, Alabama—population, 3,000. There were only fifteen or twenty members in the Church and the housing shortage was so great that Andy was shipped from family to family to live for a week at a time. The week he spent with Mr. and Mrs. Norman Childs was to change his life, and his mind about celibacy.

Andy Young was immediately impressed with the Childs' family. Mr. Childs was a man of many talents. Once a baker and candy merchant, he abandoned that business to open an overhaul shop. He and his partner boasted the ability to fix anything from a "baby buggy to a battleship. . . . If you can get it to the store, we can repair it," was the shop's motto. Mrs. Childs, a schoolteacher, earned extra income for the family by taking in sewing.

There were five offspring in the Childs' family, and the new minister found himself growing interested in the youngest daughter, Jean, before he ever laid eyes on her. "I got to nosing around," examining the books on her shelves, noticing the marked passages in her Bible—"She had underlined some of my favorite scriptures. And then there was a senior life-saving certificate on the wall. I was on the swimming team in college and there aren't that many women who are good swimmers." It was an irresistible combination: a spiritual mermaid. "I decided this must be the reason that the Lord sent me to Marion, Alabama."

When Jean Childs arrived home from Manchester College in Indiana, he was not disappointed. She was a beautiful girl with thick waves of glossy black hair, delicate features and expressive dark eyes. Underneath her low-key, unassuming manner was a serious, highly-tuned mind of great depth.

Jean, however, who had been chosen May Queen by her white classmates at Manchester, was not immediately bowled over by the young man who seemed to know all about her. "I didn't think he was too good-looking. His hair was too short and his nose and his ears were too big." She later suggested that if he grew more hair there would be less ears—a suggestion he took to great effect. "I'm the best thing that ever happened to Andrew Young," quips Jean.

What she did admire was the fact that Andy was "so understanding" and "so reliable. If he told you he'd be there at three, he'd be there at three." She was also amazed at his talk of celibacy. "How many young men do you hear say something like that?"

By the end of the summer, Andy and Jean were deeply in love. A steady stream of correspondence flowed from Hartford Seminary in Connecticut to Manchester College in Indiana. ("Andrew writes beautiful letters.") When Jean expressed a desire to transfer to Howard University, Andy told her such an event would take place over his dead body: "Too many wolves there."

Jean and Andy dreamed of beginning their married life as missionaries in Angola, but instead found themselves pastoring two churches in Georgia.

"When Andy graduated from Seminary," comments Reverend Hood, "he wasn't looking for a great mainline church. . . . We got him a job in Thomasville, Georgia, with a little church that had been closed up for a number of years. There weren't more than five or six members, but he was content to go there, because he just wanted to work." Since business was very lean in Thomasville, Young was also able to pastor a country church with seventy-five members in nearby Beachton, Georgia.

It was a happy beginning for Jean Young. She liked the "sense of community" in Thomasville. "Andrew was home constantly. Since he was pastor of the church, he was in and out of the house during the day." He had time to spend with their baby daughter, Andrea, and there was time to spend with their many friends. "We were all part of a big family."

It was while the Youngs were living in Thomasville that Jean was able to renew an acquaintance with a former fellow citizen of Marion, Alabama—Coretta Scott King. Both Andy and Coretta's husband, Martin Luther King, were speaking on a program at a little college in Taladega, Alabama. Young had heard about King's bus boycott in Montgomery, Alabama, but he had never met King before. Since Andy and Jean were driving on to Marion to see Jean's folks, King invited them to come on by the house and see Coretta.

"I felt like he was kind of shy," Young says of that first meeting with King, "very sort of introverted. I'd heard him speak. . . . and he was a powerhouse in the pulpit, but in the living room he was really very quiet. . . . I mean extremely reserved. And I remember being disappointed because I was trying to find out about him and he made me do all the talking." Coretta King, meanwhile, found Andy Young "very warm and friendly. He felt like someone I had always known."

The visit lasted about a half an hour. The Youngs and the Kings said goodbye to one another with no indication that their futures would some day become intimately intertwined. According to Young, none of them envisioned "this movement could spread and become anything regional, much less national."

The idyllic existence in Thomasville, Georgia, was to be short lived. While conducting a Bible study conference in Florida, Andrew Young caught the eye of officials from the National Council of Churches who offered him a job in New York City working with youth.

Jean told Andy she would support him in whatever he wanted

to do, but she urged him to think the offer over very carefully. She wanted him "to be sure this is what he really wanted, because I was very happy in Thomasville and so was he." Andy took himself for three days to a log cabin in the woods to ponder his decision alone. When he emerged, he told Jean he felt he ought to make an effort to help the troubled "beatnik" generation.

Life in Queens, New York, was a thousand light years from residence in Thomasville, Georgia. The sense of community was gone. "You built up a few friends," Jean points out, "but you were just another struggling young couple on the street." And Andy deplored the hour-and-a-half subway rides back and forth to work.

In New York, Jean Young glimpsed a side of Andrew Young she had never seen before—an Andrew who liked to dance, an Andrew with a sense of humor, an Andrew that Howard University students remembered. It was a side of himself he had repressed in the years that Jean had known him. And she was not sure she liked what she saw. The first time she saw him "jiving," she was "embarrassed."

Nevertheless, there were definite "learning experiences," one of which was the acquisition of more sophisticated tastes. "Neither of us ever drank," Jean recalls, before they came to New York, but in Queens friends introduced their palates to fine French wines. Jean went back to school for her master's degree. Andrew was working in the National Council of Churches' department of youth. "We were leading a nice, relaxed kind of life."

One evening they were sitting on the living room floor, sipping some "fine French wine" in front of a roaring fire, watching television. The evening news was showing students from Fisk, Tennessee State, and other surrounding colleges holding sit-ins in Nashville, Tennessee. "What are we doing here?" Andy and Jean Young asked each other. "We need to be back in the South. We need to be involved with what's going on there."

Andrew Young's mother begged him not to leave New York. "Andrew, please don't go," she pleaded. "You are working for God now. You are working for the Council of Churches. Stay up there."

"I don't feel comfortable," her son replied. "I feel guilty that I'm not there helping to get rid of a situation that's wrong."

"You have your children and you're buying a home. You're doing your part."

He was going to demonstrate, Andy told his mother, against the kinds of conditions that he had resented all his life. "They were wrong, mother. You said they were wrong."

"I did say they were wrong," she had to admit.

Daisy Young could remember all too clearly the pain of explaining segregation laws to her son when he was little more than a toddler. "Very early they asked questions. When we got on the streetcar, there were those little screens, little pieces of board that separated white customers from colored patrons. Andrew . . . would say 'give me the money, mother and let me pay the fare,' and then he'd pay the fare and run and grab a seat. Inevitably, he would go to the front where he saw a vacant seat, because sometimes there were only three or four seats in the back. I'd have to go up and get him back and he'd say, 'Why can't we sit here, Mother? There're seats here. There are no seats back there.' I'd tell him that we had to abide by the laws of the state. They were unjust laws, but until they were changed, we would have to abide by them."

"Well, aren't we as good as they are?" Andy wanted to know.

"In some cases you're better. But this is just one of those unfair situations in this state we're living in."

"Well, I don't like living down here."

Mrs. Young remembers taking her boys shopping. "Let's go get a soda," they would beg her and she would have to tell them there could be no soda because it was against the law for black folks to go into white peoples' eating places. "Aw, pshaw," one of the boys would snort, "I don't want to stay down here. I don't like their laws. Even if you have the money, you can't do what you want to. These laws are so unfair."

But Andrew and Daisy Young never left New Orleans. "My roots are very deep down here," Mrs. Young explains. "I tell you, the people in New Orleans are very warm, you know. In other places that we went, we didn't encounter those kinds of people." For many years, the Youngs lived in a predominantly white neighborhood, "and the white people were very warm and cordial." Dr. Young's office was attached to his home and gradually his white neighbors began to patronize him. They thought they were paying Dr. Young the ultimate praise when they would tell his four-year-old son, "Oh, Andrew, your daddy is such a nice man. Just like a white man." Daisy Young worried about the effect of such statements and her fears were justified one day when she and Andrew were walking down the street. Coming toward them was a black friend. "Oh, Andrew, here comes Leonard. He's such a nice young man."

"Is Leonard a white man, Mother?"

"These people," Daisy Young despaired to herself, "they're brainwashing my children. They are equating 'white' with 'nice'."

But the brainwashing did not last. When Walter and Andrew were teenagers riding the streetcars back and forth to school, they occupied themselves pitching the segregation screens out the streetcar windows. Sometimes they would wrap them up and bring them home. The prank worried their mother, who watched the collection of screens growing in her living room. She knew if the bus driver ever caught them, the next voice they would hear would be a police officer's.

Now, Daisy Young reasoned, her son had escaped the oppressiveness of segregation. He had a fine job in New York. He had started a television program, "Look Up and Live." "Why do you want to give up everything and come back to that?"

Andrew Young was gently adamant, "Don't worry about me, mother. God's going to take care of me. You know, mother, if you worry, you don't have faith."

For Andrew Young's wife, the sacrifice to come back to the South, "was the easiest we ever made." She shared her husband's desire to eliminate the conditions they both had grown up under. Her family's prominence in the black community of Marion, Alabama, had afforded her no privileges in the white community. She had not been able to attend Jubson College near her home because she was black. When she went downtown, her father's bakery store was the only place she could be served food. She had been denied the right to borrow a book from the public library to research a college term paper. Once, when her mother, who was a seamstress, was fitting a white girl in the living room, the girl had noticed that Jean was reading *"The Robe."* "Jean," the girl had exclaimed, "you mean to tell me you're reading *"The Robe"*? I can't understand that myself. I don't see how you can understand it."

Andy Young wrote Martin Luther King of his desire to return to the South, seeking his advice on where he might be most helpful. King was so impressed with the letter that he asked Stanley Levinson, a New York lawyer and an active participant in King's movement, to interview Young for a job with SCLC as Dr. King's assistant. Andy turned it down. "By that time," he recalls, King had been "on the cover of *Time* magazine. He was a national figure and I just didn't feel like I knew enough. I figured that he needed someone with more experience and training than me."

To Coretta King, the refusal revealed maturity. "He recognized the awesome responsibility that was involved and the kind of commitment that was required. He realized that you've got to prepare yourself for that. A lot of folks didn't even think of that. Most times they thought about what kind of recognition they were going to get working with Martin Luther King."

Instead, Young signed up for a position with the Highlander Folk School, which was educating black citizens in order to make them eligible to vote. One of the faculty members was a lady named Septima Clark, who had been fired from the Charleston, South Carolina school system after forty-one years of teaching: "I was found guilty of belonging to the NAACP." When Mrs. Clark heard Andy Young was joining the Highlander School staff she felt he was a very "courageous guy to come up in those mountains. . . . I was up there and I knew it was very tough. . . . very hard . . . and he had planned to bring his family there and send the children to the all-white school to integrate it. I thought this man had great stamina and great moral conviction."

The Young's "stamina and moral conviction" were to go untested in the Tennessee mountains; the Highlander Folk School was closed down on the grounds that it was "communist." The citizenship-education school took up residence in Atlanta, Georgia, the funding handled by the United Church of Christ, and the staffing by the Southern Christian Leadership Conference. The United Church of Christ hired Andy Young as the administrator of the program. For a year Andy Young, Septima Clark and Dorothy Cotton traveled through eleven of the deep South states recruiting blacks to attend their citizenship school.

Working with SCLC brought Andy Young and Martin Luther King in close proximity with one another, and "gradually" Young found himself becoming Martin Luther King's assistant, the job he had turned down many months earlier. From 1961 until King's death in 1968, Andy Young as chief of staff and Reverend Bernard Lee as personal aide were to accompany Martin Luther King on almost every major campaign.

Signing on with Martin Luther King meant more than righting the wrongs against the black man in the South; it meant a total commitment to accomplishing those ends nonviolently, no matter the personal risk. As King wrote in the book *Why We Can't Wait,* no one would be sent out "to demonstrate who had not convinced himself and us that he could accept and endure violence without retaliating. To this end, potential demonstrators were trained by SCLC to be prepared for the obstacles they would face: the verbal abuse, the beatings, the police dogs, fire hoses. If volunteers could not respond nonviolently to violent situations, they were not allowed to march. Finally they were required to sign a ten-point pledge, which included among its "commandments" promises to:

- Meditate daily on the teachings and life of Jesus.
- Pray daily to be used by God in order that all men might be free.
- Walk and talk in the manner of love, for God is love.
- Sacrifice personal wishes in order that all men might be free.
- Observe with both friend and foe the ordinary rules of courtesy.

- Seek to perform regular service for others and for the world.
- Refrain from the violence of fist, tongue and heart.
- Strive to be in good spiritual and bodily health.
- Follow the directions of the movement and of the captain on a demonstration.

Martin Luther King wrote that the black struggles were grounded in the Sermon on the Mount interwoven with Mahatma Gandhi's method of nonviolent resistance. "It was Jesus of Nazareth that stirred the Negroes to protest with the creative weapon of love."

And it was Jesus of Nazareth on whom Andy Young relied for protection during the demonstrations. "The Lord will take care of you," he was frequently heard telling other demonstrators. And indeed, Andy always seemed to escape being clubbed or wounded despite his constant marching. "Stand next to Andy," other SCLC staffers came to quip, "the Lord's taking care of him."

It appeared, however, that the Lord was busy elsewhere when Andy was leading a demonstration to the old slave market in St. Augustine, Florida. Bernard Lee witnessed the beating. It was, according to Lee, Andrew Young's real "baptism of fire. This was the first time he had really been beaten. He had the hell knocked out of him with a blackjack . . . They knocked him out. But he got up and the only thing that was in his mind was getting the people out of the area, keeping the march from breaking up, getting fragmented and being siphoned off, and keeping others from being hurt."

No sooner was Young back on his feet than he was hit again, "but that time I didn't fall and I started preaching to the guy. . . . My idea was that demonstrations were always educational opportunities and that what we were demonstrating for was to try and explain to the nation that there was something seriously wrong. So I always talked to the police and to the mob and to everybody else to try and help them understand. . . . that we weren't marching just to help black people. . . . The reason that the South was so poor was that blacks and whites were fighting each other and nobody was getting anywhere. The people who were beating on us were basically unemployed men who hung around the Ku Klux Klan because they didn't have anything better to do. So I was trying to tell them that our marching was going to help them too."

Despite the severity of Young's beating, he felt no pain. "My body was bruised all over, but I didn't have so much as a headache the next day."

One of the most dramatic moments of the movement came during a march in Birmingham, Alabama. A series of demonstrations had filled every jail and even the State coliseum with arrested blacks. During previous protests, firemen had blasted the demonstrators off their feet with firehoses. For this march, which was slated to be the highlight of the Birmingham campaign, five to six thousand people were gathered to march at Kelly Ingram park, and they were facing firemen with high-powered hoses. Police dogs were snarling at the end of their leashes. The demonstrators began to pray. "And I mean," recalls Andy, "good old fashioned country prayin' where one old lady was prayin' and everybody else was moanin', and when she finished and then somebody else took it up. . . . and everybody in the background was moanin' and you talk about a powerful feelin'!

"It failed to move the Police Commissioner who had been mumbling throughout the prayers, 'We gotta break this up. We gotta break this up.' Finally, one of the marchers stood up and cried, 'God is with this movement. We're going on through.' "

With that, the Police Commissioner ordered the firemen, "Turn the hoses on the niggers! Put the dogs on 'em." But the firemen, who had watered blacks down only days before, just stared at the demonstrators as they came forward, and the dogs remained still. "Turn those hoses on!" the Police Commissioner was now screaming. "Turn those hoses on! Didn't you hear me? Dammit! Turn the hoses on." But the firemen, some with tears in their eyes, moved the hoses aside and the marchers continued forward. "Great God Almighty done parted the Red Sea one more time," Andy Young cried jubilantly.

Despite the constant danger during the marches, Jean Young claims she felt no sense of fear. "It was very remarkable. It was like a strength that you acquired by the association of the people you were with. They were never the learned or the professionals. Oh, there were some of those, of course. But the masses of the people were very uneducated and religious kind of people, who had great spiritual strength. . . . You'd be next to a seventy-year-old woman who was having trouble walking and you're looking out and there are people with bottles and steel bars screaming and yelling and it didn't affect you. Particularly when you heard the seventy-year-old woman look at the mob and comment sorrowfully, 'Aren't those people sad? So much hate in their hearts.' "

According to Andrew Young's chief aide, Stoney Cooks, a former civil rights worker, blacks felt their greatest terror during a demonstration in Chicago where angry mobs hurled bricks at the marchers from the tops of buildings. The north, says Cooks, was fond of pointing a finger at the south, totally oblivious to its own subtle prejudices. "The northern liberals," he contends, "want to do all sorts of things *for* those poor southern blacks, but they don't want to do many things *with* them. A southern liberal wants to do it *with* you."

Jean and Andy Young were reconciled to each other facing danger, but they never fully came to grips with how they would react if anyone hurt their children. The Ku Klux Klan were very busy burning crosses on front lawns. Jean used to worry about how she would protect the children. She had been raised on a farm and learned at an early age how to use a rifle. "Well," Andy kidded, "you can always sit and point your .22 out the window."

"All of our nonviolent philosophy seemed to break down when the children were involved," Jean admits. "We could deal with that with each other, but we couldn't really deal with it with the children."

That is not to say the Young children never marched. Andrea Young remembers walking the first seven miles from Selma to Montgomery. To a girl of nine, it was like being part of a festive parade. "I really don't remember the jeering much. . . . I thought it was fun. It was really an adventure."

The incident that stands out most clearly in her mind about the days of segregation happened one Sunday when they stopped at a Holiday Inn for dinner. "It was virtually empty and they told us there were no seats available. They were all reserved. By that time, I sort of knew what was going on and I thought, 'Oh man! Is Daddy going to make us stand around here and go to jail.' " She was greatly relieved that her father passed up that opportunity to strike a blow for integrated dining rooms.

Even now, no matter that her father is Ambassador to the United Nations, Andrea is sometimes abruptly reminded of the tone of her skin. Like being "challenged" in the lobby of the Waldorf Towers, which houses the apartment of the UN Ambassador. It wasn't that anyone was impolite. It was the surprised looks and the too solicitous "May we help you?" as she made her way to the elevator. "And you know," Andrea says with some humor, "you're just trying to go home. . . ."

She appears to take such affronts philosophically. Her father, she says, taught her "you ought to be nice to people. . . . I remember once in particular, this girl seemed to have it out for me for one reason or another and his response was 'Well, be nice to her and take an interest in her.' I thought he was crazy. But that was the kind of thing he would always say. If people are mean to you, it's because they have trouble. It's not directed at you. It's just that they're upset or that they feel unhappy about something. So the only way to deal with it is to be nice to them so that they won't feel so bad or bitter. And sometimes, it was hard to do. But I did do it and it worked."

It was Young's ability to follow his own rule that made him such an effective negotiator during the civil rights movement. Often, while the marchers were making the headlines, he was in the back room with the white establishment patiently explaining and cajoling and convincing city administrators that only justice would bring the demonstrations to an end. Nicholas Hood remembers Young coming to the Detroit City Council with the Poor People's Campaign. "I was a member of the City Council then. Our public auditorium was jammed with the participants. They were ranting and raving and carrying on, but Andy was sitting down on the floor behind the podium reading and studying. . . . He was down there, planning and thinking for the next move. He was not the type of person who was mouthing off all the time. When he opened his mouth, he was saying something. He was willing to stay in the background. He was willing to give the honor to others. And always willing to take the second role."

"Andy is not the kind to push himself ahead," says Congressman Walter Fauntroy. "Looking back over the campaigns that we had, you rarely saw Andy up front, though Andy was doing a lot of the basic work. We never saw him clamoring to get into a picture, clamoring to be the spokesman. I think that spirit was not only a function of his basic humility, but also a function of his faith in God—that he did not have to push himself, that in God's own time, if it was His will, it would be very obvious that it was his role to speak or act."

It is an attitude that has enveloped Young's entire lifestyle. "I've never worried about what I was going to do. I just figured that my life really isn't my own. . . . I figure you do your part. . . . You work hard and you do your best today; tomorrow will take care of itself. My grandmother used to say that all the time. I learned the Bible, reading it to her, as a kid. She was blind. So everyday, my job was to read the paper for her and read the Bible. And she used to say, 'let the day's own trouble be sufficient unto the day thereof. . . . Consider the lilies of the field, they toil not, neither do they spin, yet none are arrayed such as these. Be not anxious for your life, what you shall drink or what you shall put on. . . .'"

Easier said than done, particularly when the better portion of a decade has been invested in total commitment to the betterment of your black fellows and the leader of your movement has been assassinated. Andrew Young's family and friends remember the years after Martin Luther King's death as being, according to administrative assistant Stoney Cooks, "a crucial period when Andy debated with himself about what he should do to continue Dr. King's work. . . . He resolved it by deciding to run for Congress."

But like every other step in his career, Young's decision to run for Congress seems to have been engineered by someone's design other than his own.

"I never thought of being a Congressman until the very day I decided to run. John Lewis and I were trying to convince Julian Bond to run. And we put together a committee that had agreed to raise money and recruit workers. Generally, we had decided that it was time for the movement to get into politics and that Julian was the best candidate and we'd set up a meeting with Julian to discuss it."

Young and Lewis presented their case in person to Bond, who was a Georgia state legislator. Lewis had penned a persuasive case in a letter designed to be the advance man for their cause. Essentially, the letter said that a number of things were needed for a black man to wage a successful campaign in the fifth district of Georgia, which was predominantly white: a candidate who could raise a great deal of cash, a candidate who was well known, a candidate who could appeal to young people, a candidate who could talk comfortably with white people and not be afraid to campaign in the white community. Julian Bond, the argument went, obviously qualified on all points.

Julian Bond, however, was not interested in running. "Look," he said to Young, "all those things in the letter apply to you too. Why don't you run?"

"Well," replied Young, "maybe I will."

"I didn't make up my mind at that moment," Young recalls. "I was on my way to New York and I had a meeting with Harry Belafonte and I told him about the conversation." Belafonte thought the idea of Andy Young running for Congress was "wonderful." With that pronouncement, he picked up the telephone and called his wife. "Right there on the spot they planned a dinner and they said they would raise fifty thousand dollars to get me going."

Not all of his friends were so immediately enthusiastic. "Oh, no! no!" was Coretta King's first reaction. "Anybody else but Andy." She thought he would have to compromise too much.

"Somehow," Mrs. King explains her initial dismay, "you tend to use my husband as a norm because he never ran for an office. He was nonpartisan. But he was evolving to a different point when he left us." Now she is not so sure that he might not have taken a similar step himself had he lived. "He was coming to believe it was important for blacks to get into the political process. . . . When I realized that, I got on board with Andy."

Her concern that Young not step into the wrong arena was so acute "because Andy is one of my favorite people." In her mind, he comes from the same mold as her husband. "They have a lot in common. Just as Martin felt the weight of the world on his shoulders, Andy now feels that. . . . I had great admiration for Martin as a person. He was my husband. But he was a great human being. I've been looking for people that you can depend on, that you can trust. To me, that is so important. I guess . . . in the absence of Martin . . . my hopes and dreams have been transferred to Andy."

Young was defeated, but undismayed, in his first bid for Congress. "I wasn't at all depressed or discouraged. When I decide I'm supposed to do something, then I just keep on until I do it. It might not happen the *way* I want it to happen, or *when* I want it to happen, but I know it's going to happen." If he is convinced that God's will is behind his efforts, "I just keep on until I find a way to make it work."

In 1972 it "worked," making Young the first black congressman from Georgia since Reconstruction days. For the first time in his career, Andy Young found himself the man out front instead of the backstage negotiator. He felt more comfortable, he told a reporter, "behind the scenes."

"Andy was never a bomb thrower in the House," points out Massachusetts Republican Silvio Conte. He seldom antagonized adversaries, but, according to Congresswoman Yvonne Burke, a black Representative from California, he sometimes had to "take it" from his philosophical kin. "When Andy Young served in Congress, people who were more liberal were often critical of him. . . . The great strength that he has is that criticism apparently doesn't bother him."

He surprised and annoyed an otherwise consolidated Black Caucus by announcing that he would vote for the confirmation of Gerald R. Ford as Vice President, despite the fact that the caucus was very unhappy with Ford's civil rights voting record. To a packed and unusually silent House of Representatives, he explained that he had as many reservations as his black colleagues about Mr. Ford's political philosophy and voting record, but he knew from his own Southern experience that people could rise above their own parochial views and develop a broader perspective which takes "into account the interest of all people. Decent men, placed in decent positions of trust, will serve decently. I believe that Mr. Ford is a decent man."

When the confirmation vote was taken on the House floor, Andrew Young was the only member of the Black Caucus to cast an aye.

Several years later, shortly after being appointed United States Ambassador to the UN, Young was quoted in a magazine article as calling the man for whom he had walked a limb a "racist." Was he sorry that he voted for Ford? "No, not at all."

When he used the term "racism," he says now, if analyzed in a religious sense, "I would say that I was talking about original sin. All men sin and fall short of the glory of God. And women, too. The tendency is to put one's self first and to look at the world from one's own perspective rather than trying to look at the world from God's

perspective. You are just one person as a child of God and everybody else is your brother and sister. And I don't think we're brought
up to look at the world from that universal brotherhood perspective.
We're brought up, we're trained, especially in this country, self-
centeredly. But it's true in almost every country. You either look
at things through your own selfish eyes, or your cultural, regional,
or racial biases. Until you get that overall perspective, you tend
to discriminate one way or the other against other people. It might
not be black people. It might be people of a different nationality.
Some folk get upset about fat people."

Nevertheless, his liberal use of a dynamite word like racism to
define truth of far gentler connotations produced an avalanche of
media and colleague abuse. "Sometimes," Young explains, "the
only way you get people to pay attention to themselves is to be
inflamatory."

Andy Young's first year as Ambassador to the UN proved at
times to be the most tortuous. He said what he liked and let the
flak fall where it might. "He's so honest," Coretta King admits,
"particularly about himself. Sometimes I tell him he's too honest."
So did the press corps. He was labeled everything from a "disaster"
to an "unguided missile." Hardly anyone noticed when Republican
Congressman Charles Whalen, sent to observe the United Nations
for several months, hailed Young as one of President Carter's best
appointments. Speculation was rife that Carter would rein his Ambassador in, but the President, who first met Young in 1970 when
he was Governor and Young was Chairman of the Atlanta Community Relations Commission, seldom indicated anything but the
highest approval of Young.

He was publicly irked, however, by Young's assertion to a Paris
newspaper that United States jails contained hundreds, possibly
thousands, of political prisoners. But Carter softened even that re-
buke with warm plaudits for Andrew Young's accomplishments in
Africa. The President seems wedded not just pragmatically to the
United Nations ambassador; his praise of Young in conversation
clearly reveals a personal spiritual bond. "If I ever knew a person,"
the President told a Congressional wife, "with whom I can't find fault,
it's Andy Young. He's honest, decent, unselfish, compassionate. . . .
All the things that seem to be, are really there. And," the President
added with emphasis, "I *know* him."

The political prisoners flap was only a link in a long chain of controversial candor such as Young's observation that Cubans in Angola
lent a stability to that country. What was never known was the fact
that Young equally irritated Fidel Castro by sending him a private
message applauding the presence of Cuban medical and technical advisors but deploring Castro's deployment of military troops. "Africa!

Africa!" the Cuban President exploded in response, "It's none of the United States' business!"

But Africa has been the business of Andy Young since the days he dreamed of becoming a missionary to Angola. Wisconsin Congressman Henry Reuss and his wife remember accompanying Andy and Jean Young on their first trip to the land of their ancestors. The Congressional party was taken to the Island of Goreé, where twenty million Africans were warehoused in small cells carved out of stone walls, waiting to be shipped off to the colonies as slaves. "I remember Andy," says Mrs. Reuss, "looking into those little holes where his ancestors had been kept, all shackled, waiting to go they knew not where. Oh," she winced at the recollection, "it is just so incredibly painful to remember." Later on, the Reusses and the Youngs journeyed to a remote country village in Senegal. Standing in the midst of the hundreds of tribesmen who had assembled for the VIP visit, Young said with tears in his eyes, "I feel as if I've come home."

He had not planned to come as a celebrity. He had planned to come as a minister—a posture, his friends insist, he has never abandoned. "That's the kind of role he played inside SCLC, that's the kind of role he played outside SCLC," says Stoney Cooks. "It just so happens that he has chosen not to have a nice, little church in Atlanta. . . . He has decided that the world is his parish."

Does that mean that some day he would like to be President of the United States? "Not at all," Andy says with considerable emphasis. "The main reason is, I don't think it's fun. One of the things I really like about this job is that it really is fun. . . . I have the freedom to be creative and expressive—in a way, shaping the world—but I don't have the ultimate responsibility. I've got Cy Vance and the President and everybody else to blame, and also to check me when I'm going too far." He likes working on what he wants to work on, he says and "I would get sick at my stomach working on the tax code." But he adds, "the truth of it is, in a larger perspective, all those things will fall into place."

Whatever the position, it seems likely that Andrew Young will carry his informal style with him. The Waldorf Astoria is an "embarrassment" to him, he says. He is more comfortable in his little house in Atlanta. And there is evidence he means it. When Cooks and Young were in South Africa, they stayed at the palatial estate of multimillionaire Harry Oppenheimer, where even the help are housed in sumptuous quarters and provided with their own swimming pool and tennis court. Cooks went to Oppenheimer's tennis court, while the United Nations Ambassador, clad casually in a sweater, strolled over to the employees' court. A young girl engaged in a game noticed him. "Are you new here?", she asked.

"Well, sort of," Andy Young replied.

"Are you going to be around for awhile?"

"Yeah, I guess so."

"Oh," the girl wanted him to know, "you're going to like working here!"

It is still, as Stoney Cooks points out, so easy for a black man "to be snatched back in his place."

That is a fact unlikely to disturb Young's tranquility. No matter where he goes, Andrew Young seems disinclined to want to forget where he came from or to whom he owes his dues.

"I feel like I belong to God," he remarked, hastening to add that doesn't mean he "blames God" when he goes wrong. Rather, he sees himself as an instrument in a large orchestra. He likes to recall his Old Testament professor, who used to say, "God spoke through Balaam's jackass and so maybe he might speak through some of us preachers. It is always in that context that I view my preaching and my religious life. Maybe God can use me. But there's nothin' special 'bout me. . . . Everything good I do is because I'm in tune with God."

He publicly acknowledged his debt when he was sworn in as the first black Ambassador to the United Nations, a milestone never imagined when he left the sidewalks of New York to battle the backroads of segregation. Then, in Jean Young's words, "All we wanted was the right to vote and the right to sit in the front of the bus." It was "inconceivable" that, scarcely a decade removed from a dinner denied at the Holiday Inn, the Youngs of Georgia would stand in the East Room of the White House before an integrated throng of admirers and hear a southern President of the United States proclaim a black man the "finest public servant" he had ever known.

Andrew Young responded to his triumph with simple words from old hymns: " 'Tis grace that brought us safe thus far and grace will lead us on. Pray we do not let this Harvest pass."

P. Stanton

# 2 | JOHN McCORMACK

It was a mean, blowing, snowing Boston December day, the kind of weather seemingly ordained for funerals. The eight hundred seats in St. Margaret's Church were filled. Several hundred people who could not get into the Church stood patiently outside, letting the wet flakes slide down their cheeks and the soggy cold seep through their skin, clinging to their bones like a damp claw.

Silently, they watched former President Lyndon Johnson, still tall, still commanding, but with whiter, longer hair and deeper shadows in his face, walk into the Church. He and his daughter, Luci Nugent, had come all the way from Texas for this funeral. A steady stream of limousines were depositing well-known faces at the curb: First Lady Pat Nixon, Boston Mayor Kevin White, Massachusetts Governor Francis Sargent. Among the sixty-three Senators and Congressmen who had flown in from Washington, D.C., the Representatives from the Massachusetts delegation were the most easily recognizable: Thomas P. "Tip" O'Neill, his usual shock of silver hair drooping over the right eyebrow; Eddie Boland, slicked-back black hair, gentleman Irish, whose bachelorhood didn't give way till after he was sixty, just when he thought he was safe; Senator Edward Kennedy, his youth disappearing into his jowls. A colorful group of men who had survived the turbulent, sometimes murky waters of Massachusetts politics, they were assembled today to pay tribute to a romance that had passed into legend long before it passed into history.

There was no sound except for the rushing of the wind, as a tall, gaunt figure in a homburg hat slowly mounted the steps. The hollows in his face were hospital gray and his proud bearing bent with loss. He was alone, except for his immediate family. His late brother "Knocko" McCormack's wife, May, clutched the crook of his elbow. His two nephews, Edward and Jocko, followed with their wives and children. He was John W. McCormack, forty-fifth Speaker of the United States House of Representatives, and he had come to bury his sweetheart.

John Monahan stood at the Church door, watching his former boss approach him. McCormack spoke first, "How are you today, John?"

Monahan felt his throat tighten, "I'm fine, Mr. Speaker. I'm very sorry to be here under these circumstances."

"I know, I know, John. No one knows that better than you and I."

The formality had a peculiar ring since the two men had been together almost constantly since Mrs. McCormack's death three days ago. Images of the last seventy-two hours tumbled through Monahan's mind like a broken kaleidoscope. A ride through the darkened streets of the nation's capital—past the White House, past the House of Representatives, past the monuments, past Hains Point—reliving fifty-two years of married life, tears curving down weathered cheeks. Flying on Air Force One, returning Harriet McCormack to her beloved Boston. The casket, flanked by a marine honor guard, resting in the rear of the plane. Touching down at Logan International airport, the plane taxiing to a stop, the former Speaker of the House rising from his seat . . . walking slowly down the aisle . . . placing his hand on his wife's coffin and whispering, "We're home again, my dear, just as I promised you" . . .

John Monahan had the turned-up face of an Irish choir boy. Only the gray overtaking his bushy brown hair betrayed his maturity. He had been one of McCormack's chief assistants until the Speaker resigned his office. When the news of Mrs. McCormack's death reached him, he was one of the first friends to reach Providence hospital. He knew McCormack would need someone to take over for him. He found the old man sitting on the bed where his wife had lain ill for a year and a half, trying to grasp the fact that she was gone.

Round, cherubic Patrick Cardinal O'Boyle sat small beside him, consoling and comforting. McCormack had walked such a long gauntlet; one would have thought he would be relieved that at last it was finished. He was not; he told Monahan he would rather have Harriet in any condition than not have her at all.

The word spread quickly through the nation's capital. The hospital switchboard lit up with sympathy. Calls from the Senate, calls from the House of Representatives. In the late afternoon, a call from the President of the United States. Richard Nixon did most of the talking. In the history of the country, the President told McCormack, the people with real character, almost without exception, had had wives who were very supportive. He knew Harriet McCormack had been such a wife to John, and had made it possible for him to be the fine Congressman, Majority Leader and Speaker that he had been.

When the President finished speaking, he turned to his Chief of Congressional liason, Clark MacGregor, "Do you know Eddie McCormack?"

MacGregor said yes, he did know the Speaker's nephew, the man who had engaged Ted Kennedy in a tumultuous first campaign for the Senate.

"Get in touch with him," Nixon directed. "Tell him that we want to put a presidential aircraft at the disposal of Speaker Mc-Cormack." The President further instructed MacGregor to make a White House plane available to Members of Congress and anyone else who wished to fly from Washington to Boston for Mrs. Mc-Cormack's funeral. He would not be able to go himself because he was scheduled to be in Canada that day. Mrs. Nixon would represent him.

Never had there been such Executive concern for the death of a Congressional wife. "One would have thought that she was the Speaker," Clark MacGregor commented later. It was even more of a mystery why a Republican President would be so anxious to please a Democrat who no longer held the reigns of power. "I think," MacGregor conjectured, "the McCormack's extraordinary relation-ship touched Richard Nixon. . . . He was always acutely con-scious of things that other people had that he didn't have the capacity to duplicate. . . ."

In the corridors of the Capitol, up the stairwells and down the elevators, the legend of that "extraordinary relationship" passed from page to policeman, from Congressman to committee aide, till there was hardly anyone who knew anything about politics in Wash-ington, D.C. or Boston, Massachusetts, who didn't know that John and Harriet McCormack had never spent a night apart in fifty-two years of married life. Everyone knew that. What no one could comprehend was how they did it. What kind of stuff was this woman made of that she commanded so much devotion? And what kind of rare politician could put his wife ahead of his career?

John McCormack never went anywhere without Harriet. If a President called him to the White House for a consultation in the afternoon, the Speaker would order his driver to detour to the Washington Hotel, so that he could have Mrs. McCormack's com-pany on the ride to 1600 Pennsylvania Avenue. If he went to a reception, if he gave a speech to a high school group, if he attended a fund raiser, Harriet was either at his side or out in the limousine waiting for him. He sent polite regrets to out-of-town speaking re-quests, pleading pressing business. The pressing business was dinner with his wife. When he was elected Speaker of the House, the Wash-ington Press Corps gave an event in his honor. After the reception and before the dinner, he rose and thanked the news media for their kindness and excused himself to go home and have his meal with Mrs. McCormack.

"Always be sweethearts," he would advise young newlyweds who came to see him at the Capitol, "You're sweethearts before you're married. If a husband and wife would carry the sweetheart stage prior to marriage *into* marriage, they wouldn't have many difficulties and troubles, despite the fact that life, at best, is a stony, steep, uphill journey. . . . Being sweethearts," he insisted, "is a state of mind."

Younger Congressional wives, whose couture and coiffures conformed to the latest decrees of *Women's Wear Daily,* eyed Harriet's long sleeved, high-necked, ankle-length dresses and wondered what magic potion she was slipping into her husband's orange juice. Their husbands used to tell them that they learned to read the Speaker's mind by watching his wife's comings and goings. Until recent years, in the tangled web of operations in the United States Congress, it was one of the inexplicable facts of life that members of the House of Representatives did not know whether they would be working from morning till night or morning till morning. It was also an inexplicable fact that the man least disposed to dispersing such information was the only man in possession of that knowledge, the Speaker. When John McCormack controlled the gavel, his wife gave away the timetable. The Congressmen soon began to notice that if Harriet McCormack was sitting in the limousine under the arch of the House around five o'clock in the evening, the Speaker was closing the shop on time. If she came inside the Capitol dining room, there was a collective sinking of hearts. They, for whom the bells toll, knew they would hear that tolling far into the night. For Harriet would have dinner with her husband in the House restaurant and then wait in his office, sometimes till three or four in the morning, until John was ready to go home.

John McCormack sat in the front pew of the Church, his fatigue as heavy as his sorrow. His sleep had been on call for two years. When Harriet fell ill and entered Providence hospital six months after their fifty-second wedding anniversary, John McCormack resigned his seat in Congress and relinquished his job as Speaker of the House, the third most powerful post in the United States government. He could have stepped down as Speaker and still retained his seat, but he said no, he would give it all up, because his wife needed him and he wanted to be there.

His friends and colleagues and relatives pleaded with him not to take such a drastic step. "He squashed me pretty flat," said his nephew Jocko McCormack. "He said, 'I've dedicated fifty years of my life to my country and I feel I owe this year or two to your aunt.' "

"I begged him," recalled a close Chicago friend, Joe Meegan, "to stay on as Congressman. I said, 'Mr. Speaker, you know she will become progressively worse and there will be a time when she won't even remember you.' "

"He would look at those people like they came from Mars," asserts John Monahan. When people talked about sacrifice, he scoffed at them. What did they mean? He *wanted* to be with Harriet. He was annoyed when anyone suggested duty. Duty wasn't love.

He took the hospital room next to Harriet's and kept the door between the two rooms open at all times, so he could hear her if she called during the night. When she was warm he bathed her forehead. When she was weak he fed her. When she could no longer eat solid foods, he did not; if she had to endure roast mush, he would endure it with her. In the small hours of the morning her soft moan would come, "John, John, where are you?" and he would scuffle into his slippers and tug on his bathrobe, "I'm right here, Harriet, don't worry."

When she slipped into the past, he was not impatient. He went with her. "I'm so glad I can help her there," he told John Monahan, "I can remember her brothers and sisters."

"He sat there day after day, hour after hour," according to Joe Meegan, "and would repeat everything. He would recall all their early life together with great fondness."

There was, after all, considerable pleasure in remembering how they met at Nantasket beach in the summer of 1919. Just one of those accidental meetings. Nantasket, which was twenty-five miles south of Boston, down along toward the Cape, was a popular resort in those days. John McCormack felt he owed himself a rest from his burgeoning law practice, so he rented a room in a beach cottage. Tired as he was, he had enough energy to focus in on two young ladies who were also renting accommodations at the guest house. One of the young women was the daughter of Henry Naphan, a former Congressman from John's district. Her companion was a raven-haired girl with dark eyes and startlingly lovely skin. Her name was Harriet Joyce and she was an opera singer who had sung with the Metropolitan opera company and who gave concerts in churches and sold out houses around the country.

The day that Miss Naphan and Miss Joyce planned to return to Boston, a severe storm developed. John helped put the convertible top back on Miss Joyce's Buick roadster. Then he got to thinking that a gentleman wouldn't let those young women tackle such inclement weather all alone; he thought he had better ride as far as Quincy with them. Miss Joyce rewarded his courtesy with her phone number and permission to call.

It was an unlikely pairing. Harriet Joyce came from property, John McCormack came from poverty. She was thirty-four, he was twenty-eight. She had a career. He was a struggling young lawyer. . . .

His law business celebrated its fifth birthday that summer of 1919. The very existence of that company was a minor Irish miracle. McCormack grew up on Anderson Square in South Boston. The McCormacks were the poorest family on the block. John's grandparents had arrived in America in the 1840s, fleeing the starvation of the potato famine in their native Ireland. The union of his parents, Joseph and Ellen McCormack, produced twelve children, nine of whom would die before they reached maturity. It was the age of galloping tuberculosis. John's life had been saved by a little Jewish doctor who was so proud of his achievement that he would holler across the street whenever he spotted young McCormack, "you are mine exheebit numbair one!"

His father died when he was thirteen, and the task of breadwinner fell to John. He quit grammar school less than a month before graduation and went to work as a newsboy. His salary was so small, it was necessary to supplement the family income with a "pauper's basket." Young McCormack's only solace from the grinding poverty was escape into fantasy. He was "a nut", he admits, for reading Horatio Alger and Dick and Frank Merrywell nickel novels. "I couldn't afford a nickel, so I'd buy them second hand, and I wouldn't swap any novel that I had unless I got another Merrywell novel that I hadn't read. Dick and Frank Merrywell were the boys who went into the game with three men on base and three runs behind and they went up to the plate and knocked a home run and scored four runs. That was very uplifting for someone who lived under poor conditions."

John relinquished his newspaper job to become an errand boy in a brokerage firm because it paid him $3.50 a week. Soon he heard about another job in a law firm that would increase his weekly pay by $.50.

More importantly, it expanded his ambitions. One of the clients in the William T. Way law firm was a lady named Mrs. Sam Helen. Mrs. Helen was a schoolteacher and she took an interest in the young office boy. She told him he should study for the law. John thought it would be impossible for a lad who hadn't graduated from grammar school to pass the bar, but Mrs. Helen persuaded him to try.

So he began studying law books, and Mr. Way counseled him in spare hours. Soon he was putting out $2.00 a week to take Charlie Innis's law classes. Charlie Innis was a prominent Boston attorney who taught law in the late afternoon to disadvantaged boys who couldn't afford a regular law school. He didn't teach for the money, but he charged each boy a dollar a course, "just so," according to McCormack, "you'd have respect for yourself."

After five years of Charlie Innis's classes, John McCormack, grammar school dropout, age twenty-one, passed the Massachusetts bar. He became a trial lawyer and a good one, but it wasn't long before the scent of politics lured him into the arena. He took part in the Massachusetts Constitutional Convention in 1917, and in 1920, the year he was wooing Miss Joyce away from the opera, he was elected to his first term in the Massachusetts House of Representatives.

Harriet Joyce's parents were "propertied," the Bostonian phrase for modest personal affluence. Mr. Joyce owned a several-storied brick townhouse on Fourth Street. Geograpically, Fourth Street was but a quarter of a mile from Anderson Square. Economically, that distance was multiplied several times over. Harriet's dramatic contralto voice was schooled at Notre Dame Academy in Roxbury. Her future husband thought that voice "one of the most beautiful in the world." In the early 1900s, female opera singers frequently housed powerful vocal cords in large frames. John was proudly appreciative of the fact that Harriet was an exception to that rule and that her slender five-foot-five figure earned her the title "the little girl with the big voice".

Not all of Harriet Joyce's talent resided in her throat. Considerable ability flowed through her fingers. She played the piano with skill and she was a painter of merit. She was fond of taking her brushes and canvas and setting up studio wherever an appealing scene presented itself. "You see that sheep over there," she commnted to her suitor upon completion of a pastoral scene, "that's the one that gave me the most trouble."

It took just one year for the young Irish lawyer to earn precedence over Harriet's many creative pursuits. She gave her last concert in Little Rock, Arkansas. "When I married John," she later told her nephew Jocko McCormack, "everything else stopped. I gave it all up for the greatest boy in the world." She had seen too many marriages sink, she later explained to her nephew, because both partners were seeking publicity. There would be only one career in the McCormack family.

Half a century later, John McCormack would still speak with pride of Harriet's gift. "She didn't *have* to give up her career," he stressed, "she *gave* it up. I had nothing to do with it."

She never sang publicly after their marriage, although, as John quipped, she would occasionally "let notes out" as a "courtesy" to guests. From the beginning, Harriet went everywhere with John. It was the era of the outdoor campaign, when politicians would climb on the back of a peddler's wagon or on top of a tree stump to address the crowds. Those were the days when a politician could still draw a crowd. If the fabled Boston Mayor James Curley were going to speak on a Saturday night at the corner of Harvey street and North Cambridge, five thousand people were at the intersection to hear him. Sometimes twenty-five thousand spectators would fill Andrew Square. Harriet attended all the rallies with her husband. John was a vibrant speaker who, according to a campaign aide, "could take an audience over when he really got rolling." Sometimes he wound on for an hour and, by the end of the exercise, he had acquired a healthy froth on the neck. Harriet kept fresh collars in the car, taking note when necessary that his present encasement looked a "bit shabby". It's time for a change, she would advise her candidate. No, John said, he couldn't be bothered.

But Harriet was undeterred by a single negative. "I think you'd better change your collar, dear." And John was wise enough to know when to bend to the winds of gentle persuasion. "Yes, dear," he would eventually concede. He was fond of telling people that he and Harriet never argued because of a compact they made when they were first married. "We agreed that if there was a major decision affecting the family, I'd make the decision and if it was a minor matter . . . Harriet would make the decision. And in fifty-two years of marriage, we never had a major decision." He added, however, that he occasionally warned Harriet of a possible uprising. "I have the inherent right to revolt," he teased. "Every human being has. And even for you, I will not abdicate my academic right of revolution."

Harriet did not confine her sartorial concern to wilted collars. She immediately assumed the role of total wardrobe mistress. Their close friend and companion during the campaign, Jerry Taylor, noted "She looked out for him like a mother looking after a child." She laid out his clothes in the morning, she bought his shoes. She bought his hats. And she advised him when it was time to abandon the old for the new, "Now, John, those shoes look kind of shabby. Now why don't you put on a new pair. I bought you a new pair."

If Harriet hadn't looked out for John, Jerry Taylor was sure of one thing: he would never have looked out for himself. "You wear a suit day after day, and it's just a suit, but you know, it's nice to have a press once in a while. She was the one who would see that that was done . . . because those things didn't matter to him at all. All that mattered to him were his job and her. No doubt about it, she was the woman behind the successful man. She always had a lot of faith in him. She always thought he was going to make it."

And she did everything she could to assist him in the ascent. She was "outstanding looking," Jerry Taylor thought, "She had a beautiful complexion, black hair and penetrating eyes. When you looked at her, you looked twice." She possessed a superior intellect, but she never let it get in the way of a good glandular reaction. Her instincts were so acute that Taylor and McCormack used to kid her that she was fortunate not to have lived during the days of the Salem trials. "They'd have burned you at the stake, my dear," John would josh her. When Harriet McCormack said something was going to happen, Jerry Taylor was sure "it was going to happen."

Her uncanny intuition, nevertheless, was very helpful to a rising young politician. It tended to give his career direction. One night in 1921, just a year after they were married, John and Harriet were returning home in what he referred to as their "second-hand car of the fourth degree," the only thing he could afford. John had just been nominated for a second term in the State legislature, after a spirited contest. One of his competitors was a man named Eddie Sullivan.

"Dear," Harriet announced without preamble, "you're going to run for Congress some day. You'll run against Eddie Sullivan and you'll lick him." McCormack stared at his bride, "Why, my dear," he exclaimed, "that's the farthest thing from my mind. I haven't got a thought along that line."

"Well," said Harriet firmly, "it's going to happen. Some day you and Eddie Sullivan will be running against each other for Congress and you'll win."

In 1928, they were and John did.

Harriet assessed people by instinct. Her politically astute vibrations were touched off with the first press of the flesh, often sending out a warning signal to her husband as to who his friends really were. They were alighting from their car, one evening in Boston, when McCormack spied an acquaintance coming down the street, a fellow he thought very highly of, a fellow he had cloaked in glowing colors to Harriet, who had never met him. After introductions and pleasantries were exchanged and the man was on his way again, John turned to Harriet for her opinion. "Well, what do you think, my dear?"

"Do you really want me to tell you?"

"Yes, I would be very interested."

"Well, I wouldn't tell him anything that you wouldn't want the whole world to know."

Five years later, McCormack's "friend" opposed him for Congress.

Harriet never made speeches, but she was not above mending small fences. Once a voter approached her to inform her that he would never support her husband again. "I wrote him a letter and he didn't answer me."

Without blinking, Harriet replied, "You didn't put a stamp on it." Later on, the gentleman told McCormack, "You know I voted for you, but I didn't do it for you. I did it for Mrs. McCormack. You know, maybe I *didn't* put a stamp on that letter."

There is no breeding ground for politics equal to Massachusetts where it is the staff of life for the populace as well as the practitioners.

From that fertile ground came some of the most colorful, charismatic politicians of the century. Raconteurs all, the only thing they love more than their job is reliving it in every detail for a roomful of cronies. Sometimes the tall tales were spun in a colleague's living room. When John McCormack was first elected to office on the state level, many of the legislators turned "their homes into a club." But John determined he was "not going to submit Harriet to those conditions." He told his friends politely but firmly, "I'll see you up in the legislature or I'll see you in my law office . . . but Harriet and I are going to be together every night." It was a commitment he never broke for fifty-two years. "That's how I started out, that I wasn't going to make my home a club. When I was elected to Congress, I was pretty well innoculated. And starting this way, it's hard, but you've got to stick to it. There was no one I would enjoy more than Mrs. McCormack or she enjoy more than me, so I'd rather be with her than going around to a dinner. To me, it was always first things first. Am I going to let politics dominate where it might interfere with family life? What's first? Family life. Let politics follow. I'd gear myself into the politics, the exigencies, the necessities of politics without letting politics dominate the family life."

There were fellow politicians who felt McCormack's sacrifice was too great. John Monahan vehemently disagreed. "Mr. McCormack was the single most political man I have ever seen. He really loved politics. And there was nothing denied him in the fellowship of political beings. He knew every President he ever served and he knew every Member with whom he served. There was nothing in his life that he would add to it now or any other time."

Love, John McCormack firmly believes, is the power that moves men to build personal relationships, to build countries. "Where are we without it?", he asks. "The very fact that you and I are sitting here with our form of government comes from the word love. The origin of our way of life and our form of government comes from the love of God and love of neighbor. . . .

"Now take the opposite way of life, the Communists. The origin is hate. When a man is willing to go to jail because he has written a book, where did he get that thought? He may not realize it in his conscious mind, but he got that thought because he has a *right* to write that book. What's the origin? Love of God. When you see Jewish people willing to demonstrate and go to jail to get a piece of paper to go to Israel, to escape oppression. What's the origin of that? Love of God."

Love in a marriage, he asserts, should effect the completion of two people. Neither one should dominate. A husband and wife are two separate individuals and that should be respected, but their love for one another should bring about the welding of those personalities.

"Two individual personalities into a unit of one as contemplated by God. They don't lose their individuality, but in the eyes of God they become one."

In 1926, after three years in the State Senate, John McCormack decided to make his first bid for residence in Washington, D.C. So he challenged the incumbent, James Gallivan, for the twelfth Congressional seat in South Boston. The twelfth district was known as a "nomination district." If a man could win the Democratic primary, he was assured the general election, as Republicans were never invited by twelfth district voters to represent them.

James Gallivan was a popular Boston politician. He and James Curley were forever contesting each other at the polls and the results were nearly always the same. When Gallivan ran against Curley for mayor, Curley always won. When Curley ran against Gallivan for Congress, Gallivan always won. John McCormack became the prince of peace between the two rivals when he announced his entrance into the 1926 contest. James Curley did not want to face McCormack some day in a mayoral fight, so he teamed up with Gallivan to beat him in the Congressional race. One morning, McCormack opened the newspaper to find the two mortal enemies pictured on the front page, strolling arm in arm down the street. It was all over for McCormack, he knew then. What little chance he had was wiped out by the photographed State Street rendezvous.

But John McCormack was back on the hustings sooner than he or anyone else expected. James Gallivan died before finishing out his term in Congress, and a special election was called to fill his seat. It cannot be said that McCormack went unchallenged; nine men jumped into the fray, seven from South Boston. McCormack's strongest competitor was the man Harriet had predicted back in 1921 that her husband would defeat—Eddie Sullivan. Sullivan was a key figure in the city and well liked. But John McCormack had spaded the ground well during his previous battle with Gallivan. When people told him then that they couldn't vote for him because Mr. Gallivan was their friend or Mr. Gallivan had done a favor for their mother-in-law, McCormack had been very understanding. "Well thank you," he would say politely, "I appreciate your frankness. I'm sorry you can't vote for me, but some day you may be able to vote for me, and I hope you will."

The soft sell repeated time after time in 1926 paid off well in 1928. Thousands of Gallivan's former supporters poured into the polls to give the courteous young Irishman the vote they had reluctantly denied him two years earlier. None of his nine opponents could catch him; only Eddie Sullivan even came close. After that, the district was John McCormack's private property.

Future contenders for the twelfth Congressional seat found their efforts a journey in wasted energy. Congressman James Burke recalls his own fruitless challenge. "I heard McCormack was going to be appointed a federal judge. Being young and ambitious . . . I said I think I better take a chance at that position. There's an old saying, 'On the beaches of hesitation, lie the bleached bones of thousands'. So I didn't hesitate; I had four hundred workers out ringing doorbells from one end of the district to the other. Every night they'd come back and they'd plead with me not to send them out again. About three out of four people would be outraged at the fact that anybody would oppose the great John McCormack. Some would even slam doors in our faces."

That may have been the reason McCormack preferred low-profile campaigns. "I started my campaign yesterday," he joked to an aide. "I sent out a penny postcard."

Harriet did not always approve of the low profile approach, however, particularly if the opponent was standing in front of her own house, tossing harpoons at her husband. In the early days of McCormack's career, the candidates traveled from corner to corner, pleading their case. Once when a competitor was attacking McCormack through a bullhorn, just a few feet from the McCormack front yard, Harriet turned indignantly to John, "What are you going to do about that man?"

"Well," her husband replied, "you always ignore someone like that."

"Well, you don't ignore *him*. You go out and answer him."

"So," McCormack later told his nephew Edward, "I went out and answered him."

John and Harriet drove to Washington after that first campaign "in that fourth-hand car of ours. It was a one seater," according to John. "Two of us could get in and you could carve in a third." The "carved-in third" was a Boston terrier named Bobby. The newcomers drove around the nation's capital until they spotted the Washington Hotel. They decided to see if the management was kindly disposed toward Boston terriers. It was, so they checked in. They didn't check out for forty-two years.

They hadn't meant to stay so long. It was just that the Washington Hotel was so convenient. It was in the heart of the Capitol. You could look out the window and see the White House. The United States Congress was just minutes down Pennsylvania Avenue. Across the street was Garfinckel's, the best department store in town, and St. Patrick's Church was only five blocks away. Harriet devoted her first weeks in Washington to looking for an apartment or a house, but nothing else ever quite combined so many attributes. "I could have a nice little house on the Hill," she once commented to a friend who repeatedly asked why she didn't have just that, "but then we'd have to worry about people smashing the windows and breaking in when we're in Boston."

Hazel Bradley was a chambermaid in the Washington Hotel. She was in the lobby when the McCormacks arrived. "Beautiful. She was beautiful. She had coal black hair. He was beautiful too. A stately man. . . . She always greeted you 'honey' or 'dear' and she'd always tell you a joke to make you laugh. She'd always be buying you something. 'Hazel,' she'd say, 'do you want me to send down and get you some ice cream?' You could talk to her," Hazel claimed. "You know some people in her high-up position, you know, they don't want an ordinary maid to talk, but she didn't want you to think you were beneath her. She treated me like I was right alongside her." (The friendship that developed between the chambermaid and the Congressman's wife was to span forty years. When Harriet lay dying in southwest Washington, Hazel Bradley, by then retired, traveled from Falls Church, Virginia, every day to sit by Mrs. McCormack's side.)

Almost from the beginning, John McCormack's presence was felt in the House of Representatives. Former Vice President John Nance Garner dubbed him the "best talker" in the House. Joe Bartlett, the man who bawled out the roll calls in the House of Representatives for twenty years, agreed with Garner. "I remember the way John McCormack and Frank Keefe of Wisconsin would argue. We have no one in the House today who can argue with the spirit they brought to a contest. McCormack, in his youth, was an imposing figure. Tall and strapping, he looked like he would be a tough man in the ring. He was not that heavy, but he was big. He was formidable. They would argue in the center aisle, shaking their fists at one another. Everyone was just waiting, because they figured if those fists ever touched, it would just be all over the well."

But even in anger, "He was always in control of himself," according to John Monahan. "There was a case one night, when another Member violently abused him on the House floor. . . ." Instead of returning the invective, McCormack rose and quietly informed the man, "I will have you know, sir, that you are a former friend of mine and you are the one who has put yourself in that category from which you will never escape."

McCormack did not always confine his acerbic tongue to House debates. An avowed anti-Communist, who told the legendary Speaker of the House Sam Rayburn that he would resign as Majority Leader if Rayburn invited Nikita Khruschev to address a Joint Session of Congress, he once challenged a Russian to a debate about the hereafter. "You're just guessing," he told the Communist. "I'm not guessing. I have over four hundred incidents in the Bible chronicled by eyewitnesses. I have reason. But you, you're just guessing. Suppose you guess wrong? . . . Where the hell do you think you're going to land?" The Communist visibly "whitened," McCormack proudly claimed.

John McCormack became a close friend of Speaker Sam Rayburn. And after only twelve years in the Congress, he was elected Majority Leader, one of the youngest men ever to attain that post. Rayburn remained in possession of the gavel for so long, however, that McCormack never gained hold of the hammer himself until twenty-one years later. He would, however, play a role in relieving a depression and incorporating New Deal legislation. He would advise and consent in three wars, become close to and be consulted by every important leader in the United States in the next forty years, including four Presidents. He revered Franklin Roosevelt, who at the time of his death was wearing a St. Christopher's medal Mrs. McCormack had given him for his birthday, and who frequently found occasion to counsel with McCormack, as he did on a Sunday afternoon in 1941 when he telephoned the Majority Leader in Boston and asked him to return to Washington immediately.

"There's been a dastardly attack," Roosevelt shouted through the receiver, his voice so loud that it reverberated around the McCormack living room. The Japanese had attacked Pearl Harbor. "I need you, John," the President said. The next day Franklin Roosevelt addressed a joint session of Congress and John McCormack offered a resolution declaring war against Japan.

McCormack was offered both the Republican and the Democratic nominations for the United States Senate. He was asked to run for Governor of Massachusetts. And once there was a groundswell movement at the Philadelphia Convention to put him on the Presidential ticket with Harry Truman. He turned aside every chance to leave the Congress for higher positions. "I liked the work of the House," he explains. "My purpose in going into politics was to render public service and when I got to Washington, I found I could render the maximum public service in the House. . . . My friend Sam Rayburn used to say, 'when a man goes to the Senate from the House, he starts puffing up in the Rotunda.' "

"Harriet played a key role in every decision. She wanted to know everything," said her nephew Edward McCormack. John McCormack's method of keeping his wife in touch with his working day was writing notes to himself. "He was a walking file cabinet," according to Edward. "He used to have notes coming out of every pocket. He'd have them in the vest pocket, in the side pocket, in the back pocket, in the inside pocket. Half of those notes he wrote to himself about things to tell Harriet that night."

She amazed her husband's close friend and protege, Congressman Thomas P. "Tip" O'Neill, with her political knowledge. "She would reminisce with you about John McCormack and John McCormack's life like John McCormack would reminisce with you himself. And the reason for that is that she was in on every little intricacy." Harriet could recount the commas and the colons of every political disagreement her husband had ever been engaged in, according to O'Neill. "The feud between the Kennedys and the McCormacks, she knew everything that was taking place—why it happened and why there were arguments. . . . This is Mrs. McCormack telling you about the machinations that take place in the backroom . . . things that the ordinary wife would never know about!"

Sometimes, she knew things that even the ordinary politician, including her husband, didn't know. In 1948, when it looked as if the "little man on the wedding cake," Tom Dewey, was going to ride Harry Truman out of the White House on a landslide, Harriet went to special lengths to see that her husband's poker-playing pal wouldn't have to vacate the Presidential premises. She promised God that if he could arrange Harry Truman's victory she would attend Mass and communion the first Friday of every month for nine consecutive months. John, who was equally anxious for a Truman triumph, was less enthusiastic about Harriet's campaign plan. The only Mass on Friday at St. Patrick's Church was 7:00 A.M. As McCormack was a devotee of the opposite end of the day, the beginning of each month formed the archietecture of an ordeal.

Harriet, having charted her course, never doubted the outcome. All through the seemingly doomed campaign she would predict to anyone who would listen that Harry Truman was going to win. Not many were willing to listen. Least of all her husband. He didn't want her criticized for lack of political acumen. "Now, Harriet," he told her, "don't tell that to anyone."

"I will! I will!" she insisted. "Something's going to happen."

"Now, Harriet, nothing's going to happen."

"Something," Harriet maintained staunchly, "is going to happen."

The night of the election, the John McCormacks and their friends sat out the results in his Boston office. The television and radio stations were calling the Democratic Majority Leader for comment on the demise of President Truman. One of the radio stations was just down the corridor from McCormack's office. As he was walking over to make a statement, Harriet spoke up, "You tell them that President Truman is going to be elected." McCormack restrained his incredulity, "Why my dear, according to the returns, he's a million votes behind."

"Never mind. Something's going to happen. You tell them." So McCormack told them. He didn't believe his wife, but he said, "I wouldn't let Harriet down. I'd rather have all the political columnists ridicule me forever than let Mrs. McCormack down." Instead of being ridiculed, when the final results came in, he was touted as a great seer. For years after the election, people would ask him, "How did you know Truman was going to win? He was a million votes behind when you were on that radio station."

"I didn't know," McCormack would chuckle warmly. "It was Mrs. McCormack's intuition."

Small wonder that HST developed a special affection for Mrs. Mc-Cormack, always referring to her, as he did his own wife, as "the Boss." After his victory, he said to McCormack, "I hear Harriet did some praying for me."

McCormack conceded that she had and then added, "I'll tell you frankly, Mr. President, the next time you have something to pray for, make it three months, not nine."

Harriet's intuitive astuteness made her "a great sounding board" according to her nephew Edward McCormack. "John would come home and say, 'I'm going to do this.' She would say, 'Do you really think that's wise? What would the reaction be here or the reaction be there? Would it be misinterpreted? Are you hurting this group?' She'd ask the penetrating questions that would cause him to rethink, not necessarily reverse the position, but certainly to know what the weak points of the thing were. If he had a speaking engagement, she might not always go, but she'd read the speech beforehand and she would sit in the car while he made it. When he came out, he would tell her everyone he met inside."

Harriet's involvement was in no way "haphazard," according to Edward's brother Jocko. "She believed all along that she was contributing to his career. She used to quote, 'behind every great man, there's a woman.' She is proof of the puddin' of just how strong a woman's role in marriage really is."

It was a sorrow to Harriet and John McCormack that they were never blessed with children. A sorrow and an irony. Both loved children and young people. Harriet was irresistibly maternal. She never failed to ask after the welfare of friends' youngsters. She fought for the chance to have a child's company, and she lavished concern and gifts on all her husband's friends and colleagues. She adored her nephews Edward and Jocko McCormack. When they came to Washington, they were her charges. "Even when I was in my thirties and early forties," Jocko half complained, "I had to stay next door to her. She thought she was lookin' out for me. I couldn't convince her that I'd grown."

Harriet was a man's woman. She preferred masculine company, frequently entertaining several of her husband's male companions in the Washington Hotel suite for dinner. For reasons most people cannot identify, she had few close women friends. Her nephews

speculate that her lack of interest in gossip and society may have
been part of the reason.

"She never liked to hear persons criticized," according to her
husband. "She'd say occasionally to someone, 'Well, let's talk about
all the nice people we know. There's so many of them that we
won't have the opportunity to talk about the other type.' "

"She passed that on to me," he claims, and as a result, "I was like
Rip Van Winkle" when it came to knowing gossip that was bandied
around his office. "She had a brilliant, brilliant mind," according to
Jocko. "Honest to gosh, there'd be five or six men sittin' around the
office and she still dominated that room. She would sit there quietly
and we'd be bangin' somethin' out that we thought was for the good
of the country. She'd say just one word and everything would stop
and every head would turn. She'd offer an opinion. A lot of times
that ended the discussion. That was the final opinion."

Edward McCormack agreed with his brother that his aunt had a
keen intelligence, but he added, "She had great instincts. Sometimes the instincts are more important than the intelligence. She was
good. She had beautiful thoughts. . . . She had inner beauty that
you just don't find. That was the secret of his devotion to her."

But she was not without her eccentricities. Her mode of dress
caused a great deal of comment and wonder in the Nation's capital,
even among Presidential daughters. Luci Johnson Nugent, who fre-
quented the Capitol as a little girl when her father was the Senate
Majority Leader, recalled seeing Mrs. McCormack on the elevator.
"She had a hat and a dress that I remember most vividly. I can
probably recall it better than any garment that I have in my closet
today—A blue dress and a black or navy hat with some netting
around it." The severity of the outfit sometimes made her seem
"foreboding" to young pages working at the Capitol.

"She always dressed very simply," said Jocko. "She had the same
style dress, I think, from the day she came to Washington." For that
reason, the general belief was that she owned very few clothes. In
fact, Harriet McCormack had a closet full of dresses and dozens of
hats, all exactly the same style. At some point in her life, she
developed an affection for high necked, long sleeved dresses and
little bonnets that tilted jauntily to one side of her head. Her millinery
was custom made and she would stride out of the Washington
Hotel, announcing to Hazel Bradley that she was going to purchase
a new hat. And when she returned, Hazel chuckles, "She was wearing the same little hat on her head she had on when she left, only it
might have a few more flowers on it."

Even Cardinal O'Boyle was moved to inquire as to the nature of
her fashion tastes. "This," she informed him, "is the way people in

Boston dress." She was more specific with her friend Jerry Taylor: "I'm an individualist," she proclaimed. "I don't dress for other people. I dress to please myself."

If she was not up to date in the eyes of Washington society, she found no disapproval from her spouse. "A lady," said John McCormack, "who is dressed in a manner showing respect for herself will always be modern."

When Washington wasn't wondering about Mrs. McCormack's outfits, they were speculating as to what she did with her time. She shunned parties, never gave interviews; it was an effort even for Presidents to get her to attend White House state dinners. What only family intimates knew was that she spent a great amount of hours working for charitable causes, although, according to her nephew, Edward, "No one was to know about her works of charity." She would give money or clothes to Jerry Taylor for someone she knew was in need, with the precise instruction that they were not to know where the gifts came from.

"She never wanted people to know," according to her husband, "that she was doing things." And they didn't. While most of official Washington thought she was roombound in her hotel suite, she was visiting the sick and the elderly, sending food baskets to the impoverished in Boston, lobbying for appropriations for new hospital wings, promoting operettas for charity, counseling and helping troubled friends. "She never liked," recalls Jerry Taylor, "to see anybody in want."

Despite her efforts at discretion, her friend Cardinal Cushing "leaked" her good deeds, including efforts in behalf of Chinese refugees, to Pope Pius XII, who awarded her the Pro Pontifice Eclessia medal, the highest honor accorded women in the Catholic Church. Only one other American woman, Rose Kennedy, had received such recognition from Rome.

The McCormacks' affinity for the tillers of the Almighty's vineyard was almost a point of amusement to their friends. John McCormack was not infrequently referred to as the "Archbishop." But the affection for the cloth extended beyond his own church to include all denominations and nondenominations. Billy Graham credits the former Speaker with launching his evangelistic mission in Washington. When Graham began his ministry in 1950, he was just the president of a small mid-western college. McCormack hosted a luncheon for Graham in Washington and later got permission for the budding preacher to speak on the Capitol steps to a crowd of forty-thousand people.

"John McCormack was the first person to introduce me to a President of the United States," Graham recalls. "He asked me if I wanted to meet Harry Truman." The then obscure Reverend Graham was "thrilled" at the prospect of meeting a President. The encounter lasted forty-five minutes, and when it was over, Graham and McCormack walked straight into the waiting pens of the White House press corps. No one had ever briefed the naive clergyman as to what to say to the media and he held nothing back. "I told the press what the President said. I told the press what I said." He went on to relate to the raised eyebrows of the gathering that he had asked the President if they could have a "prayer together," to which Mr. Truman had agreed. "The press asked me if I would mind reenacting that prayer and, like a fool, I knelt right down on the White House lawn."

That unique sight played on the front pages of every newspaper in the country. To Graham's dismay, a column reported that he was *persona non grata* in the Oval Office. As for his benefactor, John McCormack, "He never said a word," says Billy Graham. "He always treated me like it never happened."

Dr. Graham only met Harriet McCormack on a few occasions, "But I heard people talk about their relationship and that it was one of the great love stories of the generation. Especially in the pressures of Washington, where it seems marriages have a very difficult time. There was a very deep, spiritual affinity between them," Graham added, "and that was far more binding than the psychological or the physical."

Certainly it was no longer the physical. Harriet McCormack was eighty-seven years old when she died, and age had worked a cruel toll in her declining years. It had narrowed her vision, and forced her to hide her dark eyes behind glasses. Arthritis, stemming from a leg injury, had slowed her walk to infant steps. Even eating had become a chore, the food having to be soft and in small pieces. Once, at a White House state dinner, John McCormack was observed cutting his wife's meat. But even in her eighty-third year, she had seen John through the longest session in the history of the Congress, thirty-two hours and seventeen minutes, retaining her forty-two year old habit of waiting for him in his Capitol office until he was ready to go home. And still, as Harriet tottered down the hall on John's arm, they "were just like newlyweds," exclaims their chauffeur of twenty years, Roger Brooks, "they seemed like they had just met."

There were more than a few people in the church who were surprised to see President Johnson's youngest daughter attending Harriet McCormack's funeral. Almost no one outside the McCormack and Johnson families had been aware of the close relationship between the two women.

When Luci was a small girl, traveling the elevators back and forth to her father's Capitol Hill office, the Speaker's wife "was a walking legend." According to Luci, it never occurred to her in those days that she would one day share confidences with Mrs. John McCormack.

Luci was thirteen when she moved into the White House. Both of her parents were so occupied that a teenage girl felt guilty about her need for them. She began to look for support elsewhere. "As close as our family has always been . . . there was a lot of division in our household. I went to school half a year in Texas, half a year in Washington. My parents were frequently gone. . . . I think I looked for something that was strong and consistent: these are the rules . . . and if you do thus and such, this will be your strength. . . . Something that stayed . . . that didn't go to Texas to campaign. . . ." Luci quietly began attending Mass regularly. "Once I became close to the Catholic Church, it helped support me and I didn't drain my parents."

The developing closeness to God allowed her to depend on another security. "I liked me better. I liked them better. I was able to love them more honestly . . . and give to them. My love was more of a give-and-take relationship, rather than a gimme, gimme, gimme relationship."

Becoming a Catholic was a radical departure from her upbringing. Nevertheless, the President and the First Lady did not try to still Luci's interest in a religion different from their own. Instead, they asked her to think carefully about her course of action and to wait until she was eighteen. President Johnson was extremely concerned that conversion from one faith to another not be as divisive as his own conversion, at the age of eleven, from the Baptist denomination to the Christian Church. "It broke my grandmother's heart," Luci recalled. Lyndon Johnson, who was extremely fond of "Miss Harriet," as he referred to the Speaker's wife, asked her to counsel his daughter. He had sometimes sought counsel from Mrs. McCormack himself, telephoning her to confide his feelings of "loneliness in command."

"As we gained something very real in common," Luci declared, "I found that her outer appearance melted into a very warm, very real, very loving, very genteel personage. There was something about her exterior and her interior that made no pretenses. She was a character and she had character. She was Harriet McCormack at all times. . . . Sometimes religion is taken so seriously that it becomes very cold and foreboding, 'thou must do this'. Religion was not that way for her. Religion was joyous. And so when she discussed it with you, she discussed it with a sense of humor and it was joyous for everybody."

Harriet told her young friend that she shared the President's view that a religious conversion was not an experience one vaulted into without a great deal of "thought and prayer." Over the years, Mrs. McCormack restrained Luci's youthful impatience, while at the same time providing a willing ear and a source of advice and information on the Catholic Church. As a result, when Luci was baptized after five years of deliberation, both she and her parents were convinced that her desire and her commitment were real. During that same period of spiritual dilemma, Luci was undergoing the happy emotional upheaval of falling in love. She was more than passively interested in the success of the McCormack marriage. Through constant exposure during her childhood to some of the most celebrated personalities and egos of the era, Luci was well aware of the fact that marriages in the Nation's capital faced "a lot of challenge. I saw a lot of them that may not have ended in divorce, because at that time, politics and divorce were awfully difficult to sustain. But the quote 'closed doors' couldn't be closed to people existing in that environment." It amazed her to learn that the McCormacks really *did* eat dinner together every night. "I thought nobody in public life ever ate dinner regularly with anybody. The fact that that marriage made it in the way that it did frankly awed and intrigued me."

So much so, that she finally worked up "the nerve" to ask Harriet McCormack how she and the Speaker were able to live that kind of life. Well, Mrs. McCormack replied, you have to make great sacrifices to attain what you want in life. She and John had decided that they both wanted this portion of their life to be shared, that this was the most important priority. Her work with the Church had been like John's work with the Congress. But we never, the old woman told the young girl, let these loves divide our love for each other and for our God. And that is the mistake a lot of people make. And when you do, that's when the whole thing becomes so confused that you sometimes can't put it back together again.

Luci never forgot that conversation. "In a world of indecision, especially the world of politics, where choosing priorities is so often excruciatingly painful, Mrs. McCormack had made her decision and was consistent about where her priorities stood. It wasn't as if she had no alternatives in terms of personal choice. . . . I think this sustained and flattered the Speaker . . . to have been chosen over a very promising career . . . as her number one priority and to know that no matter who else deserted him or who wouldn't stick with his vote; no matter how inconsistent things might get, his Harriet would always be there."

The funeral party threaded slowly through the worsening snow to St. Joseph's Cemetery in Roxbury. The temperature had dropped to twenty degrees and the wet flakes were crystallizing into a serious storm.

Lyndon Johnson had come from Texas in a private plane. He should have left the church and headed for the airport. Instead, he drove to the cemetery and stood next to John McCormack at the graveside. "He never left McCormack, despite the bitter cold," says John Monahan.

When the ceremony at the cemetery was over, Johnson's obligation to his friend and former colleague was more than completed. It was after three; the sky was growing dark; cars were beginning to drive with their lights on. Only immediate family and very close friends were going back to Edward McCormack's apartment. The former President asked if he and his daughter could come too.

Perhaps thirty people gathered in Edward McCormack's living room, among them his wife Emily, their two sons Edward and John who had been coaxed there by John Monahan when he heard LBJ was coming, Walter Flaherty, Cardinal O'Boyle, John and Jean Monahan, Luci Nugent. Few people there had ever seen Johnson except as a public person. They were astounded by his performance as a private friend. He transported John McCormack from the desolate moment to the lustrous past and he took everyone in the room on the journey. Luci and Edward desperately searched for a tape recorder. "It is the single greatest regret of my life," she said, "that we could not find one."

"He came for a few minutes," says Eddie McCormack, "and he ended up staying for hours. He did not say much about Harriet. It was a great testimonial to Lyndon Johnson the man. He knew the loss to John McCormack, knew the feelings John McCormack would have after the funeral. He spent four hours talking about things other than Harriet McCormack. He told jokes. He told anecdotes. He told things that were of great historical significance, and he brought everyone in the room into the conversation by a story that touched on them." `

"It was Lyndon Johnson à la carte," says John Monahan.

For the administrator of Providence Hospital, he had a tale of his stay there. He had been just a boy, "working the doors" at the Capitol, and he had contracted pneumonia. For hours he lay in a coma in Providence Hospital. When he finally came out of it, he turned over to discover a man with no hair and a dead cigarette dangling between his lips, sitting sound asleep in a chair near the bed. Hearing young Lyndon roll over, the visitor opened his eyes and announced, "I'm Sam Rayburn, and if I had a son who was sick in Texas, your daddy would be there. Your daddy's my friend and I'm here."

"Sam had a heart of gold," said John McCormack.

For all the Democrats present, Johnson had an appreciated thrust at the opposition party. No one told a joke better than Lyndon Johnson, full of accents and gestures and eye-rolling.

"There was this old cowpoke in Texas. He was sick and he went to the Texas Center in Dallas and the doctor told him he had some good news and some bad news. 'The bad news is you have a very bad heart.'

" 'What's the good news?' asked the cowpoke.

" 'Well,' said the doctor, 'we can give you a replacement. You can have the operation now, and it just so happens we have three potential donors. The first is the heart of a twenty-one-year-old beauty queen, a wonderful young girl. The second is the heart of a great male athlete. He won the Olympics. The third is the heart of an eighty-year-old Republican banker.

"So the cowpoke thought it over and he said, 'If it's all the same to you, I'll take the heart of the eighty-year-old Republican banker.' So the operation was performed and it was a success and when it was over and it came time for the cowpoke to leave the Center, he went in to see the surgeon and thanked him profusely. 'Can't imagine what an old cowpoke like me can do for a doctor like you, but you only got to ask.'

" 'Well,' said the doctor, 'you can do one thing for me. You can explain to me why you turned down the warm, compassionate heart of a beauty queen and the heart of a strong, powerful male athlete to take the heart of an eighty-year-old Republican banker?'

"The cowpoke said, 'Well, doc, ah ain't the smartest hombre in the world, but ah allowed as how ah's gonna git another heart, ah's gonna get me one that ain't never been used before.' "

Johnson finished the story slapping his knee and hooting with laughter. "You almost had to kick him in the lungs," says Monahan, "to stop him. Everyone was roaring . . . the nuns . . . the Cardinal . . ." Most importantly, John McCormack. It was exactly what he needed. It was legislative triumphs and near misses, poker games . . . and laughter in the White House. "The years that those men shared together just flashed before everyone's eyes," said Luci Nugent. "It was one of the single most moving experiences of my life."

The hours flew by. Johnson kept talking and smoking. Outside the snow was growing thick on the ground. The former President and his daughter could afford to wait no longer. Johnson took Edward McCormack aside, "Eddie, I've got to go. Now don't let the Speaker come with me. You keep him here, he's dead tired."

Then he turned to John McCormack, "Now John, you've had a very tough and trying day and I'm going to have to go. I can't delay my departure any longer. They tell me that the plane won't be able to fly out if I don't go now. I want you to stay here in the bosom of your family and your friends who mean so much to you." He concluded his little speech by insisting that McCormack not accompany him to the airport.

John McCormack stood up as if he were in the Well of the House of Representatives. Everyone in the room was transfixed. It was no longer "Lyndon" and "John". Suddenly it was Speaker John W. McCormack addressing President Lyndon Baines Johnson.

"I'll have you know, Mr. President, that no President has left the city of Boston in the last forty years without being in my company."

The 36th President of the United States looked long at the 45th Speaker of the House of Representatives, "In that case," said Lyndon Johnson "I will be honored to have your company, Mr. Speaker."

John was, after all, only doing what Harriet would have expected.

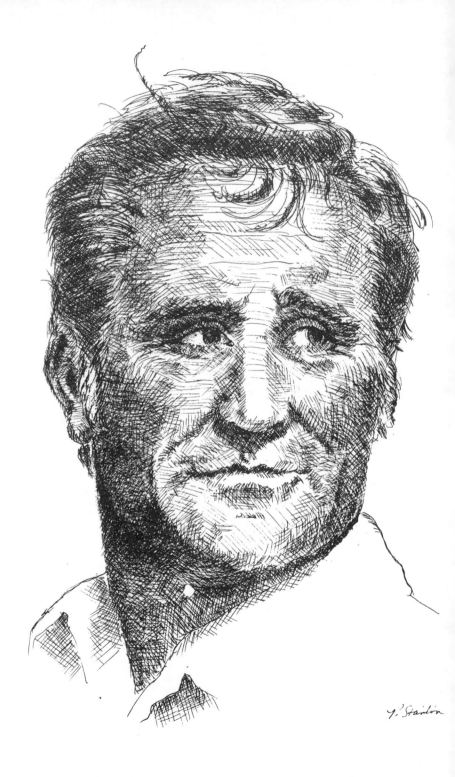

# 3 | DON SHULA

They stood on the balcony of their motel room in Long Beach, California, watching the roll of the Pacific Ocean. "Well," he said, his large muscular hand slipping down to cover hers, "here we go again."

"Yes," she smiled up at her slope-nosed, chisel-chinned husband, "but this time we know the outcome."

They had come a long way, this team within a team—Dorothy Bartish and Donald Shula of Painesville and Grand River, Ohio. But not far enough. They wanted one more thing—the World Football Championship. Twice before they had been to a Super Bowl. Twice they had left as losers.

"Loser." It was the term Don Shula had spent a lifetime avoiding. Most of the time he had succeeded. He was the first coach to win a hundred-plus games in ten years. He was the first coach to command a professional football team through an undefeated season. But if his Miami Dolphins bowed to the Washington Redskins in the Los Angeles coliseum tomorrow, he would be the first coach to lose three Super Bowls. And that would be the first that would live on.

The memories of the two Super Bowl defeats were permanently, agonizingly, and vividly filed in Don and Dorothy Shula's memory bank. And now, the night before their third try, those files of failure kept springing unbidden out of the drawer. The most painful folder was labeled Super Bowl III. . . .

The year was 1968, and Don Shula was the coach of the Baltimore Colts. He had been guiding the Colts for seven seasons and, at the age of forty-one, was considered one of the game's most successful practitioners. Under his leadership the Colts had compiled a record of seventy-one victories, twenty-three losses, and four ties. Three times in seven seasons he had been named Coach of the Year. The natural conclusion of the sporting world was that this young football genius would have an easy time adorning his finger with the Super Bowl ring.

But Dorothy Shula was not so confident. Her antennae had been picking up bad vibrations about Super Bowl III right from the beginning. She could remember expressing her uneasiness to Colts owner

Carroll Rosenbloom as he excitedly described the lavish party he had planned.

"Carroll," she had said, "did it ever occur to you that there is a loser in every game and we could be it?"

"Of course," Rosenbloom had answered off-handedly, "I shouldn't expect that it couldn't happen." But in fact that was exactly what Rosenbloom expected. His powerful, prestigious squad of veterans would surely make lasagna out of the New York Jets, a team barely out of diapers. The sportswriters had anointed the Colts seventeen point favorites. No one, it seemed, had sufficiently reckoned with the flamboyant on-and-off-the-field talents of the Jets' quarterback— When Joe Namath wasn't honing his golden arm, he was unleashing a lethal tongue. His team was certain to win, he predicted; some of the Colts wouldn't be playing that well. And he named names.

Baltimore fans anxiously awaited the silencing of the shaggy-headed Broadway Joe. The night before Super Bowl III, at the annual Touchdown Club dinner in Washington, D.C., Don Shula was again named Coach of the Year. A close friend, accepting the award for Shula, told the audience, "He's in Miami, as you know, preparing to give Joe Namath a haircut."

But the following day it was Don Shula who got trimmed. The upstart New York Jets toppled the mighty Baltimore Colts sixteen to seven. When it was all over, Dorothy Shula, who had watched her husband's humiliation surrounded by her five children, a sprinkling of Kennedys, singer Robert Goulet, and the Vice President of the United States, rushed for the locker room. Win or lose, she had never left a stadium without seeing Don first.

Police dogs were being used to keep the crowds at bay. Dorothy saw Carroll Rosenbloom emerge from the locker door with his eyes fixed on his shoetops. When Don came out, he was immediately engulfed by reporters eager to hear an explanation of his embarrassment.

"Let me through," Dorothy pleaded, "I'm his wife." When she finally reached the coach, she put her arms around him. "I'm sorry," she whispered. She was offering as much empathy as sympathy; she liked to win almost as much as he did.

But the bad news was only to grow worse. The Shulas had scarcely entered their hotel room when they heard shrill screams filling the corridor outside. The cries came from the wife of Colts player Rick Volk. Volk, who had been hit in the head twice during the game, was having convulsions. The coach and the team doctor rushed to Volk's room. Shula stared at his stricken safety, who was turning blue and losing consciousness. Shula held Volk down in the bathtub while the doctor prevented the player from swallowing his tongue. Outside in the hallway Charlene Volk, who was pregnant, was standing in a corner, raising and lowering herself on the wall in rhythmic panic. Dorothy Shula was afraid she would pass out.

"Charlene, remember this. If you want to get into the ambulance and go with your husband, they'll let you go, but only if you can control yourself. If you cannot, you're not going to be able to stay with him. Make up your mind right now to come out of this and handle yourself, no matter how hard it is, because you can help, or you can just stand there and be emotional. God knows you have a right to be emotional. But you have got to be able to handle this!"

The shock treatment was effective. Charlene Volk gained command of her terror and rode in the ambulance with her husband to the hospital in North Miami. The Shulas followed by car. In Golden Beach, Carroll Rosenbloom was holding his "victory" party. Don and Dorothy Shula were two of the most important guests. But the Super Bowl had fled their consciousness. "Defeat was out of our minds completely," Dorothy recalls, "no one even talked about it." For several hours Rick Volk's life hung in the balance. This is the worst night of my life, Shula thought to himself. But, around ten o'clock in the evening, the doctors finally assured the coach that his player would recover, and the Shulas knew their next obligation was an appearance at the Rosenbloom party. Walking on the beach behind his home, Carroll seemed philosophically resigned to the Super Bowl loss: "Remember," he told the Shulas, "out of every bad situation something good comes."

But the next morning and many mornings after, philosophy had to face the sports section, which to Rosenbloom and Shula read like the obituary page. Don Shula returned to Baltimore the first National Football League coach to surrender a Super Bowl to the "upstart" American Football League. "Did you throw the game?" one fan wired, "Or were you just not coaching?"

The harrassment was equally hard on Rosenbloom, and Don Shula could feel the temperature dropping in their relationship. So when one season later the owner of the Miami Dolphins, Joe Robbie, came after him proposing a lucrative salary and part ownership of the Dolphin team, it seemed like a financial and psychological offer Shula couldn't refuse.

The change marked a new beginning not only for Don Shula but for the Miami Dolphins as well. Only four years old, the team had scored just three victories out of fourteen games the previous season. In one year, with Shula at the helm, the statistics reversed dramatically and the Dolphins claimed ten wins out of fourteen games. The following season, to the amazement of football fans, they were participants in Super Bowl VI, and Shula was proclaimed a miracle worker. But expectations that Shula's squad could carry home the World Championship were slim. This time Shula's charges were the neophytes and the opponents were the veterans. The young team was subjected to considerable scoffing and incredulity from the sportswriters. How did this crowd that nobody ever heard of manage to get to the World Championship? These "no-names," as they were christened, didn't belong in the same stadium with the powerful Dallas Cowboys.

Nothing undergone in the regular football season had prepared the uninitiated Dolphins for the rigors of the Super Bowl rites. The opposing squads were required to arrive in New Orleans one week before kick-off, so the players could be scrutinized by reporters, photographers, and fans for seven days. Celebrities from every profession—astronauts, golf champions, boxers, movie and television stars, not to mention present and former pigskin heroes—poured into town for an endless round of pregame festivities. From Texas, on trains, planes, and campers, came the white-ten-gallon-hatted Cowboy fans, who playfully jeered at the orange-bonneted, turquoise-shirted Miami loyalists.

Customers lined up for blocks to dine at New Orleans's most famous restaurants, Antoine's and Brennan's. Jazz bands snake-danced through the downtown at all hours of the day and night. Every state in the union seemed to be represented on Bourbon Street. And in the middle of hotel lobbies stood middle America, pencils poised, anxiously awaiting the appearance of Someone. At the Super Bowl, Someones are recognized by size rather than by face. Anyone over six foot two, with a deep chest and broad shoulders, was likely to be assaulted for an autograph.

To Don Shula and his rival Tom Landry fell the task of trying to keep their players' minds on the game. Landry's job was easier; the Dallas Cowboys had tried and failed to gain the World Championship the previous year. Having once tasted defeat, the Cowboys were far hungrier for victory than hoorah and hoopla. They wisely housed themselves in a motel near the airport, far away from the distractions. The Dolphins, on the other hand were ensconced uncomfortably close to New Orleans' downtown area, like guests at a banquet forbidden to partake of the feast.

The pressure was too much. In Miami, the Dolphins had performed to perfection during practice sessions. Once in New Orleans, Shula could see his players tightening up and was frustrated by his inability to unleash their tension. When the game was over, the press was reaffirmed in their belief that the contest had been a woeful mismatch. Dallas dealt Miami a merciless flogging.

Once again, Shula had to face a mob of reporters and cameras. Once again, he had to explain his failure to "win the big one." Once again, he had to slink into a "victory" celebration. A victory party without victory is like a wake done in rococo. There are flowers. There is drink. There is music. There is abundant food. There are finely-gowned ladies and brightly-blazored men. There is everything but joy. Nobody knows what to say, least of all the defeated coach. But the silent crowd of noncelebrants had only to study Shula's anguished face to know what he was thinking. He was not just disappointed at being vanquished. He was crushed by the force of the annihilation: twenty-four to three. He blamed himself for the team's pallid performance. He had failed to properly prepare the players emotionally. He had gotten them charged up too early and they had left their high voltage in Miami, bringing only their nerves to New Orleans.

Shouldering the guilt only increased the pain. Reflecting on the two Super Bowl defeats, Shula recalls many hours of "searching for inner strength. . . . you can put on a show of being calm, cool and collected, but deep down, you have your own doubts. *Can* you win the big ones? Is it possible? Or am I always going to be the guy who's led up to the altar and let go? What I made myself do after those frustrating losses was get off alone, make a visit, light a candle, and ask God for help. . . .

"The thing that I didn't want to develop was the 'why me?' syndrome—the self-pity, the thinking that God has aimed something directly at you. Because of my faith, I was able to get by that and just charge ahead to believe in what I was doing and hope the next time I would be the one who would end up the winner." Since his rookie playing days with the Cleveland Browns, Shula had made a habit of daily Mass: "I had all this pressure on me then, and I'm a conscientious guy. When I set out to do something, I work hard not to fail, and I try to solicit help from the Man Upstairs."

After the Super Bowl VI disappointment, Shula emerged from his talks with the Man Upstairs with renewed determination. He would return to the Super Bowl with his Miami Dolphins, this time to win. File this experience, he told his dejected players; lessons learned in Super Bowl VI would be valuable for Super Bowl VII. The following July in training camp, Don Shula was as keyed up as Secretariat at post time. He laid down three goals for his team: Get into the play-offs. Win the American Football Conference Championship. Win the World Championship.

The last target was the most important, he insisted. If the Dolphins failed to achieve the third goal, the first two might just as well not have been accomplished. "Two teams go to the Super Bowl," he said, "but only one team leaves—the winner."

And as the season unfolded, Shula watched his team achieve what no other professional football squad had ever accomplished—

a perfect record of sixteen wins, no losses. But as they plowed through game after undefeated game, the Dolphins had only one goal before them, the seventeenth contest—Super Bowl VII.

This time they faced the Washington Redskins, who had whipped the Dallas Cowboys out of contention in the final play-off game two weeks earlier. Despite their sixteen-zero season, the Miami Dolphins were again the underdogs. It stood only to reason, according to sports gurus, that a team who had trounced the World Champions would have no trouble polishing off a squad the Cowboys had decisively licked in last year's Super Bowl. Then of course there was Don Shula's unfortunate habit of clutching in "the big ones," a fact that his former boss Carroll Rosenbloom was fondly recalling on the sports pages. "I'll believe it when I see it," Rosenbloom remarked about the possibility of a Shula Super Bowl win. The remarks angered Shula, but according to Dolphins' safety Tim Foley, the coach never revealed his frustrations or his anxiety. "Nobody picked that up," Foley recounted, "Coach Shula was handling himself so well. Like it was just another game. And you see, players feel that. I mean if he had been walking around with his hand around his throat. . . . they might start to think 'uh oh,' he really doesn't think we can do it."

All week, says Foley, Shula projected a casual, confident, amused air at his daily press conferences. He was calm and patient when continually second-guessed about his decision to start the game with quarterback Bob Griese instead of Earl Morrall. Griese, the Dolphins' number-one quarterback, had been inactive most of the season due to injury. Morrall had taken over the team leadership and guided the Dolphins through most of their perfect season. It seemed, on the surface, only fair and wise to let him clinch the final victory. "Earl had played well," Shula conceded to the doubters, "but he started to slip." In a game with the Pittsburgh Steelers, the coach had turned to Griese "and he helped us win it. It looked like he was completely healthy and he was our number one and there was a big age difference, so I went back to doing it the way I had planned all along."

Still, it was anything but easy to tell a man who had quarterbacked a team to eleven consecutive victories that he was not the fellow who would captain the biggest game of all. It is even tougher when the player is a person for whom the coach has genuine affection. Shula knew the decision would hurt Morrall and it did. "It was a setback," Morall admitted, "you know, you had come so far and now it's turned over to somebody else. During the practice, . . . you just don't have the same feelings you did when you were playing all those weeks before when you knew you were going to be in there. . . . The best thing that Don did was to hit it head on. He didn't let everyone wonder all week who the quarterback would be, so people would choose up sides."

Softening a blow is not one of Shula's gifts or desires. "I'm about as subtle as a punch in the mouth," he concedes. Coaching is full of unpleasant choices and only one man can make them. "This is where credibility is important. You sit down and look the guy in the eye and say, 'This is what I think. You may not agree with it. But this is the way I feel and this is why I'm doing it. I know it's tough to swallow, but I just want you to try and understand what I'm thinking and what my purpose is.'"

All of these reflections flashed continually before Shula's sleepless eyes as he tossed and turned his way toward the dawn of Super Bowl VII. His mind seemed powerless to shut off the instant playbacks of his past defeats in Super Bowl III and Super Bowl VI. If he lost this third Super Bowl he felt sure the sports world would try to "bury" him. Sixteen straight victories would be forgotten because of one loss. Fears and prayers mingled freely in his anxious mind. "It was the most pressure I've ever felt," he later acknowledged.

The morning glowed with warm temperatures and clear skies. Before he turned them loose in the Coliseum, Don Shula gathered the Dolphins around him for a "chance to bring the Lord into their lives." He led them in the Our Father and then gave them a few moments of private supplication. The Coach followed the prayer with his pregame talk, outlining the first series of plays as carefully as a director cuing actors for their positions on stage. Shula is a detail man, not an orator. He does not tell his team to go out and "win one for the Gipper." He tries to prepare them for every eventuality they will encounter on the field. But even he could not have foreseen the bizarre conclusion to Super Bowl VII.

From the start of the game, it was obvious that Shula's decision "to go with Griese" had been a wise one. The first Dolphin touchdown was accomplished easily when the quarterback surprised the Redskins with a perfect spiral to Howard Twilley, who carried the pass into the end zone. Then the frustrations began. Another Griese pass earned a large yardage gain only to be nixed because the Dolphins had linemen downfield. Miami fans went wild when Griese sailed a touchdown pass through the air into the waiting arms of receiver Paul Warfield. They went even wilder when the referee announced the touchdown was no good because another Dolphin receiver was offside.

And so, although the Miami Dolphins were playing nearly flawless football, penalties were holding a score that might easily have been a safe twenty-eight to zero to the uncomfortable margin of fourteen–zero. Each setback was heartstopping for the Dolphins.

Football, like every sport, is as subject to the whims of luck as it is based on practice and skill. Never was this more apparent than the startling sequence that took place in the last two minutes of the game. Though the score was still fourteen to zero in Miami's favor, Shula, well aware that touchdowns can be made in the final phase of the game, sought to widen the point spread by attempting a field goal.

The strategy was thwarted by the Redskins, who succeeded in blocking the kick. They failed, however, to grab the ball, which fortuitously bounced towards the Dolphins and was recovered by kicker Garo Yepremian. Just as Shula was lifting a grateful gaze to the Almighty, his eyes were diverted by the incredible sight of the kicker attempting to become the quarterback. The crowd was on its feet in disbelief when Yepremian, instead of falling down on the ball to protect it, raised his arm to throw a pass. Shula was close to cardiac arrest as he watched the football slip from Yepremian's fingers into the eager hands of a Redskin who lovingly trotted the little orphan into the end zone.

There are more than a few times in football history when such a break has changed the outcome of the game, even with only seconds left to play. But on January 14, 1973, the Redskins failed to follow up their opportunities. And Don Shula, his third time in the Super Bowl, at last had it all. Never again could anyone say he "couldn't win the big ones." There was no way, Shula later wrote in his book *The Winning Edge,* that he could accurately describe his elation. "I just felt relieved of a lot of pressure, like a steam pipe bellowing smoke into the sky."

Before the champagne corks flew in the dressing room, Shula told his euphoric squad they had some "business to attend to," and each player bowed his head in silent thanksgiving.

Shula was, he said, grateful for something besides victory. "I took a great deal of pride in the fact that we were the least penalized team in professional football. That meant we accomplished within the system. I've always tried to do things within that framework and not look for the cheap, easy way to succeed."

That night at the huge celebration in the Century Plaza hotel, as the Miami coach listened to himself being lauded by a galaxy of sports figures including the widow of Vince Lombardi, his mind was already setting new goals. Turning quietly to a long time friend, he wondered how he could best "use" his success.

Later he explained the question. "I was all of a sudden placed in a position of recognition. I was looked up to. And I knew the influence that professional football has on the family. . . . I wanted to take great pains to live my life in a way that, hopefully, would set an example for anyone who was looking for one."

He has only to read his mail to know that the national preoccupation, which is televised pro football, has made heroes of its principal participants. "He gets an awful lot of letters," says his personal secretary Lynn Brandom, "from people of all ages asking for advice on how to live their lives and how to attain the goals that he has. And he takes the time to respond to these people."

But he is no saint, he is fond of reminding admirers. Sometimes he proves it when he least expects, as he did on national television during a heated game with the Los Angeles Rams. Unhappy with the referee's call, Shula enunciated his displeasure with several whacks at the First Commandment. Unbeknownst to the coach, an open microphone was carrying his blasphemy into millions of American living rooms.

According to Shula's secretary, the reaction was numerous, instantaneous, and vociferous. The coach's fans, in no uncertain terms, made it clear that their idol had let them down. "I have never," declared a lady from Merritt Island, Florida, "written a letter with so much sadness before. . . . You see, I was always under the impression that you were a Christian (possibly a misunderstanding) and during yesterday's game the announcer mentioned that those choice words came from none other than Don Shula. . . . I pray God will bless you and not return to you the disrespect he received and doesn't deserve." Some of the rebukes were issued in language far stronger than the phrases being protested. Most were unsigned.

But to those irate pen pals who did initial their distress, Shula wrote his regret without excuses. "Thank you for taking the time to write," ran a typical response, "Please accept my apologies for the remarks; I value your respect and will do my best not to let it happen again."

Recalling the incident, Shula admitted, "I felt bad about it. But it did happen. . . . It just pinpoints the fact," he chuckles ruefully, "that I'm earthy." That does not, however, negate the fact that "I do have strong beliefs and I do take pride in trying to do what's right. But I'm a long way from the guy who wears religion on his sleeve or the guy who's done everything right all his life. I've lived the other way and gone through almost every experience. And I still have moments I'm not very proud of. But that doesn't distract or keep me from trying to live my life the way I believe that it should be lived."

He grew up, he says, "around some pretty rough guys" and he didn't "miss much." Painesville, Ohio, was a working man's town, population 16,000. Shula was born two miles from Painesville, in Grand River, once a fishing community with fewer residents than Plains, Georgia.

Whatever "roughness" Shula encountered outside the home, his principles were buttressed by the bedrock morality of Mary and Dan Shula. Dan was a Hungarian immigrant who left his fifteen-dollar-a-week nursery foreman job to become a Lake Erie fisherman when the birth of triplets unexpectedly doubled the number of his progeny. A small man, he spoke little, but his children learned that his few well-chosen words were not to be disregarded. Mary Shula's round face and ready laugh masked an iron determination and rigid discipline. "My dad and mom," says Shula, "were God-fearing, churchgoing. I had a tremendous religious background. There wasn't anything false about it. I really believed."

"We always made sure," Mary Shula declares, "that they said their morning and evening prayers, said grace before meals, and never missed Mass on Sundays." There were also some restrictions that chafed—home when the street lights go on, no playing in the living room (an order that so aggravated Don Shula that he now allows his own children to frolic freely all over his own house).

Still, he seldom disobeyed, according to his mother. "He was always willing to do anything that he was asked to do. He must have been in the seventh or eighth grade when the triplets came along. And I used to say to him, 'You take care of those kids at recess time. See that they don't get hurt.'" The admonition took, according to St. Mary's pastor, Monsignor William Galena, who reported to Mary Shula that he observed "Donald on the playground wiping the nose of one triplet and tying the shoes of another."

On one memorable occasion, however, Don disregarded a maternal decree, a decision with which she now concurs. After a bloodied nose, Mrs. Shula ordered young Don to give up football, refusing to sign a school permission slip. "You know what he did?" she laughs, "he signed it himself."

In the summers, Mrs. Shula recalls, her son "used to caddy for the golfers on Lake Shore boulevard. He'd even carry two bags, one on each shoulder, so he could get more money." Mrs. Shula carefully squirreled away his earnings, and when Don expressed a desire to own a car, she surprised him with enough of his own money to make the purchase. Much later, he repaid Mary Shula's frugal concern for his funds. While playing football for the Baltimore Colts, he worked in the off season as a car salesman for a Painesville Lincoln-Mercury dealer. One year he saved all his salary to buy Mary Shula a black two-door Lincoln.

It was while standing in the display window of the Lincoln-Mercury dealership that he caught the eye of a lively, dark-haired, hazel-eyed Painesville schoolteacher named Dorothy Bartish. When customer traffic was light, Shula and his boss—also a handsome bachelor—spent their time appraising the passing parade of Painesville pulchritude.

Twenty-two-year-old Dorothy Bartish hadn't been in love since she was fourteen, but it only took one date with Don Shula for her to realize that Cupid had revisited with a large arrow. "I had some pretty solid objectives set for the man I'd marry. . . . There was never really anyone that was the right one because I didn't respect men. Their morals and my morals weren't the same. But with Don it was a little bit different. . . . God and what comes from God was part of our relationship from the very beginning."

One Saturday night, Shula shocked Dorothy's Irish grandmother by showing up for a date wearing a hat. "What does he have a hat on for?" she asked Dorothy. "Are you going to a wedding?" "No," Dorothy answered, "We're going to confession together before we go out this evening." The news so surprised Mrs. Hammond she could only stammer, "Oh." It wasn't "the normal thing to do," Dorothy chuckles. Particularly since couples sometimes felt more need for confession after a date than before.

Shula was strongly attracted to the young teacher's nonstop personality, which he admitted helped to coax him out of his shyness. On their first date she had him dancing, the only exercise he had previously avoided. He liked the way this totally unself-conscious, candid girl encouraged him to new ventures, but he was a long way from marriage vows. At John Carroll college he had so admired one of the Jesuits that he now claims he thought of entering the priesthood. This revelation is received with some skepticism by a former classmate, Roy Kropac: "The closest Don would ever come to being a priest would be coaching at Notre Dame." Shula, had a healthy appreciation of feminine company, Kropac recalls.

So does his mother, who offered ready opinions on the many girls brought home for inspection. One young lady she refers to as the "Baltimore woman." She seemed "like one of those kind of girls that could go up on a stage," Mrs. Shula sniffs. "When she went upstairs to get ready, it took her hours. I said to Don the next day, 'she sure spent a long time up there. She'd drive you out of your mind if you ever had to wait for her.' "

That was the end of the "Baltimore woman."

Speed at the mirror was not the only Shula requirement. Flexibility was also clearly indicated. One female companion who had come to watch Don play for the Cleveland Browns spent the remainder of the date in the dentist's office while her hero had his broken teeth repaired.

Sensing after a year of dating that home and hearth were not on the immediate Shula horizon, Dorothy Bartish departed Painesville for a teaching job in Hawaii. While she was gone, Shula's career with the Baltimore Colts ended. After one season with the Washington Redskins, he joined the coaching staff at the University of

Virginia. The move convinced him that his life's work lay in the teaching end of football. And more and more his thoughts turned to Hawaii, absence having fueled his ardor. When word came that Dorothy was seriously dating another man, Shula quickly dispatched a note reminding her that Easter was approaching, urging that she make no hasty moves during Paschal season.

Another letter followed soon after that entreaty. Page one was a recitation of the latest football happenings. Page two, second paragraph, contained a proposal.

It was a mail-order marriage, with Don making all the wedding arrangements and offering to pay for some of the expenses. With the same concern for detail so evident in his game planning, he picked out the wedding date, reserved the room for the reception, worried over alternate menus, worked on the guest list and researched the ring. ("Are you sure you want the marquis cut? The jeweler seems to think we could get more ring for the money in one of the other cuts.") When he was not organizing, he was analyzing. He investigated his bride-to-be as thoroughly as if he were recruiting a rookie for the University of Virginia football squad, making a special trip to visit her grandmother and father for an in-depth critique. "They've told me a lot about you," he wrote Dorothy, "so now I think I'll be able to handle you pretty well."

The intense appraisal continued on the honeymoon in Wildwood, New Jersey. One day, as they were walking down the beach, the groom turned to the bride and requested, "Let's see how fast you can run backwards."

"What?" Dorothy gasped.

"Run backwards. Let's see how fast you can run backwards. Here I'll show you."

It was obvious to Dorothy that her new husband was dead serious, so she began chugging to the rear. "Hmmm," said the coach, "not bad. Maybe. . . ."

"What do you mean, 'maybe'?", Dorothy demanded. "What did you have me do that for?"

"Well," he answered, "in football you have to do a lot of back-pedaling. I just wanted to see what your moves were like so I'd have an idea how our children will be as football players."

It has been like that ever since. "We talk football all the time," Dorothy Shula asserts, "in season and out of season." She is his best friend. She inhales and exhales every run with the same intensity as her husband. Sometimes she has to control her nerves with a tranquilizer during a crucial game. And when she thinks Don Shula is unjustly criticized, she does not hesitate to rush in where muscle men fear to tread.

"One time in Baltimore," she recalls, "Don was rightfully mad at an official for miscalling a play that cost us the game. Don backed up the player and said it was a bad call. This is a no-no in the NFL." The result was a reprimand with a three-hundred-fifty-dollar price tag from Commissioner Pete Rozelle. As chancellor of the Shula exchequer, it was Dorothy's job to pay the fine. She refused. "Why should you be fined when you were right?" she stormed to Don. Skip the self-righteousness and send the money, Shula ordered. She ignored him. "Notices kept coming that we were in arrears and Don kept telling me to send the check or we would have to pay more." Finally she agreed, but not without throwing a few of her own flags on the play. "Enclosed is the check for my husband's fine," she wrote Rozelle, "However I do not believe we should be paying this. It was, after all, a first offense. Secondly, three hundred fifty dollars is a lot of money. Thirdly, the referee was wrong, not Don." Fourteen newspapers, she added, backed up her analysis. She concluded her arguments, with the assertion that Don Shula couldn't help but act the way he did: "He is incapable of not defending the truth."

Shortly thereafter, this response arrived from Commissioner Rozelle: "Dear Dorothy, Taking into consideration all that you have said, I am making a small refund." Enclosed was a check for one hundred fifty dollars.

Don Shula's sense of concentration is total, according to Dorothy. "He can crowd out someone screaming in his ear. One time I had to turn off the television set and throw my shoe to get his attention."

But it's not all helmets and cleated shoes. "Tender moments are tender moments to Don. He's a very romantic, loving husband. He's a very private person about it. That's why someone on the outside might not see this side of him. He has a niece named Judy; I told her that Uncle Don was a real romantic and she giggled and said, "Uncle Don romantic? I can't picture Uncle Don romantic!"

Indeed, most football fans familiar with the jutting jaw, the mouth that roars, and the determined scowl striding up and down their television screens would greet Dorothy Shula's description with the same askance as niece Judy. There is, however, a decidedly gentle side to the coach, capable of easy banter and self-criticism. It is most apparent in a personal conversation with good friends. Relaxing over dinner or chatting in his Miami Lakes living room, the strong chin recedes in prominence, overshadowed by a youthful face and an almost acolyte innocence in his blue eyes. The softer side of Shula is especially apparent when he speaks candidly about his own vulnerability.

"I'm a very sensitive, high-strung person," he admits, "I hate to be criticized. I hate to have anything negative said about me. I'm conscious of everything said or written. If it's uncomplimentary, I get upset about it, worry about it, think about it. Maybe too much.

If anything, I'm too sensitive, too high-strung. But I don't know how bad that is. If you didn't worry. . . . then you might not have the commitments you have."

It is this sensitivity that leaves him open to being wounded by his players, as he was when three of his stars—Paul Warfield, Larry Csonka, and Jim Kiick—left his fold for the more lucrative World Football League. According to Dorothy Shula, the departure of Larry Csonka was almost as painful to her husband as the loss of a son. "We stayed up," she recalls, "and we both cried that night. . . . I think Larry Csonka and my husband had a very special relationship. They had a great bond. They would make any sacrifice to win. . . . It was not a case of 'oh boy, these guys are leaving and my empire is falling.' It was a case of personal hurt worse than anything I can think of that's ever happened to Don."

Shula admits that he had thought of his team as his 'family'. He was, he says, "going through this fantasy of everybody being a part of a whole. . . . the beautiful feeling of everybody pulling together. . . . the fans feeling they're a part of it. . . . enjoying the accomplishments as much as the players. All of a sudden, there's a stark realization that loyalty isn't a two-way street. . . . It's a business and people are in it for a living. It's human nature to get whatever you can. These players are in the marketplace. It's supply and demand. And they're in demand. They negotiate to the best of their ability. . . . I was hurt more than anything that they didn't come back and give us the courtesy of sitting down and discussing it. I felt that enough of a relationship had been established that they owed us that courtesy."

Ironically, according to former Dolphins quarterback Earl Morrall, it was the closeness of that relationship that prevented Larry Csonka from extending "the courtesy" Shula expected. "He had so much love and respect for Coach Shula," says Morrall, "he knew that if he sat down and talked with him, Shula would talk him out of [leaving]."

Morrall, who can remember the days when football salaries were only a quarter of the sums players make today, analyzes the seeming greed for astronomical salaries. "You're looking for security. You're looking for the rest of your life because you know that it's short term. How much do you sacrifice for loyalty? It's a difficult thing to answer."

Though Shula earns a handsome salary now, career insecurity is as integral to coaching as it is to playing. A losing coach is soon an ousted coach. But grabbing all you can get is not part of Don Shula's philosophy, according to his lawyers. Dorothy Shula agrees. "When Don's salary came up in this last contract, we had very good advice from accountants and attorneys that Don could have gotten more than he did." But Shula refused to take the advice. When his wife quizzed him as to the reason he did not press Dolphins owner Joe Robbie for the ultimate, the coach replied, "Why should I? I'm not out to break a man's back. We can live on this."

Neither Larry Csonka, who wound up with the New York Giants when the World Football League collapsed, nor Jim Kiick, who joined the Denver Broncos only to be cut later, have to date exhibited the playing splendor of their Dolphin glory days when they were known as 'Butch Cassidy and the Sundance Kid'. It will "never be the way it was," Kiick conceded to a reporter, "There will never be another 17 and 0. It's something that I will always have. It gets better as I grow older. Guys from Denver, guys from Oakland ask me how it happened, how the Dolphins did it!"

How Don Shula took the losing Miami Dolphins and turned them into undefeated World Champions in three years has already become part of football legend. His techniques have been studied on every major sports page, in books, in films. He has been a *Time* magazine cover story. There is no magic formula, he has told anyone who will listen. Just hard work. Anyone who has the wisdom to surround himself with a superior coaching staff, is ready to put in eighteen-hour days, study game films hour after hour appraising talent, organize team schedules and practices down to the second, cover every player's move in detail, make any physical and mental sacrifice to win can accomplish the same results.

But football is not just a game of passing and running, offense and defense, scoreboards and strategy. It is first and foremost a game of men and teamwork—human beings trying in the most intimate of circumstances to understand, to relate, to work with and for one another. It is the success or failure of that effort that ultimately separates the winners from the losers.

"See, I play for the guy," explains safety Tim Foley, "because I like him. I think he's a fine fella. I think he's as consistent as a man can be in his position. He's honest and he's open. There's nothing that goes on with this football team that we don't know about, that he doesn't announce to us. There's nothing undercover. Nothing goes on behind anybody's back. He just tells us all there is to know."

One of the things that Don Shula wants his players to know is that he is adamantly opposed to maiming a star opponent in order to eliminate him from a game. Football, he is frank to admit, "is a violent sport, but the violence in professional football comes from bodies running full speed in one direction meeting bodies coming full speed in the other direction. It's clean and it's tough. It's hard-fought and to me, it's part of the American way of life, the struggle to succeed." However, he emphasizes that there is no place in football for "unnecessary violence," as when a defensive back strikes a pass receiver across the head. Shula is concerned that more and more such "cheap shots are creeping into the sport. . . . Some of the coaches are teaching it as a method of intimidating the opponent." As a member of the Competition Committee of the NFL, Shula worked on methods to prevent the further encroachment of calculated injuries. As a result of the committee's recommendations, the NFL membership in 1978 passed a new rule providing a seventh official, whose chief chore during the game will be screening out unnecessarily rough play.

The fact that Don Shula is concerned about the well-being of his players is part of his coaching success, according to Tim Foley. "If a guy's going to go to war for you, put his body on the line—and that's a very real thing for us—a player has to feel that the coach cares about him as more than just a left cornerback or a number 57. If the player doesn't feel that the coach cares about him as a person, there is, I think, a percentage of that player that the coach isn't going to reach."

"He treats everybody equally," states Earl Morrall, citing an example of a star player who balked at attending a Boy Scout banquet. Shula, who is an active participant in the community and urges his players to be the same, had made attendance at the dinner a mandatory team function. "The fans," he pointed out, "come to support us. They're behind us. We owe it to them to show up." The admonition took with all but one member of the squad. At the next team meeting, Shula informed the players that their absent comrade would be fined five hundred dollars. Because Shula refused to let one player make his own rules and because he discussed the problem in front of the entire Miami squad, "the team," explains Morrall, "backed Coach Shula."

The player, despite his talent, ultimately had to be traded because of his recurring attacks of rebellion. Such failures in human relationships bother Don Shula. "If I am dealing with forty-three players and I know forty-two of them are gung-ho and the forty-third is questioning or doubting—not really behind me one hundred percent, I worry about him more than I do the forty-two who are going out and doing battle. There are forty-three different personalities that make up a football team, and as a coach you've got to get inside each and every one of them and find out what makes them tick, what motivates them. If I feel a player is too tense, I'll try to loosen him up. If I feel somebody is too loose, I'll chew him out."

Thanks to what his mother refers to as his "hair-trigger temper," Shula is better known for the "chewing out" than the "loosening up." Tim Foley thinks the Shula bark is merely an effective tool. "I think people don't give him as much credit as they should for his famous temper. He calls on the famous temper. . . . I'm not saying that he's acting. I'm saying he knows when to turn himself loose. I think if in that point in time he wanted to control himself, he could."

Shula does not agree. If he used his temper as a device, "then that would be a challenge to my credibility. . . . and I want the players to believe that everything I do is authentic." When he projects anger, it's because the fuse is truly hot. "I think I've learned to live with it a little better than I did in my early years. I had a vicious temper as a youngster growing up, and as a coach in my early years, and still occasionally as a coach in my later years." He is impatient, he concedes, a characteristic he suspects goes hand in hand with low boiling points.

"Hey," laughs Painesville pal Roy Kropac, himself of Hungarian origin, "he's a hot Hunky! I can remember some thirty years ago, when we were playing softball and he was playing centerfield and the umpire made the wrong call. Before you knew it, Don was in from center field in ten flat."

Shula wryly points out there are some benefits accruing to immediate sound-off. "I'll never have an ulcer." Instead he gives them. Friends who traveled to Havanna with him in the fifties think there is a Cuban who is still on a milk diet after a close encounter with Shula, who was then cornerback for the Baltimore Colts. When Shula gave his name at the immigration desk, the clerk burst into uncontrollable laughter. Grabbing the man by the collar, Shula lifted him several feet off the ground with just one arm. "What's so funny?" he growled. When the airborne Cuban explained that Shula in Spanish was the description of a criminal occupation, Don quickly returned him to ground level and joined in the laughter.

The Painesville friends who went to Cuba with Don Shula over twenty years ago are still among his closest friends today. "I could call him tonight," says Roy Kropac, "or I could call his secretary, and if I ask for something, it's there. If I go to a Super Bowl, the tickets are there, the rooms are there. He'll take care of his friends before he'll take care of big wheels."

"He never has forgotten his old pals," says Lynn Brandom. "They are important to him. Anytime any of these people call, I know to put them right through to him. . . . If Bob Hope called and the coach were looking at films, I would let him know that Bob Hope is on the line and find out if he can talk to him. But if it were Roy Kropac, I would just tell him Mr. Kropac is on the line."

Shula has always seemed anxious to share his successes with friends and family, all of whom were present in force when his teams played in the Super Bowls. "We all love football," says Dorothy Shula of herself and her five children, "and he tries to bring us into it as far as we want to go." The Shula's oldest son David performed odd jobs for the team. Number two daughter

Sharon was a member of the Dolphin cheerleading squad. All five children regularly attend the games unless they have more pressing activities of their own, in which case their father urges them to pursue the event of their choice.

He is proud of the fact that two of his daughters, Donna and Annie, have become experienced horsewomen. Participation in sports, he thinks, teaches children a great deal about living. "There is the perparation; the actual competing; the finality of it, whether you succeed or fail; trying to learn something from having succeeded, so that you can succeed again; learning to walk away from failure without making excuses or worrying about it." He is fond of summing this philosophy up in the phrase, "Success isn't final. Failure isn't fatal."

"There's one thing he really hates," notes David Shula, "and that's when you give excuses why you didn't do something. You didn't do it and that's all there is to it." David says he finds himself emulating his father in very small ways. "If something is wrong with my car, I've got to make sure it's fixed right away. If it's not clean, I clean it right away. That's the way he is too."

The genial side of Shula is most evident with children. He likes to tease and spar with them in conversation. When he is home, his youngest daughter Annie is frequently tucked under one wing. "Annie's my girl," he grins.

Sharon Shula says the characteristic she likes best about her father is the fact "that he cares so much." Once, while talking about her father, tears flowed unashamedly down her freckled cheeks. She was crying, she said, "because I never get to see him as much as I should. He's not home enough really, but it's his business and you have to live with it." But, she adds plaintively, "I like to be in his company."

He is full of what she terms "stupid, corny" jokes. "Oh, they're so dumb!" she grimaces. "One day, he came down to breakfast and he said, 'I wrecked the car. I hit a henweigh." And I said, 'what's a henweigh?' and he said, 'three-and-a-half pounds.' "

Shula frequently turns family humor on himself. He relates with relish the story of buying a horse for his daughter Donna. Before making the purchase, the coach took a turn in the saddle and wound up on the ground. Donna raced over to his side. "Daddy, daddy," she cried anxiously, "are you all right?" He was fine, he told her. "Are you sure? Are you sure?" Donna persisted. Shula was deeply touched by his daughter's effusive concern. "Now I told you I was fine, honey, don't worry." Donna's face immediately brightened. "Then can I still have the horse?"

Shula demands the same excellence from his children that he tries to extract from his players. He was a regular observer of David

Shula's high school football games. He was also a ready critic. "He doesn't say," maintains David, " 'You blew it. You lost it. You're a jerk.' But if I was the cause of a major goof in the game and we ended up losing, he's going to say, 'You made a dumb mistake. Do you know why you did? Do you realize that you did it so you can correct it in the future?' Constructive criticism," David adds wryly, "is what he's best known for, I think."

There is another characteristic, however, that David thinks he will remember more about his father. "You know those times when we lost the Super Bowls or we lost players that were real valuable— things that really hurt my father and, as a consequence, our family? I could see his devotion to God by the fact that he didn't lose faith, that he didn't give up, he didn't quit. And the reason that he didn't was because he had confidence that Someone was watching over him."

In 1976, David again had the opportunity to observe his father's reaction to adversity when Coach Shula suffered his first losing season. Not only had he lost some of his biggest stars, Csonka, Kiick and Warfield, but he also saw twelve of his starting Miami Dolphins retired to the bench due to injury. "I think a losing season was extremely difficult for him," asserts Tim Foley, "he'd never gone through anything like it before. But I think it's easy to win. A guy with just a little bit of class can win with style. With what Shula had to cope with this year, he could have really gone bananas and gotten irate with everybody. But he maintained his composure through most of the season. I really gained respect for him."

In 1977, there were dire predictions on the sports pages that Miami would have little chance to recover significantly from the '76 setback—Too many injured players, too many lost stars, too many rookies. The Dolphin team, wrote *Miami Herald* sports editor Edwin Pope, was facing "turmoil." Other sports gurus declared that the Dolphins would be lucky to garner a seven–seven season. They ate their typeface when a team full of eager young players wound up with ten wins and four losses, nearly capturing the American Football Conference championship. Network sports announcers like ABC's Howard Cosell continually expressed their amazement at the feat: "If you don't look at this man and say this is one of the greatest coaches in modern football history," crowed Cosell, "you're not being fair to him."

Shula, however, might be inclined to agree more with the observation of Edwin Pope in the *Miami Herald:* "Somebody up there is looking over the Dolphins and it isn't the Goodyear Blimp."

Don Shula has been successful, according to Miami defensive coach, Bill Arnspargar, because he knows how to separate "what's important from what's not important. . . . Don is great because of the decisions he has made. And the decisions he has made have been based on his religion. His faith has made him the tremendous person he is."

Don Shula's faith is just that—faith. It is not an intellectual exercise. "I don't try to dive into the Bible and understand the verses. I don't claim to be an expert on God's word. But I'm interested in listening to the readings at Mass every morning. . . . I believe that God is up there. . . . I try to live in His likeness. That's my prayer every day—to do the job to the best of my ability in a way that will reflect on His image and likeness. It would be easy," he points out, "to be a disbeliever, if you're looking to be a disbeliever. If you want proof of everything and you want to question everything that is written in the Catechism or said in the pulpit or talked about in the gospels. . . . But that's not what faith is all about."

"Faith," he told a Biscayne College graduation class, "is the greatest force in all humanity. It is greater than intelligence, charm, physical beauty. It is greater than strength, political power, money or social position. There is practically nothing a man can't do for himself if he has faith. Supreme self-confidence is based on faith, and without self-confidence, success is an impossibility." When a man has faith, Shula contends, he is without limits. "Faith gives you a definition and a purpose." It makes football more than just a game. Men engaged in competition, he believes, are men contesting for excellence.

"I think the worst thing I see, the thing that bothers me the most, is an individual with great ability who doesn't have what it takes to make that ability come to the front. . . . In order to get the most out of the gifts that God has given you, I think you've got to reach as far as you can reach.

Some people are so afraid. Some people never play the game. They never enter into the arena. They never give themselves a chance to accomplish. They go through life without ever knowing how good or how bad they are. I want to find out."

F. Stanton.

# 4 | GERALD FORD

"I've got to give a State Dinner! I've got to give a State Dinner!" Betty Ford wailed to her children. It was not enough that she become First Lady on twenty-four hours' notice. Within one week of her boost in social status, a King and Queen were coming for dinner. In the midst of organizing a move from 514 Crown View Drive in Alexandria, Virginia, to 1600 Pennsylvania Avenue, Washington, D.C., Mrs. Ford was expected to provide a scintillating evening for Hussein of Jordan and his glamorous Alia.

The Nixons, who had hoped to be hosting the royal pair, had already invited the dinner guests. But Betty Ford had heard that the King and Queen loved to dance, an exercise she was rather fond of herself, so she decided to add some of the more agile couples from Capitol Hill for a little after-supper swing and sway. Frosting on the King's cake, so to speak.

Since the King was relatively young and attractive, and the Queen was objectively so, Mrs. Ford thought the dancing group should be likewise. She also wanted an even distribution of Democrats and Republicans, and she did not care whether they moved to the left, right, or center of the political spectrum.

Her orders produced a set of visitors stunningly different from anything seen in the previous administration. It was "pass the Maalox please" in offices still peopled by former Nixon staffers who feared Mrs. Ford had stumbled over the "enemies list." Senators and Congressmen who had not been seen on the premises for over five-and-a-half years were being invited to the White House. There were Democrats in profusion, liberal Republicans, a Republican turned Democrat—even a Democrat who had voted against Gerald Ford's nomination for Vice President.

Mixing the political menu provided an electrifying social feast. "I've never seen so much joy in the White House," mumbled CBS commentator Eric Severeid with a kind of numb amazement, as he was coaxed into the middle of a group performing the Mexican Hat dance. The austere East Room took on the air of a cabaret: small, round, candle-bedecked tables and gilt chairs surrounded a dance floor made almost invisible by the solid mass of feet moving continuously to the thumping sounds of the Howard Devron orchestra.

There were fox trots, rock-and-roll numbers, latin rhythms—even a Charleston.

Former outcasts hailed each other across the dance floor, swapping length-of-exile stories: "It's been six years since I've been here." Adversaries were dancing with each other's spouses. "Who was the genius who did the guest list?", marveled G.O.P. Congressman Henry Smith's wife, Helen. "Look at this magnificent crowd," beamed Democrat Lud Ashley. "There are no enemies here!" John Seiberling, an Ohio Democratic Representative, who had cast a dissenting vote against Ford's confirmation for Vice President, said he had thought Jerry Ford too partisan to be Vice President, but he was changing his mind because of Ford's actions as President. "Tonight shows he really wants an open administration. Last week, we ended the Watergate; this week, we ended the war."

For Gerald Ford, the evening was like a release from a self-imposed solitary confinement. As the weeks of June had passed into July and the increasing inevitability of a Ford presidency loomed on the horizon, the Vice President had completely withdrawn from any discussion of his future. "That was really a hard time," recalls John Byrnes, former Wisconsin Congressman and longtime Ford crony, "because he couldn't even talk about it to close friends. . . . I broached the subject to him a couple of months before August when things were deteriorating pretty badly. I said, 'Gol,' you've got to do some thinking and reorganizing of your staff . . . putting yourself in the posture of being President."

"Oh no, no, no," Ford insisted. "Nixon's not going to be out next month or the month after."

Ford maintains he was not being coy; he was sincerely uncertain about Nixon's criminal involvement in the cover-up. Colleagues claim this attitude has to do with Jerry Ford's lifelong habit of looking for the sunnier side of human nature—a trait Ford himself admits to. "I've always felt there was far more good in people than bad," he says, "and I try to work with the good side and perhaps ignore the bad side." Since President Nixon had claimed innocence, Gerald Ford accepted his statements at face value. "I felt, based on his comments and based on the comments of John Mitchell at the time of the break-in, that there was no complicity by Nixon. Trust in politics to me is the highest commandment. . . . From my own point of view, I try to be honest with people in politics. So when I was told by various people that there was no involvement, I believed it until I saw evidence to the contrary."

John Byrnes could well understand Ford's reluctance to disbelieve a friend. He had known Richard Nixon as long as Jerry Ford had known him, preceding the two of them to Congress by one term. And they were all members of the Chowder and Marching Club, a group made up mostly of conservative Republican Congressmen.

Chowder and Marching met once a week on the Hill, mainly to discuss legislation. "But," notes Byrnes, "there was a certain social aspect to it. The wives would get together and we'd have parties." Even then Richard Nixon was a loner. "I liked him," says Ford. "But I never felt intimate, because I don't think Dick Nixon had many, if any, intimate friends. . . . I don't think anybody that I knew—John Byrnes, Glenn Davis—ever felt a closeness [with Nixon] like we had with each other." John Byrnes agrees. "He never really let his hair down. I always used to say that the thing Dick Nixon needed most was a good drunk once a month."

On the other hand, Jerry Ford could easily, on weekends, substitute the well of the House for the green of a fairway. Though he astounded his colleagues with his stamina for long working hours, he was equally adept at applying all his energy to the end of a golf club. One Chowder-and-Marching member, former Wisconsin congressman Glenn Davis, wryly dubbed Ford his "trained gorilla. . . . He drives the ball a mile," joked Davis, "and that's exactly the way he putts, too."

While possessed of a certain amount of desire to mount the political ladder, Jerry Ford was not, according to John Byrnes, "a guy with insatiable ambition. . . . During the battle for the minority leadership, I remember Jerry coming to me and saying, 'Some of the boys are talking to me about being a candidate for minority leader, but first I want to know if you're at all interested in it.' I said, 'No, absolutely not.' That was typical of the kind of thing Jerry would do. He'd kind of look around and make sure that he wasn't going to be doing end runs around people."

For that reason, Byrnes was astounded when Ford expressed an interest in the Vice Presidency after Spiro Agnew's demise. What Byrnes, who had retired from the House, did not know was that the idea had originated, not with Jerry Ford, but with his colleagues in the Congress. New York Congressman Barber Conable kept a careful account in his journal of the amazing ascension of the Minority Leader into the Vice Presidency.

According to the Congressman's chronicle, there was a populist uprising on the floor of the House within ten minutes of the announcement that Spiro Agnew had resigned—a drive to make Jerry Ford his successor. New York Congressman Jack Kemp and Tennessee Representative Dan Kuykendahl immediately began circulating petitions of support for Ford, a move discouraged by the Minority Leader, who told Kemp he welcomed honest enthusiasm but not organized efforts in his behalf.

Amazed by the speed with which the Ford-for-Vice-President boomlet was ballooning, Conable, who is one of the most respected House G.O.P. leaders, telephoned Bill Timmons, Chief of the White House Congressional liaison office. Conable was aware that Nixon leaned heavily in favor of John Connally as his successor, and he warned Timmons that if the President had someone other than Ford in mind he had better move quickly or face another confrontation with Congress. Since Nixon needed a two-thirds vote of approval to confirm his Vice-Presidential choice, confrontation was a luxury he could not afford. Connally, who had recently turned his coat from Democrat to Republican, was unlikely to garner a plethora of votes from the rejected party, Conable reasoned.

By late afternoon, the winds of favor blowing in Ford's direction had taken on hurricane force and Conable again called the White House. "I told them the only way such a draft could be avoided would be for Ford to make a clear statement that he was not interested. Bryce Harlow [Special Assistant to the President] argued with me at some length about it."

Later that evening, Conable received more argument via a phone call from White House Counselor Mel Laird, who declared Ford could not possibly be interested in the Vice Presidency. Conable quickly disabused Laird of that impression and, according to Nixon's personal secretary, Rosemary Woods, the message finally came through loud and clear to the Oval Office. "Mel Laird told us," says Miss Woods, "that the only man we could get through the Congress was Ford."

Nevertheless, Nixon put the veracity of Laird's prediction to the test with a kind of informal election. He asked members of the House from both sides of the aisle to submit to him their top three choices for Vice President. When the letters were delivered to the White House, the President repaired to Camp David to ponder their contents. Letter after letter, from Democrats and Republicans alike, placed Ford at the top of the pack. Later, when he reviewed the affection with which Capitol Hill greeted his choice of Ford, Nixon realized the wisdom of his accession to Congressional wishes. "Well, finally," he sighed, "we've done something right."

Only Betty Ford seemed disenchanted with the turn of events. When Barber Conable walked through the receiving line at her husband's swearing-in ceremony, she quipped, "I ought to kick you in the shins."

But her husband had not altered his plans for retirement. He just thought bowing out as Vice President of the United States was a rather splendid exit. Finishing out Spiro Agnew's term "still fell within the time limitation of our previous commitment. . . . and I felt it would be a good way to end a career. I'd tried to be Speaker of the House and never made it, and so I thought if you can't get number three, number two wouldn't be bad."

But by the end of July, it was becoming obvious that he would soon be number one. He still refused to discuss the potential with his top staff assistants. "Up until the last minute," Ford says, "the decision could have been changed, so to talk about it on a broad basis, I thought, would have been inappropriate."

"We respected the fact," says Jack Marsh, a former Democratic Congressman who became one of Ford's top aides, "that he was establishing a wall of privacy around himself on this subject and he wanted us to establish a wall of privacy around ourselves on the subject, too. . . . The one thing we were concerned about was not creating a feeling or an attitude in the West Wing of the White House that the Prince was seeking to topple the crown. The example was set by Ford and it was a disciplined thing."

Part of the discipline was a total embargo on contingency plans for a move to the White House, a fact that deeply concerned Ford's first law partner Phil Buchen, who had come to Washington from Grand Rapids, Michigan to serve as Counsel to the Domestic Council on the Right to Privacy. Without telling his long-time friend, Buchen assembled a small group of men to act as an underground transition group. "Never," Buchen insists, did he so much as allude to his clandestine activities in the presence of the Vice President.

Though his intentions were noble, Buchen admits the restriction of size and secrecy hampered substantial achievement. "We didn't prepare very well," he smiles. "Four of us would meet as soon as we could conveniently get away from the public eye and we would always meet in a private home. We just sat around and began to make checklists and speculate on what kinds of things should be prepared for. Our timetable turned out to be wrong. We never expected it to come that soon and we were caught short."

Despite the fact that all summer Washington was like a city with a tight throat, almost no one was prepared for the sudden appearance on August 5 of the "smoking pistol," the June 23rd tape, which proved that the President had been aware of the cover-up only four days after the Watergate burglary. Now it was no longer a question of whether Richard Nixon, despite his emotional fluctuations on the subject, would resign; it was merely a question of when. From August 5 until August 9, crowds gathered in Lafayette Park across from the White House like flocks of vultures hovering over a corpse. Citizens never strayed far from their radios or television sets. Phone lines between Capitol Hill and the suburbs hummed. "Have you heard anything?"—"No, have you?"

Everywhere he went now, Gerald Ford attracted crowds of reporters and the curious. On Wednesday, August 7, he drove down to the Capitol for a meeting in House Minority Leader John Rhodes's office. His presence there spread through the ranks of the Congressional press corps like a prairie fire with the wind at its back. The Vice President meeting with the Minority Leader seemed a certain signal that a transition was imminent.

What was happening inside John Rhodes's office, however, was not an exchange of power, but an exchange of prayer, the continuation of meetings that had begun when Jerry Ford was a member of the House of Representatives. Included in the group were Mel Laird and Congressman Al Quie. "What we would do," explains Al Quie, the originator of the group, "was just go in and sit and talk about whatever came to us, and then we would take turns praying whatever came to our minds. At the end we would just say The Lord's Prayer."

For years, the meetings had been a secret even from Betty Ford. With the exception of Al Quie, none of the men were perceived as being particularly religious. And that was the way they preferred their image. All were fiercely opposed to waving the banner of religion in an effort to garner salutes. Now, while they were praying in the office, the press were preying in the hall and there would be no way of evading their questions.

"Jerry," said Al Quie, "now's the time. You've got no other way of going but to talk about it. I think you ought to consider what you're going to say."

"Well, I'm not going to say anything," retorted the Vice President. "I'm not going to make any comment at all." He didn't like to wear his religion on his sleeve, he added.

Mel Laird also announced his intention to remain silent. Finally Al Quie and John Rhodes decided they would be the spokesmen. When the four men stepped outside the Minority Leader's office, there was an instant chorus of "What's the meeting about?"

"We were praying," replied Rhodes.

"You were what?"

Of all the astonished reporters, Al Quie remembers CBS' Daniel Schorr being the most insistently inquisitive about the proceedings. "He must have thought," Congressman Quie chuckles, "we were something like the Moonies."

The decision the reporters thought might occur on Wednesday actually took place the following afternoon, when Gerald Ford sat across the desk from Richard Nixon in the Oval Office. "I know you'll do well," Nixon said to his successor.

Suddenly the Vice President's office was in the path of the hurricane. "Let me tell you," says Jack Marsh, who was trying his best to buffet the winds, "when you get an announcement that the President of the United States is resigning and you're working for the guy who's going to be President, you get a number of calls!"

All night long, Jack Marsh worked on the invitation list to the swearing-in ceremony. "There were certain things you had to do when you were seeking to restore confidence," he points out. "Meaning you've got to think in terms of Democratic leaders, national leaders and cabinet officers." Ford especially wanted former Speaker John McCormack, his opposite in the House for many years, to be present. But he did not want McCormack, who was in his eighties, to make the trip alone. So the Ford staff hunted down McCormack's former assistant John Monahan. "We found him jogging along the road at 6:30 A.M. and got him on a plane," recalls Marsh.

The night of August 8 was almost as short for the Vice President's Chief of Staff Bob Hartmann, an ex-*Los Angeles Times* bureau chief and an excellent writer. "I have to say something when I'm sworn in," Ford told Hartmann, "but I don't want it to be very long. Just something very simple." From three until eight in the morning, Hartmann worked on "something simple" for the new President to say to the American people.

On August 9, 1974, at 12:03 P.M., scarcely two hours after Richard Nixon's departure from the White House, Gerald Ford delivered the "simple message" Bob Hartmann had prepared for him. He wanted, he said, to engage in a little "straight talk among friends. . . . I am acutely aware that you have not elected me as your President by your ballots," he said to the millions of Americans anxiously scrutinizing their new leader. But, he reminded them, "If you have not chosen me by secret ballot, neither have I gained office by secret promises. I have not campaigned for either the Presidency or the Vice Presidency. I have not subscribed to any partisan platform. I am indebted to no man and only one woman, my dear wife, Betty." One month later, that statement would be questioned.

With Ford's swearing-in, an excitement charged the Nation's Capital, which only the week before seemed slumped in a permanent depression. Congressmen who had been dreading the ordeal of impeachment, loathing to cast judgment on another government official and particularly the President of the United States, were almost giddy with relief. Newspapers which had been sparring with the White House for almost two years dropped their dukes and took up their harps, discharging continual lilting praise to the new Chief. Everyone agreed he was the most lovable of men—a man with no hang-ups, no enemies lists, who carted his own fat briefcase up the driveway and toasted his own English muffins. No Lord Ford in the Oval Office. Al Average at last.

And when former Congressman Jerry Ford returned to the House of Representatives as President Gerald R. Ford to deliver a speech before a Joint Session of Congress, the roof came close to departing its stately pillars, so great was the roar of affection from the men most responsible for his new job. In Chicago, where Ford traveled to address the Veterans of Foreign Wars, the curbs were lined with cheering citizens. A touch of Camelot was in the air.

It was this atmosphere that made Betty Ford's first state dinner, in the words of the *New York Times,* seem like "a gathering of Yale freshmen at the Senior Prom." As the guests departed, Senator Mark

Hatfield called out to no one in particular and everyone in general, "Happy New Year."

It was anything but "Happy New Year," however, at One McPherson Square, the building that housed Special Prosecutor Leon Jaworski and his staff. There the shadow of San Clemente fell long across the desks as Jaworski and his team pondered whether to prosecute, for the first time in history, a former President of the United States. According to Special Counsel Philip Lacavara, who would later resign in protest of the pardon, the staff was not eager to see Richard Nixon incarcerated. "The scenario that I would have scripted," he explains, "had I been Lord of the Universe (and thank heavens I wasn't), was for an indictment and a trial, just to get the evidence on the record. . . . It seemed to me, looking down the road, that the verdict of history might be open, when I didn't think it should be."

Leon Jaworski, on the other hand, worried that there was already so much evidence on the record that the former leader of the country might be denied the constitutional right of the ordinary citizen—a fair trial. For two years Nixon's conduct had been discussed on daily and nightly newscasts. The House Judiciary Committee had pored over nine thousand pages of evidence. Before an estimated audience of ninety-two million viewers, Committee members had voted to impeach Nixon. Four hundred twelve members of the full House of Representatives had accepted the Judiciary Committee's report. The former President's resignation speech was widely interpreted by the media as an admission of guilt. Could the prosecution, Jaworski puzzled, find twelve jurors with unprejudiced views?

George Frampton, one of the staff lawyers, argued against Jaworski's concern. "It seems to me," he wrote, "that reliance on prejudicial pretrial publicity to avoid prosecution altogether would be widely perceived and stamped by history as a resort to a completely novel legal theory and thereby judged a cop-out." He thought if the decision were to be based on the fate of the nation, the issue should be resolved by Congress or the White House.

But on Capitol Hill Congress had already "copped out" on the question of what to do with the former President. Senator Edward Brooke, who had originally planned to author a resolution suggesting no legal action be taken against Richard Nixon, dropped the idea because he was unhappy with Nixon's resignation speech. The rest of the Congress had gone home to campaign for reelection.

The debate at One McPherson Square soon extended to the front pages of the newspapers. Columns were written for and against prosecution. Public opinion polls took the people's pulse and found the readings uneven. One poll's results cancelled the other's. VIP opinions were equally erratic. The American Bar Association called for indictment and prosecution. Nelson Rockefeller, never a Nixon intimate, called for mercy. Nixon had already been hung, he said; there was no need to draw and quarter him.

On August 28, Gerald Ford held his first press conference, and Helen Thomas, the astute UPI White House correspondent, immediately tossed the fate of Richard Nixon in his lap. Would he, she wanted to know, use his pardon authority if necessary?

Ford replied, "In the last ten days or two weeks, I have asked for prayers for guidance on this very important point. In this situation, I am the final authority. There have been no charges made. There has been no action by the courts. There has been no action taken by any jury, and until any legal process has been undertaken, I think it is unwise and untimely for me to make any commitment."

But the Special Prosecutor's staff did not want President Ford to wait until after they had taken legal action, and his press conference initiated new flurries in what had become a memorandum blizzard. There were strong feelings that if the President had any plans to issue a pardon, he ought to do it, in the words of Henry Ruth, deputy to the Special Prosecutor, "early rather than late."

Philip Lacavara agreed. "The pardon power," he wrote Jaworski, "can be exercised at any time after a federal crime has been committed and it is not necessary that there be any criminal proceeding pending." Lacavara explained later that there had been "some discussion about whether or not the stage for the pardon would have to be set by proceeding with an indictment or a conviction or an affirmance and I said that's not constitutionally necessary." Lacavara then suggested to Jaworski that he find out from the White House whether a pardon was indeed on the President's mind. If the President had made his decision, Lacavara reasoned, "It would make more sense to grant the pardon immediately," saving the prosecution and the defense the useless ordeal of engaging in what amounted to "nothing more than a costume drama."

On September 4, Jaworski carried substantially that same message to Phil Buchen, who was now the President's legal counsel. How soon, Phil Buchen asked Jaworski, could Richard Nixon receive a fair trial? In a letter delivered to the White House that same day, Jaworski estimated it would not be possible to bring Nixon into court for at least nine to twelve months. The albatross had been neatly shifted from the neck of the Special Prosecutor to that of the President.

President Ford had never, he says, given a pardon "any thought until I was preparing for my first press conference. . . . We had a group of about seven or eight people on the White House staff who were trying to brief me on what the questions might be from the press. I was somewhat surprised they thought a number of those questions would involve what I would or wouldn't do with the tapes and Mr. Nixon's status."

He was further amazed at the accuracy of his aides' crystal ball. Over half of the press conference questions dealt with some aspect of Watergate and a possible pardon. "Just because they were so concerned in the press, I knew the public was inevitably going to be interested. And I could foresee, after that press conference, that every press conference I had from then until whatever Mr. Nixon's fate would be in the courts would be dominated by one question or another, probably many. And I just figured that I ought to start thinking how best I could allocate my time in the job. If I had to spend 25 percent of my time . . . worrying about advice from my counsel and advice from the Department of Justice concerning what ought to be done about Mr. Nixon and his problem, when 100 percent of my time should be spent on unemployment, on the problems of inflation, on foreign relations, it seemed to me that I ought to ask for God's help. Which I did, and I have no apologies for it."

It was, he admitted, the most agonizing decision of his twenty-eight years in politics. "I was the only one who could sign that document. I had to get advice on the technical aspects of it, but the real decision was predicated on my conviction as to what were the best interests of the country." He was well aware that his constituency was deeply and angrily divided on the issue. "People of course thought that Mr. Nixon was guilty and that he ought to go to trial, and that's a very integral part of our society."

But, he had to ask himself, was extracting an "eye for an eye" from Mr. Nixon worth the further carnage it would wreak on America? Was it worth the time it would take him away from trying to cure the ills that were corroding society? A coal strike was threatening. The economy was in critical condition. The bottom line had not been written under the Vietnam war. The truce in the Middle East was uneasy. Once again, Gerald Ford found himself in mental isolation. Only he could understand the problems and priorities of the Oval Office. It was a lonely perspective.

He could not even discuss his thoughts with his closest friends on Capitol Hill. It seemed to him that sharing the agony would shed no light on the dilemma. And he wasn't at all sure he would be "able to translate my problems to them. They couldn't have understood the situation as intimately as myself, for sure, or others who were working right in the White House." There was also the fact that a secret sent from the White House to the Congress frequently returns a headline. Consultation, the President decided, would "involve having the problem so broadly discussed that it would have been misunderstood."

Then too, his friends who were politicians would more than likely have pressured him to decide against the pardon. Congressman Al

Quie later told the President, "It was good for the country. It was good for Nixon. But I can't help myself, Jerry—I care about you. And it's terrible for you!" Even if Quie had been able to enter that plea before the pardon was granted, former House colleagues think it would have made little impact. "I've known Jerry Ford for twenty-five years," says Michigan Congressman Al Cedarburg. "In all my dealings with him . . . he always put the political consequences in the background." A number of Congressmen who observed Ford in the throes of a decision recall his frequently invoking the phrase, "But, what is the right thing to do?"

There would of course be many who thought dialogue would "condition" the American people, that it would be unwise to take them by surprise. But the President did not agree. No matter when or how he granted the pardon, he thought, "the shock would be there anyhow."

So he consulted with only a handful of people—Phil Buchen, Jack Marsh, Don Rumsfeld, Al Haig, Bob Hartmann. And when he announced his thinking to his White House counselers, he received less than thunderous applause.

"I was stunned," recalls Phil Buchen, but he kept his political views to himself. The President had assigned him to examine all the technicalities of a pardon and Buchen did not want any other considerations to color his legal opinions. "There was," however, according to Jack Marsh, "a free and frank exchange of views."

"Frankly," recalls Bob Hartmann, "I can't remember anybody being very strong for it. Haig was obviously pushing for it, but in his own sort of quiet way. He never came on strong. He was always very diffident in the presence of the new President."

Hartmann, the politically savvy ex-reporter, did not, however, hesitate to warn the President about the political fallout. "This will create an awful furor," he aptly predicted.

The President seemed equally conscious of the consequences. "This may cost me a lot," Phil Buchen remembers him saying, "and it may prevent me from being elected, if I choose to run."

"I hadn't made up my mind at the time," the former President recalls, but he was leaning strongly in the direction of asking his wife, Betty, to extend the lease on his career. "The more I was in office, the more I saw that to be effective I couldn't be a person who was running out a term. To be an effective President for two and a half years, people in the Congress, people everywhere had to understand that I was probably going to be a candidate. If everybody knows you're going to have an end of a term, they treat you differently in the White House. If they think you're still going to be a candidate and might be there four more years, they also treat you differently."

The fact that a pardon granted might bring about forced rather than optioned retirement was a subject discussed by the President and the First Lady. "Both of us realized at the time," says Betty Ford, that the pardon would place a great burden on the 1976 ballot. "I think, in many ways, that it may have brought about the loss of the election. It may not have been all of it, but it certainly was a main factor. . . . I know many people who said that they just couldn't vote for him because of the pardon."

Nevertheless she urged him to ignore the risks. "I could see that there was absolutely no way that President Nixon could be brought to trial at that time. There was no question in my mind or, I don't think, anyone's mind that Nixon was really a sick man. To have that hanging over your head, to have all the innuendos. . . . We'd been through so much. To have that going on and on and on for another year and a half before he was brought to trial was just ludicrous." It did not seem to her that Richard Nixon was going unpunished. She felt that he had "suffered enough" when he was forced to resign in disgrace. "That would be on his conscience and I thought the thing should be put to rest as quickly as possible and [we should] get on with getting the country back on its feet." It was time, she thought, to bring the people together again and give them "some sense of assurance."

Discussion of the pardon went on within the White House, according to the President, "for maybe a period of a week. . . . It was a broad discussion, says Ford. "Each one expressed their views. . . . My whole technique in discussing an issue where I have to make a decision is to let people express themselves freely and then I go off by myself and make the final decision."

And so, in the end, he was left alone with his conscience. He prayed continually, the President says, searching for guidance. The Presidency had only served to increase his reliance on a Supreme Being. "After all, you do represent two hundred fifteen million people in the eyes of God." Typically, Ford does not dramatize his discourse with his Creator. He says simply, "He was very helpful. . . . I think the prayers I said, when you get right down to it, were the determining factor." The decision to pardon Richard Nixon, he firmly believes, "was God's will."

He made that dependence clear on September 8, when he announced his decision to the American people in a Sunday morning televised address. "As we are a Nation under God," he said, "so I am sworn to uphold our laws with the help of God. And I have sought such guidance and searched my own conscience with special diligence to determine the right thing for me to do with respect to my predecessor in this place, Richard Nixon, and his loyal wife and family. Theirs is an American tragedy in which we all have played a part. It could go on and on and on or someone must write an end to it. I have concluded that only I can do that, and if I can, I must."

Ford then pointed out that the former President's chances for equal justice under the law were precarious due to the length of time needed to insure a fair trial. He would be "cruelly and excessively penalized either in preserving the presumption of his innocence or in obtaining a speedy determination of his guilt in order to repay a legal debt to society." The country would be enmired in a new national nightmare. "My conscience tells me clearly and certainly that I cannot prolong the bad dreams that continue to reopen a chapter that is closed. My conscience tells me that only I, as President, have the constitutional power to seal this book. My conscience tells me it is my duty not only to proclaim domestic tranquility but to use every means to insure it."

Almost instantly, euphoria disappeared in the smoke of outrage. Nowhere was anger more explicit than in the lavalike columns that poured forth from the nation's newspapers, many of whom openly snickered at Ford's reliance on advice from the Almighty. There was considerable whimsical noting of the fact that Ford chose to make his announcement on a Sunday morning after attending 8 A.M. communion services at St. John's Episcopal Church, the implication being that the decision came to the President on a beam of light descending from the Church ceiling.

But it was obvious that, however fine a Creator, God was not much of a politician. Jerry Ford's national popularity plummeted, with the swiftness of a suicide victim departing the top of the Empire State Building; his seventy-one percent rating nosediving to less than fifty percent.

Phone calls stormed the White House switchboard. Out of every nine callers, eight protested the President's action. Jerry Ford had dug himself a political pit from which he would never fully emerge before the 1976 election. "That is the only reason," declares G.O.P. pollster Bob Teeter, "that he ended up so far behind at the starting gate."

The President was given an early warning of the reaction to come just an hour before he delivered his pardon message on television. His press secretary, Jerold ter Horst, a former reporter and Ford friend for twenty-five years, who had not been consulted about on the pardon, resigned his job. Ter Horst said he could not defend a position with which he did not agree. The resignation brought ter Horst instant fame and a syndicated column.

While ter Horst was hailed a hero for making a decision of "conscience," his former boss was strongly suspected of making a deal, paying off the man who made him Vice President. "I had a letter from a friend in Europe," recalls Betty Ford, "and she said in Europe it was more or less believed that it was a deal. That really hurt because I knew it wasn't."

If there was a deal, the principal party, Richard Nixon, seemed strangely unaware of it, according to Leon Jaworski's book, *The Right and the Power.** Up until the time the pardon was discussed, his lawyer, Herbert J. Miller, Jr., had worked feverishly to persuade the prosecutor not to bring the former President to court, executing a lengthy memo to Jaworski detailing Nixon's inability to receive a fair trial. Nixon himself was using more direct and dramatic approaches. In a tearful telephone call to Senator James Eastland, a longtime friend, Nixon pleaded, "Jim, don't let Jaworski put me in that trial with Haldeman and Erlichman. I can't take any more."

Although President Ford realized that there would be allegations of a deal, he could never conceive of the fact that anyone would think the charges credible. "He had been so free of deals and his life had been laid out so publicly," says Bob Hartmann, "that he just felt good people would never really believe it." Not only had his career been marked by a lack of backroom maneuvers, there was also the plain fact that he owed nothing to Nixon. If he owed his Vice Presidency to anyone, it was to an insistent Congress which had practically arm-twisted the appointment out of the White House.

The suspicions surrounding the pardon prompted Gerald Ford to become the first President since Abraham Lincoln to testify before a Congressional committee. He flatly denied making a deal with his predecessor, answering any questions Congressmen put to him regarding the matter. But the scent of secret maneuvers lingered on. Even the assertion by the *Washington Post*'s Watergate reporters Woodward and Bernstein that they had been unable to unearth evidence of a pardon pact while researching their book, *The Final Days*, failed to dispel the odor. Americans had been badly bruised by the Watergate deceptions. They were conditioned now to believe the worst. Those who did not accuse the President of an outright deal castigated him for dispensing selective justice to a sick friend. If there was an element of compassion, Ford says now, it was subconscious; he insists the overwhelming reason was his concern for the country. "I must say," he admits, "when I went out . . . to the West Coast a month later, to make a series of political speeches during the campaign, I went down to see Nixon in the hospital, . . . I saw a man as close to death as I've ever seen anybody. When I saw him with all those tubes and all the other things the doctors were using to save his life, I think at that point—which was a month after the pardon—there was a human element. I think I said to myself, 'I'm glad I did it,' just because it could have affected whether he lived or died."

Special Prosecutor Leon Jaworski, the man who, next to Richard Nixon, perhaps benefited the most from the pardon, declined, despite

---

* Houston: Gulf Publishing Co., 1976.

strong urging, to attack it on legal grounds. Shortly after the pardon was delivered, he returned home to Texas, freed, in Philip Lacavara's words, "of the need to make that hard call. . . . He's never said what he would do and he's never shared a tentative leaning with the staff." But from all of Jaworski's public statements Lacavara has concluded, "had there not been a pardon, he would not have asked the grand jury to indict."

The sonic boom resounding over the pardon caused even Richard Nixon to telephone Gerald Ford. He was sorry he caused the President so much trouble, Nixon said. Ford replied that he had made the decision, and was willing to take the consequences. "I didn't feel sorry for myself because it was a deliberate decision. Sure, I was unhappy with the adverse reactions and certainly surprised they were so strong, but . . . when I do something and I'm convinced it's right, I'm not going to worry about the last contest. I'm looking down the road to the things we have to do ahead."

And several years after granting the pardon he could still say, "I've never backed off from it. The Nixon-Frost telecast, he asserts, only deepened his conviction. "What went on in those interviews was only a small part of a scene that would have played every day for three years, and that continuous replay of all the sordid and sad things in the headlines and in the evening news would have been disastrous for this country."

Gerald Ford was to find that support for the pardon came from the most unexpected sources. Dr. Duncan Littlefair, a minister from Grand Rapids who had often been at odds with Congressman Jerry Ford because of his political opinions, took to the pulpit to defend his frequent adversary. "I have been here in Grand Rapids all the years of Gerald Ford's public life. . . . I have had to fight him over and over again. . . . In all of those years of my opposition to him I never once had to call into question his motivations, his integrity, his honor or his honesty. . . . There is no valid reason for impugning to President Ford a dishonest or dishonorable thing. His whole life speaks against it.

And from across the political aisle in the House of Representatives, Democratic Congressman Andrew Young, who often disagreed with Ford's voting record, also stepped up to back the pardon. Being the first man in the history of the United States to surrender the most powerful office in the world was the greatest humiliation any American could ever have, Young pointed out. The country did not need to chase Richard Nixon to the door of San Clemente. The country needed to be about the business of healing itself.

Ford's ability to accept unfavorable consequences surprised his staff. "He was strange," comments Max Friedersdorf, who lobbied Congress in behalf of White House causes, "different than the usual run-of-the-mill politician. Ford taught me a lot about how to deal with people. . . . I remember the first time I worked with him on a piece of legislation back when he was Minority Leader. I would get pretty upset at certain Congressmen who couldn't help us. We lost one pretty close one time; I came into his office and was very critical of this Congressman. And he got very stern with me."

"Look," Ford told Friedersdorf, "he votes the way he did because that's in the best interests of his district and his own viewpoint. We try to persuade him to our viewpoint. If we can't do that, that's not his fault. That's our fault."

One Republican Congressman commented, "If I couldn't vote with Ford, I'd hide. Not because he'd get mad, but because he wouldn't. He was always so decent about it; I felt terrible when I had to let him down. The only time he'd get upset," adds Friedersdorf, "was if somebody lied to him."

But the President could sometimes be as stubborn as he was fair-minded. Despite his amicable, placid appearance, those who know him well attest to the fact that when he is firmly affixed to an opinion, it is difficult to dislodge him from it. The most tragic example of this trait came after his second debate with Jimmy Carter. For days, several members of the White House staff attempted to convince Ford that his statement proclaiming Eastern European countries free of Soviet domination was in need of immediate amendment. The President steadfastly refused to accede to their requests. He knew what he meant by his remarks: in their hearts, the people of the Eastern European countries were independent, even if their territories were occupied by Soviet troops.

Ford's reluctance to surrender his misspoken phrases had an emotional base, according to his former appointments secretary Terry O'Donnell, who traveled with Ford to Poland. "We visited a hospital and he had a chance to talk with a number of people throughout the hospital. . . . He was genuinely moved. . . I could see it then, by the spirit of the people and by what he interpreted as their will for freedom. . . . This is a mindset. I don't think he was really hearing what he was saying in conjunction with the question. I think he recalled those people and started talking about the fact that they're not dominated, because their spirit is not dominated. If any-one could quote you chapter and verse on the number of Soviet divisions in Poland or the types of weapons the Soviets have in Poland, it would be him because of his days on the Appropriations Committee."

For those not privileged to share O'Donnell's first-hand view, Ford's assertions about freedom in Eastern Europe replowed the already fertile ground of speculation as to the amount of intelligence nestled behind Gerald Ford's benign brow. The charge brings ire to staff members, who insist their former boss has highly adequate intellectual powers. As an example, they point to his mastering the complex and tedious subject of the budget; he once astounded the Cabinet and the press with what was acclaimed as a virtuoso recital of the facts and figures behind Federal spending in the various Government agencies. Several House colleagues who brought him a broad range of legislative problems claim that he proved a "quick study" on issues not in his area of expertise. "He is a good listener," says former Federal Reserve Board Chairman Arthur Burns, "and he has an amazing memory." Bob Hartmann points out the former President lacked the gift journalists most admire—articulation. "We are masters of words and anybody who isn't a master of words is stupid!"

There was considerable speculation as to how Jerry Ford managed to so amiably accept the continual strafing of his intelligence, particularly since he managed, while holding down a full time job, to graduate in the upper third of his Yale law class, which contained, out of one hundred twenty-five students, ninety-eight Phi Beta Kappas, two Supreme Court justices, a Senator, a Secretary of State and a former Director of the Peace Corps. Ford never made an angry defense of his intellect, even when publicly questioned about it. Friends and colleagues attribute Ford's ability to accept slights to an internal confidence.

"His kind of personal security and knowing who he is, is the most unique characteristic about him," says Bob Teeter, who directed the G.O.P. polling during the presidential campaign. "He was not threatened at all. It's almost impossible for me to emphasize how significant that was about him, particularly because that is not a characteristic you find apparent in a lot of politicians. He had it to a greater degree than anybody I know."

Teeter considers another Ford characteristic unique. "I think maybe he is the only President in modern times who really dealt with virtually every decision on [the basis of] whether he thought it was the right thing to do."

According to his former White House Chief of Staff, Richard Cheney, Ford consistently turned down political advisors who urged him to pump up the level of economic activity, arguing that rising employment would be most conducive to his election in 1976. Ford also rejected, points out Cheney, backing popular federal spending programs for short-term political gain. Instead, he vetoed bill after bill, "convinced it was not in the long term economic interests of the country. He took a lot of political heat for this."

While Ford's fiscal conservatism is a widely acknowledged fact, his actions in behalf of blacks were perceived by that community as being less than bold. Cheney disagrees, citing Ford's action in Africa as rebuttal.

"In the spring during the primary campaign, the situation in Rhodesia was obviously growing worse. . . . The President made a decision to move aggressively in Africa, to seek majority rule . . . with a caveat that he also wanted to protect minority rights. It was argued by some . . . 'Mr. President, maybe we ought to postpone that for a while because we have primaries on the southern states coming up. We may do ourselves some damage.' And his reaction was, 'I just don't want to do business that way. We've got to address the African problem. We've got to do it now.' And he went ahead and sent Henry Kissinger to pursue a policy of majority rule before the Georgia and Alabama primaries."

\*    \*    \*

It is May in Massachusetts, and that haven of collegiate activity is bustling with graduation fever. At the King's Grant Motor Inn, on the perimeter of Boston, there is an added thrust to the temperature. One of the many parents occupying a room at the motel is the former President of the United States, Gerald Ford, here to see his son Michael receive his degree from Gordon-Conwell Theological Seminary.

The motel is undergoing noisy renovation, forcing guests to walk a wooden gangplank to dinner. At the registration desk, a man in a bright green golf sweater is telling the clerk to convey a message to "Jerry" that he is ready to "play nine anytime Jerry needs a partner."

Outside Ford's suite, a long queue of people quietly observes the comings and goings from the former President's room. Gerald Ford is dressed in a maroon golf shirt and plaid slacks. He has not been in the motel more than twenty-four hours and already he has made two trips to the pool. He is Pebble-Beach brown and appears to have shed ten pounds and ten years since he left the White House. When he is told that he is looking very well, he laughs— "Why not?"

Gone is the huge entourage that occupied a full floor of any hotel or motel housing the Presidential presence. Gone are the gleaming black limousines. He does not seem to miss the majesty. He had many more years without luxury than with it, and the leaner years never faded, he insists. He could remember the time when "I used to do all these things myself—dashing to airports, making my own breakfasts—and it was a nice shift. But it didn't affect my personality or my attitudes. I always justified it on the basis that time was more important to a President than to a Minority Leader. Therefore, if these things save time and give you more opportunity to concentrate on the other problems, that was an appropriate availability of service and people. But I never felt it was a glorification of me. It was a practicality of the person who occupied the office."

He does not think his humility was severely taxed by the awe the Presidency inspires. "I never was overly impressed with people who were impressed with the so-called frills. In fact, I used to get irritated with anybody in public or private life who got an exhilaration out of goodies of one kind or another. And so I think my reaction was to sort of downgrade them."

He is in Massachusetts to give the commencement address at his son's graduation from Gordon-Conwell Seminary. Speaking to a group of theological students has given him the opportunity to view his Presidency from a philosophical perspective and to talk about his faith, a subject he is reluctant to discuss publicly.

"I strongly disagree with those who directly or indirectly try to exploit a religious conviction. Fortunately, in this country, there has been a minimum of that. It would just be so foreign to my own belief for me to try to get up and sell a political audience that they should vote for me because I have certain religious or spiritual convictions. I wouldn't feel comfortable."

Even in a small group, it is difficult for the President to lay out his relationship with God. "I feel uncomfortable whenever questions are really asked about it because I've not sat down and written it out precisely. . . . And yet it's a feeling within that's important to me. . . . something I rely on." He does not perceive God as "something formal," partially because of the devotion that his son Mike has to Jesus Christ. Now he too feels closer to God the Son than God the Father. "It's been sort of an evolutionary transition, but I think Mike's had a big impact in that regard."

"It's a very private thing with him," declares Betty Ford. "Much more private with him than it is with me. . . . Religion," she says, was born into her husband "intuitively. . . . I know because I know his family background and I know how religious his mother and father were."

"My mother," the former President reminisces, "was a very gregarious person. She was always on the move. I don't think she had an enemy in the world. She had literally thousands of friends. I think I inherited some of her characteristics. She belonged to many, many organizations—the Garden Club, the D.A.R., the Women's Club, various hospital guilds. Anything that had a relationship to people she was a part of, and she loved them regardless of their station in life."

"She was in her seventies when she died and she had had many illnesses. . . . two mastectomies. She had diabetes. She had high blood pressure. She never wanted a lingering illness. . . . She always wanted to die with her boots on, she used to say. Well, she literally did. She dropped dead in church with a heart attack. We looked at her schedule for the next month—she had a date book. She had luncheons for five days out of seven days for the next month and I don't know how many dinners. She lived a life of real action, but action related to people and trying to help people."

His stepfather, who never finished the eighth grade but rose to become the entrepreneur of a paint factory, also set an example of perpetual motion. "He was very active in fraternal organizations—the Masonic Lodge, the Elks. He was also active in what they called the sort of auxiliary to the local police; he believed firmly in the job that the police were doing and he was part of an organization of non-officers who helped the police with their problems." Jerry Ford got an early taste of politics watching his stepfather perform the chores of the Republican county chairman. "So the whole atmosphere in the home was one of doing things to help the community." The Fords preferred motion to dialogue. Religion was not intellectualized. "I wouldn't say we talked about religion per se. The family tried to live a spiritual life."

Gerald Ford, Sr.'s paint factory was a flourishing Grand Rapids business until the crash of '29. When hard times befell the Ford family, Jerry, Jr. went to work for an hour and a half a day in the local school hangout, serving food and washing dishes. It was there that a stranger walked into the restaurant and introduced himself as Jerry Ford's real father. Jerry was seventeen years old, and until that moment had never known of his mother's first marriage or the fact that he was Gerald Ford's adopted son. The trauma of that revelation seems not to have entirely faded. "It was," the former President admits, "a very difficult immediate situation. But what it really did was reaffirm my love for my stepfather, because he was a person who had adopted me and was going through great financial difficulties trying to raise a family of four. My real father was a person of some affluence and he was not doing or hadn't done as much as the courts said he should have done for a long period of time."

It may have been this experience that later provided the stimulus for Congressman Ford to promote what was known as the "runaway Pappy" bill, legislation designed to employ the resources of the Federal government to track down fathers who abandon their families and their alimony payments. "Every year," recalls former press secretary Paul Miltich, "for years and years, he introduced this bill. He tried very hard to get it enacted, but he was ahead of his time." In 1978, a "runaway Pappy" bill was finally enacted.

There were moments, however, when Jerry Ford felt like a "runaway Pappy" himself. As Minority Leader, he was besieged by his colleagues with requests for campaign appearances in their districts. "Other members," asserts former Congressman John Byrnes, "just harrassed him from morning 'til night. You know, they think they're the only ones who have problems. . . . And he couldn't say no. . . . He would go out of his way to accomodate people."

"It was a terrible strain on Betty," Congressman Al Quie points out. "And when it was a strain on Betty, you know it had to be a strain on him." Ford himself admits to anguish: "That was real tough," he says, "because we had four children and they were active. The net result was that I had a feeling I wasn't carrying my part of the bargain in raising the children. . . . and my conscience used to bother me occasionally. But I had to rationalize it on the basis that, one, she could do the job; two, I had assumed an obligation when I was elected a Member of the Congress and Minority Leader. I had a responsibility. And part of that responsibility was being away as much as I was. But it was real tough for her and I think it may have contributed to some of her physical problems."

One of those "physical problems" began with an injury Mrs. Ford incurred while trying to pry open a reluctant window. The resulting pinched nerve in her neck made Betty Ford a frequent visitor to George Washington University hospital. She was in "total agony," says close friend Barbara MacGregor. Pain killers and tranquilizers were all too often the only relief from that agony. Her growing dependence on medications was, Mrs. Ford concedes, "an insidious thing." The former First Lady's inner circle had long been concerned about the obviously debilitating effect of the drugs and they were elated when she later checked into the Long Beach Naval Hospital for rehabilitation. Most, however, were amazed when she announced an addiction to alcohol as well. "I've seen her nurse just one drink all night," insists one long-time chum. "She would never have had to make that public. But it was typical of Betty that she did."

Mrs. Ford declines to join the ranks of those who call her candor courageous. "It isn't anything great;" she demurs, "it's just that I can't lie." Though many observers excuse Jerry Ford's Congressional absences as unavoidable, they are less generous in their assessment of his travels since leaving the White House. "Why can't he stay home with her now?" they grouse. Part of the answer may lie in the former President's own extraordinary good health. "I've always thought what drives him," speculates one crony, "is just pure energy. I used to get tired just watching all the things he did." Ford smiles at the remark. "Well," he concedes, "I get bored sitting around—and disagreeable too. . . . I just can't sit still." His hope had been that his wife, now freed of family responsibilities, would be able to travel with him. In their first weeks as private citizens, she tried. But all too soon, she discovered that "keeping up with Jerry" required more stamina than her arthritis would allow. "I was not getting my physiotherapy treatments and I wasn't getting my hot packs. I just wasn't taking time for any of that. . . . I guess if I thought about it, I would have known I was due to fall apart."

For years, as a Congressional wife, "falling apart" had been the inevitable result of too much pressure. Colleagues in the House of Representatives claim the Minority Leader's concern for his wife's health was sometimes painfully evident. Once during a period of hospitalization, he wept openly in front of Speaker John McCormack. Often, according to John Rhodes, Ford would take an hour out of his working day to converse with his wife on the phone. Al Quie recalls several occasions when the Minority leader departed a political gathering after receiving an SOS from Betty. One such message came while they were traveling down the Potomac on the Presidential yacht, *The Sequoia*. "They had to send a boat," Quie recounts, "to pick him up. I know some of the guys who were close to him over the years sometimes swore under their breath, as men do when a wife appears to have a hold on a guy and breaks him loose from the fellowship. But I've never seen Jerry even show body English that would indicate anything other than complete devotion to her."

That devotion, according to Betty Ford, "is part of his religion. After all, it's one of the Ten Commandments. When I say that, I don't mean that he doesn't enjoy a pretty woman, and if he ever stopped looking I'd begin to worry, because I'd figure there was somebody."

It is perhaps the grief as much as the good times they have shared that brings a tremble to Jerry Ford's voice whenever he mentions Betty in a public speech. The display of emotion embarrasses him. "It's hard. People don't expect you to react that way."

Jerry Ford came to an unexpected and even fuller appreciation of his wife when he learned she would undergo surgery for a mastectomy. "Coming home from the hospital the night before she was to have her operation," the President found the White House cold solace. "To the best of my recollection, I was the only member of the family there." And he found himself considering the worst alternatives . . . "When you have an operation of that kind, even though the prospects are that they can perform the operation so that the cancer doesn't spread, there's always the chance that it might. If there had been some adverse development that would have been a pretty lonely place for two-and-a-half-years."

The operation, however, did not bring an end to anything; it signaled, in fact, a new beginning. The week following surgery, Betty Ford underwent what she frankly terms a "born again" experience: "It really came on sort of unexpectedly. I was not praying and I was not under any medication." The incident was so personal and so unusual that she can hardly find words to describe it. Although she was alone, "I felt the presence of Someone else in the room. . . . I was in bed and it almost seemed as if I was floating." The sensation lasted for some time—"as long as the room was quiet. It just seemed," she reflected, "as if this tremendous thing had happened to me, and I had finally reached what I had been seeking for so long."

When her seminary-student son, Michael, came to visit, Mrs. Ford told him what had happened. "I think," he muses, "if I had to describe what Mother went through—and my father did, too, at the same time on a different level—it was a new personal commitment to Christ that she had not previously had." Though his mother seemed to feel that God had "kind of miraculously delivered her from her illness," Michael thinks that "It's more miraculous the way God's spirit dwelt in her and Dad and really gave them a new life in Christ."

Despite a reluctance to ask God for favors ("I thank Him, that's what I do"), Betty Ford found herself continually praying for her husband's safety while they were in the White House. Twice she was greeted with the news that the President had narrowly escaped an assassin's bullet. The two events left the Ford family with a permanent anxiety. Whenever President Ford departed the Oval Office for a trip, he would telephone over to his wife in the mansion to tell her he was about to board the helicopter on the south lawn. "Then," says Betty Ford, "I'd go out on the Truman balcony and wave goodbye to him," always adding a prayer: "Please bring Jerry home alive." The fear for the President's life was just as real for the children.

"We were tremendously concerned," says Michael. "We wanted him to resign." He laughs, "I guess that's kind of an emotional response." The President himself candidly "expressed a real fear of a violent death. . . . I think his faith played a real part in his being able to deal with that. He felt that was where God wanted him to be. . . . And he would have to go about his life and his service to the country and just trust the Lord to protect him. But you know, he spent some agonizing hours over those times. We all did."

Whatever fears the President felt internally or expressed to his family were not apparent to his staff. Shortly after he was addressed by a gun instead of an outstretched palm in Sacramento, California, Ford was inside the State Capitol building calmly discoursing with Governor Jerry Brown, "as if," according to Bob Hartmann, "nothing happened," while outside, says Hartman, "there was pandemonium." After the second attempt in San Francisco, the President could even find some amusement in the event. As soon as the Secret Service heard a shot fired, they shoved Ford onto the floor of the Presidential limousine and piled in on top of him. In order to get the automobile up to speed as fast as possible, the chauffeur refrained from cooling the car. After some distance had been covered, a voice came up from beneath the two secret service agents. "Would somebody mind turning the air conditioner on?" asked the President of the United States, his face still flush against the carpeted floor. "It's getting a little warm down here."

The memory of the attempted assassinations provided ironic comfort to Betty Ford when her husband faced his first election failure. "In some sense, I felt a relief. . . . I figured I wouldn't have to worry about his life being destroyed."

Defeat was hardly a relief to the President. "I never like to lose," Jerry Ford admits. "Losing the election after everybody had worked so hard was real saddening inside, but I'd learned over a long period of time that you have to be as gracious in defeat as you are in victory, so regardless of how I felt inside, I projected an attitude of understanding a loss. . . . I wasn't going to sit around and be moody and disconsolate and the thing that really burned me up were those stories to the effect that I was mentally distraught. That was one hundred eighty degrees wrong!"

"It was the rest of us who couldn't accept it," recalls Michael. "I remember there were a lot of tears shed in the Oval Office. . . . He was the one who had the real sense of serenity about it. He'd give us a hug or a squeeze or a look in the eye—'It's O.K.' It was gratifying to me to see that his faith had not decreased in any way because of setbacks, but only increased. He felt that the job was really too big for one person, and that in order to fulfill it well and to do the job that had to be done, inevitably he had to go beyond himself. . . .

"He had tremendous awareness and consciousness when he was in the Presidency, of his finiteness. . . . He has a proverb that is particularly significant in his life. . . . 'Trust in the Lord with all thine heart; and lean not unto thine own understanding. In all thy ways acknowledge him, and he shall direct thy paths' " (Prov. 3:5 KJV).

It was that proverb that Michael and his father read over together in the Oval Office the morning the President learned his days of occupancy there were coming to a swift conclusion.

He had fought to win until his face was puffy and blotched, his eyes the color of a sunset, his voice lost in his larynx. He would second-guess himself with staff members for a week or more: "What could I have done differently?" But even when urged, he would not lift a finger to disturb the results.

"I was at the White House the morning after the election," recalls Senator Robert Griffin of Michigan, a longtime Ford friend. "There were some reports of election fraud in New York, West Virginia, Ohio. There was talk that busloads of people were hauled into counties where you don't have to be registered in advance. And there were pretty strong pressures that Ford should not concede the election and should hold out to launch an investigation, . . . pressures from party people around the country and some of his own people. It is possible that if Ohio and one other state had been turned around by ten thousand votes, he would have had the electoral vote. But the idea of being President by electoral vote rather than the popular vote, which was clearly Carter's, held no appeal to Ford. "We cannot do that," he said flatly.

One of the President's prime concerns about his own job loss was the fact that it affected the employment of all the people around him. Almost immediately he began assisting them in their search for reassignment. A Republican Congressman who had a staff opening was startled one morning to receive a telephone call from the President of the United States, acting as a job reference for a former press secretary. Jerry Ford was only doing what comes naturally—moving on. The great challenge to Christians, he says, "is not to become disillusioned by day-to-day problems, day-to-day disappointments. I just feel that you can't let what happens today overwhelm you. . . . You can't go into a shell and refuse to be a part of life. I think God wants man to move ahead and continue to participate, to do whatever he can, for himself, but primarily for others."

Will Ford run again? The odds are against it, he once said, adding with a twinkle, "but the odds can always change." Even if they do not, his short Presidency will have inscribed a significant sentence in history books. He held the bridge. When he left 1600 Pennsylvania Avenue, President Ford waded through the sudden flood of praise that customarily appears to carry away departing officials. But no tribute was more meaningful than the farewell editorial from a frequent critic, *The Washington Post*, which read in part:

> The President who will leave office this week brought precisely the needed temperament, character and virtues to the high offices he has temporarily held. These qualities are regularly subsumed under the familiar general heading of decency, a word that does indeed fit the man. What is so revealing about the times in which we live . . . is the vaguely condescending way in which this particular tribute is paid to him: 'Well, you have to admit, he's a decent person' . . . or 'Don't get me wrong! Of course, I think he's a decent person' and so on. Decency, in this context, becomes as an attribute something roughly comparable to good posture or punctuality. How odd that so few of us have been willing to acknowledge that decency in the White House can be regarded as a luxury or a bonus or a fringe benefit only at our own peril . . . It is central.

P. Stanton

# 5 | ARTHUR TAYLOR

"Damn it! That's not the way twelve-year-olds react! Arthur Taylor, president of CBS, exploded at producer Norman Lear, slamming his fist on the desk for emphasis. "That may be the way *your* twelve-year-old reacts, Norman, but it's not the way *my* twelve-year-old reacts!

What had occasioned Taylor's outburst was a scene from one of Lear's television shows, *One Day at a Time*. In the sequence, a twelve-year-old girl deliberately drops a bottle of aspirin on the locker room floor. "Oh," she says to her classmates, "I dropped my pills." She is hopeful the word will spread through the high school that she is on "the pill" so that a hip eighteen-year-old motorcycle driver will ask her out.

Taylor, the father of three young girls, was not amused by the implications. "What we're doing," he protested, "is feeding a lot of slimy propaganda to the American people."

Norman Lear, creator of *All in the Family, Maude,* and *Mary Hartmann, Mary Hartmann,* couldn't have agreed less. He thought he was merely showing life as it is, addressing himself to everyday situations, daring to be innovative and provocative. Since his first character, Archie Bunker, had snarled his bigotry across the home screen, Lear had been uncommonly successful in producing winning television series—all of them based on characters as controversial as Archie, all of them at one time or another engaged in probing such previously unairable themes as rape and homosexuality.

The confrontation between Taylor and Lear was the beginning of an epic battle of values, a battle which would eventually engage NBC, ABC, the Federal Communication Commission, and the National Association of Broadcasters as codefendants in a ten-million-dollar lawsuit.

The seeds of the struggle had been sown almost as soon as Taylor, a thirty-seven-year-old financial wizard, had been brought in to head CBS by Chairman of the Board William Paley. CBS had outdistanced NBC and ABC in the ratings for twenty years. But ratings were not enough for Arthur Taylor. He wanted to be able to look the public in the eye, to be proud of his product. And it was not easy, he found, to be proud of a product that was, according to rapidly accumulating evidence, having a destructive influence on America's children.

In the early 1970s, studies showed, the average child under five watched approximately 23.5 hours of television a week. If an adolescent continued that pace of viewing until graduation from high school, he would have vicariously participated in eighteen thousand murders. More than twenty-three thousand reports on the effects of this steady diet of violence had been compiled; the conclusions were mostly negative. They showed that video violence tended to produce aggressive behavior in the young in any segment of the society. What concerned Taylor most was the effect television carnage had on the underprivileged, whose access to church, school, and family guidance was severely limited. Research showed conclusively, Taylor pointed out, that "where there's a heavy dosage of television and where this may be the major input—or God help us in some cases the only imput—the correlation between it and violent behavior is very large. Who are these kids? These are black kids in the ghettoes. . . . And what we were doing was feeding a time bomb into the society."

With these facts in mind, Taylor insisted there was no time to wait. "Clearly a cure was in order. You couldn't say, 'Look we're sorry. We made a mistake and all these kids are in jail now.' We couldn't do that."

The best advice Taylor got from industry advisors was "Don't stick your neck out." But, he asked himself, "Who else was going to do it?" Was it right to thrust the wheel of a tough ship into the hands of a coerced employee? He was well aware that the sharpest cries of pain would come from the creative community, the very group upon which an entertainment corporation was most dependent. He was convinced he could persuade them that producing "clean shows" was not paralyzing their ideas, that the challenge of reaching beyond the quick fix of sex and violence would stimulate rather than stifle creativity.

While Arthur Taylor was turning these kinds of thoughts over with other television executives, the public was becoming more and more aroused over the same questions. The over nine-million-member PTA was organizing forums to channel public anger into constructive dissent. Citizens were complaining to their Congressmen. The Federal Communications Commission received twenty-five thousand letters a year protesting gratuitous sex and violence on the air. Norman Lear scoffed at the amount of mail; he maintained it was miniscule as compared with the number of actual viewers in the land.

On November 22, 1975, the clamor came to a head; the Chairman of the Federal Communications Commission, Richard Wiley, asked the presidents of the three networks if they would meet with him in

Washington to discuss the public displeasure with the television content. Thus began the FCC chief's innocent foray into what he later termed "the most frustrating thing that's happened to me in government." Wiley, a former Chicago lawyer and a highly respected figure in Washington, projects an Eagle Scout earnestness from behind his horn-rimmed glasses. "Look," he told the network executives, "we've got a problem. Something ought to be done about it and it ought to be done in the private sector because I can't regulate."

"I agree with you, Mr. Chairman," said Arthur Taylor. "And speaking for CBS, we're going to do something about it." CBS had been going through intense self-examination for many months. They had discussed various proposals with other representatives in the industry. Plans for change were well into the developmental stage.

Taylor's statement, Wiley later recounted, about knocked him and the other commissioners "off our chairs. . . . I was really impressed with him because I thought here's a guy . . . who's really got the public interest at heart. When he took that position on violence, I thought, 'Boy, something may happen.' "

By the end of December, after another month of discussion at CBS, the network presented a proposal to the National Association of Broadcaster' Television Code Review Board. In essence, CBS suggested that the hours between seven and nine o'clock in the evening should be filled with entertainment suitable for the entire family, and that all NAB members voluntarily subscribe to such self-regulation. After a three-and-a-half month gestation period and considerable labor pains, the proposal was accepted by the NAB Television Board. The Family Viewing Hour was born.

Its arrival coincided with the start of the 1975-76 television season. No sooner had the Family Viewing Hour made its appearance than it was ducking attack from all sides. The Catholic Bishops of America said the proposal did not go nearly far enough; children were often still at the set beyond nine in the evening. Other critics blasted the new regulation as a smokescreen to provide free license for murder, mayhem and rape from nine to twelve. Arthur Taylor was the first to admit that the Family Viewing Hour was not the total solution. But it was, he insisted, at least an initial step: "the first time that TV had ever conceded that there was an ethical consideration to be made. Prior to this, it was simply a question of what will attract the largest audience."

The most potent lung power came, as expected, from the TV producers and writers who would be forced to alter their material or face seeing certain shows shoved to the later, less lucrative hours of the evening. "Censorship," they bawled. The loudest voice was Norman Lear's. He claimed that the family viewing hour was "a gutless give-in," that the networks were overreacting to a situation "they helped create." Writers, he said were often just responding to the demands of program chiefs when they inserted too much "action" into scripts.

In December of 1975, Taylor took his case directly to Los Angeles. Speaking to the Hollywood Radio and Television Society, he stressed the responsibility of their all-pervasive medium. "Unlike movies or books or magazines, our product is usually watched by family members together. . . . It is thus a factor in the family's conversation, in its divergent views, in its decision-making. It follows that when the family gathers and operates as a unit, when choice is a family one and not an individual one, then we have an obligation to program in a manner responsive to the needs, the tastes, the interests of that entire group."

Rather than persuading audiences to his view, Taylor's high-toned rhetoric was lampooned by some broadcasters as "lecturing." The CBS president was "pompous" and arrogant, his critics claimed. Only the public was behind Arthur Taylor's family viewing hour; a poll commissioned by *TV Guide* showed that eighty-two percent of the citizenry favored sanitizing the entertainment hours between seven and nine in the evening.

By this time, however, Hollywood had made its own independent judgment as to the desires of John Q. Viewer. The writers', directors', and screen actors' unions banded together under the leadership of Norman Lear to bring the issue into court. Changing the name "Family Viewing" to "Prime time censorship rule," the trade unions declared it a violation of the First Amendment. We don't think, asserted Writers' Guild executive Michael Franklin, "that the government has any business telling the people what they can see and when they can see it."

Ironically, it was in the CBS news department, one of the most fervent bastions of First Amendment rights, that Taylor's efforts met with approval. While philosophically in tune with any writer fighting for unfettered expression, CBS anchorman Walter Cronkite asserts, "It seems to me that the operators of the networks and individual stations must have something to say about the quality of the material that is put on their network. I don't see where the artist can have complete freedom in this particular regard."

The Family Viewing Hour, in Cronkite's opinion, "was a valiant effort. I was rather appalled that some aspects of the industry should not have gotten aboard his bandwagon." News and entertainment are separate worlds, Cronkite maintains, but from an "outsider's view" Taylor's lack of support "looked like jealousy to me. They didn't want to follow the lead of the new boy on the block, in what was a rather radical, but sound, idea."

Taylor himself had been one of the most frequent advocates of the First Amendment: testifying before Congressional Committees in defense of broadcast journalist rights, often making the topic the central theme of his speeches, even occasionally facing off with the White House on the subject.

Below the constitutional arguments, however, was the issue of the pocketbook. The creative community did not deem it politic to publicly discuss the financial aspects of dissent, Norman Lear admitted to *Playboy* magazine, "because it makes us look like we're more interested in dollars than in the high-flown issue of the First Amendment. . . . But I'm not ashamed to admit that I care very deeply about the free enterprise system. . . . So I'm angry that *All in the Family* has been moved from Saturday night at eight to nine on Monday. I'm furious about having worked five-and-a-half long years to achieve the kind of success that *All in the Family* has enjoyed, only to have its dollar value diminished." It was equally annoying to Lear that he was unable to sell his avant garde series *Mary Hartmann, Mary Hartmann* to the networks. He registered his displeasure by suing the networks, the NAB, and the FCC for ten million dollars.

The case against the Family Viewing Hour was tried in the plaintiff's backyard, by a judge who freely admitted to Arthur Taylor, "I'm the defender of the creative community."

"God help you," Taylor responded. "These people are out for the fast buck."

"Well," the judge insisted, "they know what's going on in America."

"I defy a producer who's been married six times," declared Taylor, "and is living in a beach house in Malibu, to tell me what's going on in America!"

The conversation made little impression on Judge Warren Ferguson. Neither did the testimony of the three network officials who had attended the meeting called by FCC Chief Richard Wiley. Wiley did not coerce them into taking action against violence and gratuitous sex on the air-waves, they insisted, it was the broadcasting industry's sincere attempt to regulate itself. Wiley had been very candid in saying that there was little, indeed nothing, that the government could do. It was up to private enterprise, he had asserted.

But the judge believed the Hollywood producers and writers, who stated that Wiley had threatened the network officials, causing them to fear government retaliation if they did not heed his admonitions. In a landmark decision, the judge declared the Family Viewing Hour unconstitutional, a violation of the right of free speech as guaranteed in the First Amendment.

The decision, as well as the scorching denunciation of his behavior, stunned Richard Wiley. "I wish," he says wryly, "I had had a tape recorder at that meeting, because there would have been no loss of that lawsuit." The whole affair, he said, had been a headshaking experience. "To go through all of this for something that I thought was in the public interest. As Newton Minow has said, 'If I hadn't done it, I wouldn't have been doing my job.' "

Before the court decision was handed down, Arthur Taylor was fired from CBS. On October 9, 1975, he was called into the office of his one-time mentor, William Paley. It was nine o'clock in the morning, just two hours before a CBS board of directors meeting. With Paley were two of the directors. They would like, Taylor was told, his resignation. "Why?" asked the dumbfounded Taylor. No reasons were given, it was simply the pleasure of the board. It was all over in less than five minutes.

At eleven o'clock as the board of directors of CBS eyed the empty chair at the seventeen-place mahogany table in the CBS board room, William Paley announced to them that Arthur Taylor had resigned, effective immediately. That concluded, he proceeded to review the success CBS had achieved under Taylor's leadership. CBS's third-quarter profits had risen to a record $40.8 million on sales of $525 million, a large leap from the previous year when CBS had earned $29.1 million from revenues of $461 million. Indeed, since 1972, when Taylor had assumed command at CBS, each annual report revealed substantial financial gain. His release from the company left Wall Street as well as many CBS employees in a state of shock.

"This comes as a complete bolt out of the blue," a corporate spokesman stammered to *Time* magazine. Since neither William Paley nor Arthur Taylor would discuss their differences publicly, industry and the media were left with speculation. Initial conclusions linked Taylor's dismissal with the decline in CBS' ratings, a direct result of some rearrangement of program scheduling due to the demands of the Family Viewing Hour. One New York newspaper attributed the fall-off in ratings to the departure of many talented CBS program executives who objected to Taylor's management policies. "Taylor was hired 4 years ago to tighten corporate efficiency but apparently alienated creative personnel, several of whom are now helping competing networks overtake CBS. Paley reportedly hopes new president John Backe will improve the creative climate."

Indeed, Paley was mystified by Taylor's quarrels with a segment of the broadcasting industry that he himself had arduously courted. Observers contend that Taylor was unable to convince the CBS chairman that it was important to win the Family Viewing war. That accomplished, the dust would settle.

But Paley, according to industry sources, believes in "what works" and clearly the Family Viewing Hour wasn't working. Some sources conjecture that one of the turning points in the relationship between

Paley and Taylor was Taylor's appearance on a religious television program on the West Coast.

The interviewer was Minister Robert Schuller. From where, he wanted to know, had the motivation for the Family Viewing Hour come? Had Christ ever played a part in this? "Yes," the young CBS president answered. "There's no question about that. That's where I derive an enormous amount of strength. Whenever things in my life have been cloudy, that light has always been there." The comment seemed to intrigue Chairman Paley. He acquired a copy of the show, according to a CBS insider, and watched it over and over and over.

No one knows what was in William Paley's mind as he stared at his young protege's image and listened to his blatant Christianity. But some knowledgeable sources contend that the television show drew the bottom line under the steadily accumulating differences between Paley, the pragmatist, and Taylor, the idealist.

From his earliest days in the CBS saddle, Arthur Taylor had been riding herd on reform. "I think he felt," says Bill Leonard, CBS's recently appointed President of News, "that a corporation had to be more than a coffee grinder for money. He cared a great deal," says Leonard, that the employee receive his fair share. He worked tirelessly, according to other associates, when preparing to present a cash bonus plan, called the Executive Improvement Plan, to Paley for approval. "And I remember," says one employee, "that for literally hours and hours he would sit there and go over this list of people, trying to weigh in his own mind what contribution each individual had made to the company, increasing, decreasing, mostly increasing, fiddling with these numbers, trying to make certain everything was fair.

"I remember when he came out of his presentation, he was totally exhausted. 'You just don't know what I've been through,' he said."

"I think," adds another CBS executive, "that Paley thought he was trying to give away the store."

Few CBS employees, for obvious reasons, will speak on the record in behalf of Arthur Taylor. Off the record, there are statements such as this one made by a director: "I view Arthur Taylor as probably one of the most decent human beings I've ever met. . . . He is an extraordinary man. When I was here, he started the women's movement, which was really nonexistent before his arrival."

Working for women necessitated a good deal of friendly persuasion with men. "We had to make everyone conscious," says Taylor, "that the wrong thing had happened with women employees. There were talented, experienced women who simply had not risen through the ranks, who had been doing a fine job and had been constantly passed over. And that had to be stopped. In effect, the blinders had to go.

And in those cases where injustice had been done, we just simply cut through and solved those problems."

Taylor's advances for feminism were so widely noted that Harvard made a study of his personality to discover his motivations. The project brings a chuckle from the subject. "I'm a 'case' at Harvard." As was done with other men who showed an uncommon concern for the welfare of women, Taylor was put through a series of questionnaires and interviews examining his background. They discovered a man of acknowledged brilliance who, unlike many of his Yale-Princeton colleagues on Wall Street, was raised in a blue-collar town—Rahway, New Jersey. He was the son of a New Jersey Bell Telephone engineer who quit school at the age of twelve to become a telegraph messenger. Mr. Taylor thought that his son should also drop the books and pick up the hoe at an early age. But young Arthur, encouraged by his minister and aided by scholarships, pursued his studies, graduating with a degree in Renaissance History from Brown University, *magna cum laude* and a member of Phi Beta Kappa. Thinking his career would be in the academic world, Taylor worked as admissions officer at Brown, earning tuition money for graduate work in the field of American economic history. But the dreariness of Rhode Island winters drove him to New York, where he joined the First Boston Corporation as a trainee. In four years he was Vice President of the underwriting department. In three more years, he was serving as a director of First Boston. In 1970 he left that organization to join International Paper Company as vice president in charge of finance. Within a year, he was International Paper's executive vice president and chief financial officer. When Arthur Taylor was elected president and chief operating officer of CBS in 1972, he was 37 years old, just 11 years out of graduate school.

Taylor's early success pattern coincided dramatically with that of other men involved in the women's movement, Harvard discovered. So did his modest, middle class background and lack of membership in the Ivy League "club." Another strong influence was the fact that he was the father of three young girls. "I started when they were very young," Taylor remarked, "thinking what kind of a world they were going to have."

Arthur Taylor's initiation of the women's movement at CBS was only part of a larger effort, according to former colleagues, to create a more humane corporate environment. "He had a view," says ABC executive Sheldon Wool, who served as vice president for development under Taylor, "that the performance of the company was directly related to what was going on in people's heads, in terms of their satisfaction with their jobs. And if people were frustrated and dissatisfied, either . . . with the company or with their personal lives, it was going to be very hard for them to come and be . . .

creative." Approaching business from a humanistic view was, according to Wool, "very satisfying because . . . you were doing the thing that you thought was right; yet at the same time, in being practical, hardheaded business men, you could say that you were doing the right thing for the corporation."

"I've found," says Arthur Taylor, "that when groups of human beings have some faith in the justice of the organization in the sense that their own foibles and weaknesses and mistakes will be put into context that they won't be misused, the creativity level goes through the roof. For every ten percent you reduce the fear, the creativity goes up twenty percent. And you reduce the fear by saying to other human beings, 'Whatever position you are in, you are worthy and your contributions are worthy.' "

Kathryn Pelgrift, director of finance for Phillip Morris, worked with Taylor in three different organizations. She claims that Taylor's techniques of inspiring employees "made people want to go over the edge after him." He was, she points out, particularly effective in bringing the bloom to "wilted flowers." When he traveled to various corporate locations around the country addressing local management, he stressed the significance of each individual's role to the entire organization. He made a point of getting to know employees on the lowest levels in order to inspire them with a sense of mission.

"He started something at International Paper," recalls Miss Pelgrift, "that is really now sort of old hat. He brought outlying company people—some of them very low level—to New York for three-and-four-day seminars." For some of the employees, it was a first look at the Big Apple. The purpose of the seminars was to give the workers a chance to personally air their problems to the front line.

Another Taylor method of imparting a sense of dignity to the individual was a willingness to share the credit. A CBS employee says, "We used to have what we called Corplan meetings, and they were essentially planning meetings for various divisions. The chairman of the board would be there. Arthur would be there. A number of group presidents would be present. If one of the division presidents would give a presentation and the underling who composed the report was just sitting in, Arthur would say, 'Mr. Chairman, I would like you to know that so-and-so put together the report that was just given.' "

Not only did the promotion of human dignity promote the corporation, Taylor believed, but it had the potential of benefiting society as a whole. He often voiced a recurrent theme with Sheldon Wool. "Many of our institutions are failing around us. There is a loss of confidence in government, in families, in marriage, schools, churches. I think it's fair to say that he felt that despite a lot of criticism the American business institution was one of the institutions that was working the best—the best being defined as performing the role that it was supposed to be performing in our society. And he started to develop this idea that . . . we had to find ways in which the American corporation could perform even a larger role in catering to the issue of personal satisfaction."

One atmospheric change Taylor attempted to make met with a good deal of subterranean grumbling: his efforts to clean up the CBS conversational stream. "In some respects," says a former associate, "he was a very different type than the sort of junior or middle-level executive on the television side of CBS—the guys in their mid-thirties, the station managers, the aspiring network heads who had grown up in an environment that taught you it was clever to make cheap comments, sexually-related jokes, the Las Vegas type repartee. Arthur was very uncomfortable with that." When Taylor came down very heavily on public vulgarity, "he incurred the charge of pompousness. He was aware that he was thought pompous, but he didn't care. He wasn't about to let it go on."

The fact that Arthur Taylor worked to blend humanistic values with business achievements caused some of his former colleagues to regard him as a "statesman." Don Gull, an American Airlines executive who worked as Taylor's assistant at CBS, says, "His great depth provides a perception of man that is far beyond what most of us experience."

Corporate "statesmen" are more often than not considered a rarity, but Ambassador Sol Linowitz, former chairman of the board of Xerox and a conegotiator of the Panama Canal treaties, thinks "statesmen in business are very often the best businessmen. . . . If you are going to lead your enterprise with perspective and with a sense of where we ought to be going in the world, you have to take into account problems that go far beyond the profit and loss. . . . I just don't think it's possible anymore for us to go back to the era of 'What's good for business is good for America.' What's good for America is what business must take into account in deciding what's good for business."

It was also Arthur Taylor's conception that industry had to abandon the hierarchial chain of command. "The day when the powerful rich can get away with stomping on others, I think is coming to an end. The American corporation ought to find a new way to operate."

He advocates a more collegial decision process. "Everything is done with a maximum amount of communication—where candor is prized, where no one is penalized for their viewpoints or their counter viewpoints. So that when a decision is made everyone feels . . . their judgment has been considered. They know precisely why an action has been taken."

For William Paley, who had built an enormously successful

organization based on the traditional system of hierarchy, Arthur Taylor's "collegial" view of management was just another radical concept to swallow.

Arthur Taylor's working environment was also markedly different in style. Junior executives, blacks, outside visitors tended to wander in and out of the president's office all day long—an atmosphere totally alien to Chairman Paley's Nineteenth Century proprietorial management.

Despite the large gap in their value systems, William Paley and Arthur Taylor had almost a father-son relationship until Taylor's final year with CBS. Some daily observers of the two men weave a poignant tale around their eventual schism.

For several years, William Paley's beautiful and aristocratic wife, Babe, had been terminally ill with lung cancer. Not only did the illness place a psychological strain on the chairman; it also exacted a physical toll. It had been an annual Paley custom to vacation in Europe for several months. When it became too difficult for Mrs. Paley to travel, her husband began coming to the office every day, putting in longer hours, missing the recuperative periods he had been used to. At the age of seventy-five, the pressures were wearing down the keenness of his memory. At times, it was difficult for him to recall decisions in which he had participated. "He would forget," says one eyewitness, "that there was a meeting yesterday and he'd be convinced that people were involved in a conspiracy against him. You'd get into these situations where he would accuse Arthur directly of keeping things from him. 'Why wasn't I consulted on this,' Mr. Paley would demand and the answer would be 'But you were, you chaired the meeting.' "

There was also the fact that William Paley was the founding father of CBS, having purchased the fledgling network with stock sales from his father's successful cigar company in 1928. For nearly half a century, he had operated as the chief executive officer, lending his shrewd intellect to every major CBS decision, watching the organization grow into a two billion dollar conglomerate. His acknowledged programing acumen had contributed greatly to CBS' twenty-year ratings leadership. CBS was purely and simply his baby, and he wanted it to remain in his image. Instead, it was becoming more and more identified with the forty-one-year old president, who seemed to be operating on all fronts at once in what appeared—some say—to the aging entrepreneur as an arrogant usurpation of power.

"What the Chairman probably forgot," speculates one CBS employee, "was that when he selected Arthur, he wanted a man who was dynamic and would take the corporation someplace and had a vision of what it was going to be, but you know when you reach a certain age . . ." the employee shakes his head sympathetically, "We're all that way. It's going to happen to all of us."

William Paley replaced Arthur Taylor with a very different kind of personality. John Backe, said Paley, had never disagreed with him on any major decision. Not even, it appeared, in matters of fashion. At the press conference announcing Backe's appointment, both men wore the same color suit, the same patterned tie. Backe himself expressed a preference for working "behind the scenes." When Paley finally turned the chief executive reins over to Backe in April of '77, he retained his chairmanship, and industry speculation was strong that Mr. Paley would still be very much in control of his company.

For Arthur Taylor, who had built a reputation of unusual achievement in every line of work, there was only sudden humiliation. Leading newspapers and major news magazines carried lengthy articles on his dismissal. Chairman Paley's statement was simple—He and the board did not think that Arthur Taylor had the proper qualifications to be his successor. "When Mr. Taylor learned that, he felt he should resign." Taylor said nothing.

A year later, when Paley was asked to specify why he didn't think Taylor had the proper qualifications to be his successor despite the fact that he had brought the company to such heights of financial success, Paley replied "I'm afraid I can't."

Richard Nixon once said that the president of a network has more power than the President of the United States. The instantaneous and unceremonious stripping of such power reveals the character of many people—the victim and the colleagues of the victim.

"I really feel," says New York attorney and friend Stanley Schlesinger, "the greatest performance of Arthur Taylor as a human being, as a business man, as a renaissance man, has been since he left CBS . . . He was conducted himself with all other people and all other companies . . . in a fantastic manner."

"He's got a lot of inner courage," says Kathy Pelgrift, "that I sure wouldn't have had under the circumstances. He really picked himself up and kept going to all the things that he'd always gone to—to the Bilderberg meetings in England, to the Tri-Lateral Commission in Japan—kept his Washington contacts; went to the dinners, was moved thirty places down the dais, put up with all the people saying to him, 'Boy, you really got it! What are you going to do next?' I don't think you get through something like that," Miss Pelgrift adds, "unless you've got a strong foundation somewhere, belief in yourself or a religion or a destiny or what have you."

"What have you" was indeed his faith. Without a belief in God, Taylor concedes, the ordeal would have been "terrible, terrible. No man has enough faith in himself to sustain this. And it's particularly true because so many people turn away from you. They're not bad people. It's just that they go on with their own lives, and they consider you sort of stopped. Some of them are very bad. But most of them just don't care. There are a number of Chinese writings which say that the number of people who can share the trauma of life with you are very few. And you're kidding yourself if you think there are dozens. There are not dozens. There's not a dozen. . . . A great many people simply turn their backs on you and walk away. And that hurts."

The "walk aways" that hurt the most were former employees who were themselves saved from the guillotine by Taylor. On three occasions as CBS president, Taylor interceded in behalf of one executive, who told him at the time, "You've got to understand that if anything goes wrong, I'll never be able to repay you. I don't have any loyalty."

The disillusionment was balanced out, Taylor contends, "by the people who love you. They stick to you like glue." Indeed, Taylor loyalists—former employees and friends—frequently use superlatives like "extraordinary," "brilliant," "sensitive," to describe him, and they are full of anecdotes to refute the pompous and arrogant charges issued by his critics.

"There are," claims Sheldon Wool, "innumerable little stories such as this one about Arthur: There was a CBS executive named Ray Schwartz, who didn't know Arthur particularly well. Suddenly, one summer, he got cancer of the pancreas and died within a few months, leaving a wife and ten children. . . . Arthur was spending like a third of his day, not only making sure that all the financial issues were being taken care of, but speaking to Mrs. Schwarz to make sure she was getting moral support. . . . I remember one time we were sitting in the office and Ray's name came up and he suddenly realized that he'd not talked to Mrs. Schwarz for two or three months and he just called to find out if there was anything he could do.

"He was always sensitive to the little things," Wool continues. "He used to come in the morning and see people carrying containers of coffee into the building. Which is normal enough, except we had a cafeteria on the twentieth floor which served coffee and presumably if you could buy coffee on the twentieth floor, why schlepp it across town?" The mystery intrigued Taylor so much he began making inquiries. The reason people weren't buying coffee on the twentieth floor, he was told, was because the coffee on the twentieth floor was wretched. Since the president of CBS always has his coffee served to him on a nice tray, he is unaware of the flavor of machine brew. "When he found out," concludes Wool, "that the coffee was undrinkable, he insisted that the vice president of personnel get drinkable coffee into the organization."

In conversation, Arthur Taylor talks with remarkable equanimity about his abrupt departure from that organization and the equally abrupt change of lifestyle. One day he had a chauffeured car, a company plane, and a reserved table at The '21 Club at his disposal.

The next day, along with his prestigious title, they were gone. The morning after his execution, "I said to myself, when you came to CBS you didn't have any of those things. So you're not losing anything. You're still the same man you were five years ago, hopefully a little better."

He is frank to admit the fawning and the perequisites attached to great power are "a pull on the ego, but I don't think there was a day that went by, when I walked in that Taj Mahal over there, that I didn't say to myself, 'You've got to understand that this is temporary.' I fought identifying with those things. I never got into the car with the chauffeur that I didn't say, 'Don't get to the point where you rely on these things,' because I knew that if I ever did, when they were taken away, I would be left with really nothing."

His keenest disappointment as a broadcasting executive was the failure of the Family Hour. "They won," he says sadly, of the Hollywood community. Which means, he points out, that the values of America are being shaped on the West Coast. "What they really want to see are their own morals justified. We're talking about a hundred people in Los Angeles. But a hundred people make a difference—directors, writers, producers." They have become so powerful, Taylor contends, "because . . . the networks don't have the guts to try other people. The cost of failure is so high, people who are successful are asked to do more. Everytime I say that to groups of people, there are intakes of breath. But really, we're in the hands of a very small number of people who live among all the tinsel of Hollywood."

He is somewhat consoled that the Family Viewing Hour helped curtail TV violence. "Unfortunately, now, it's gone the other road. In the summer of 1977, he predicted the invasion of what he termed "soft porn" on the small screen. And the fall programing proved him a prophet. Near-nudity and bed hopping has become so prevalent on television that *Newsweek* devoted a cover story to the fact that "the sexual revolution has finally seeped through the looking glass." In one season, video offerings included a rape scene in *All in the Family,* the saga of a sixteen-year-old boy losing his virginity, an intimate look at the world of prostitution, the expose of a white slave ring, and an examination of incest. "The most widespread suspicion," wrote *Newsweek,* "is that prime time's new blue hue is a carefully calculated replacement for the old red-blood one."

A study undertaken by two Michigan State University researchers reveals that children view thirty-to-forty implied or explicit sexual acts in one view week. Between nine and eleven in the evening, such acts occur at the rate of 2.7 per hour, largely between unmarried couples.

Arthur Taylor worries about the effect of such scenes on the youthful psyche. "What in the world are we doing? My daughters are so vigorous. They're so vital. . . . They're into horses. They play tennis. And yet they're being bombarded on television because some producers in Hollywood find some psychological release. I find that very uncomfortable." Had he stayed at CBS, "I would have gone on struggling. There's no way that I would have let up. I either had to make the job right for me or there was no job."

He would never return to the broadcasting industry except on his own terms. "If somebody would come to me and say, 'Forget the profitability; find a new way to do mass television in America.' That I'd take. That I would accept in a second. But when they say to me, 'We want to make it profitable. We want to make it first' in the old terms, then I know there's an internal conflict with what I believe that I can't resolve. Look at the position you're in. You take on the responsibility for keeping this thing financially sound. . . . To compete and make it financially sound, you give them more of the same. You're constantly faced with the situation of putting together a product that is less than satisfying and it tears you apart. What we really need is carte blanche for two or three years to make the changes and not worry about how much money you're going to lose, because you're going to lose a lot of money.'

The episode of the Family Viewing Hour proved conclusively that the content of television is up to the customer. "We've always maintained," says Bill Leonard, "that there is nothing as self-correcting or as democratic as television. That the public really does decide in a variety of ways. . . . We're as bad as politicians. . . . People are voting for us every day. Sooner or later, if the public doesn't want violence or sex, that's the last thing you're going to see." Ratings, however, indicate that people frequently fail to put their channel tuner where their mouth is.

Reclining in a wing chair, in his shirt sleeves, his light brown hair cropped short against a forehead growing taller, soft-spoken Arthur Taylor looks much more like a college professor than a corporate executive. He thinks his academic demeanor may have contributed to his reputation for being removed. "You'll find people will say, 'My Lord, he's pompous.'

"I hear that all the time and I don't think I am." But, he admits, "There is a little stiffness. I'm not a locker room, hail-fellow well met, get drunk type. That's not my bag, and I've always stayed aloof. If anything, what they're saying is I'm aloof, and that's true, I am." If he is at a dinner party and four people get drunk he immediately backs away. "Maybe," he laughs, "I am pompous. As far as I can determine, this comes from something I can't help, which is, I feel a little apart. A lot of the stuff that used to come up in fraternity houses, I didn't like very much. I could never see the benefit of hazing, for example."

In conversation, there is little evidence to support the charges of pompousness. As he ranges over a variety of topics, his brown eyes are direct—more soulful than imperial. He is as frank about his liabilities as he is about his assets, and he is used to being misread. His own parents didn't "understand what I've been doing since the age of five. They loved me very much, but what I was doing and what I was about they didn't understand. My father is dead now, but my mother doesn't understand to this day." When he was fired from CBS, Mrs. Taylor said, "I hope you can get something now closer to home."

He is proud of the fact that his parents were "very good, very simple people." His father was an engineer for New Jersey Bell Telephone. When he retired at the age of sixty, he had given the company forty-eight years of service. "I don't think," says Taylor, "that my mother and father had ever been on an airplane or traveled more than two hundred miles from home until about six years ago when they moved to Florida. That was the longest trip they had ever taken." Their desires were as uncomplicated as their lifestyle.

He does not know where his own ambition came from. "It started very, very early. Please don't misinterpret this. It's very, very, very hard to put into words." He pauses for a long while, starts the sentences, then pauses again, afraid candor will smack of egotism. "I don't know whether I can get it right for you. I started to read when I was very, very young, like three, and by the time I got to school I was vaguely conscious of being different. That has stayed with me all my life."

He has found great understanding and intellectual companionship with his wife, Sandy, whom he met when he was a junior administrator at Brown University and she was a senior at Pembroke. "She's a very, very intelligent, very, very good person and whereas I tend not to be so optimistic, she's eternally optimistic. . . . My experience has been that when couples work, it's essentially a blending of minds more than anything. And what was really the first impression of our relationship was that it was a stimulating experience to be together. . . . I've often said about women that the sexiest part of them is their brain, as far as I'm concerned. And most intelligent men that I know feel that way."

In their seventeen years of marriage, there have been many pressures on Sandy Taylor. She was forced to assume the mantle of corporate wife at an unusually young age. They handled the difficulties, her husband explains by, "not overreaching ourselves in terms of base. If I had had a giant house, with a lot of servants and chauffeurs, it would have been rough. We opted to go small and manageable, so the kids and Sandy, when I was gone, never felt overwhelmed by infrastructure."

And gone he was, a great deal of the time. "It bothered me then. It bothers me now. When you come to a stopping point like I have, the guilt is always with you. You always wonder if you've done it right. . . . You just live with that guilt. I live with it. I've never resolved it." His period of unemployment has brought obvious family benefits. "Sandy and the children and I have never been closer—never, ever, ever. . . . The things that we do have become tremendously important. . . . And the funny thing about it, I derive far more joy out of those things." He finds himself storing the memories. "It's the strangest thing. I find myself, when we're together, saying 'Now, remember this. Catalogue it; put it away.' I'm building a file I never built before."

For he, like so many of his friends and former associates, see a day coming when his time might be severely collapsed again. "I have an abiding faith that I will be called to do something significant again. . . . Maybe not. Maybe I'll spend the rest of my life watching sunsets." And if that indeed should be his lot? "I can accept that. I can accept that. I'll go to my grave thinking there were some things I could have done that would have been helpful. But maybe I've done it. Maybe it's over."

Taylor-watchers don't see it that way. "I think he's a very unusual guy," says Ambassador Sol Linowitz, "extraordinarily able to take on responsibility, particularly in these times. . . . I can't see him doing a small thing." Don Gull sees Taylor's period of enforced retirement as "almost a serendipitous thing. You know, all great men of history, Abraham Lincoln for example, had periods of very difficult trials. It's sort of the refiner's fire. Periods when they really had to go into themselves and sort themselves out before they could make the contributions to society and the world that they did."

A statement with which the former CBS president does not necessarily disagree. Since childhood he has had an urge to be involved with matters of substance. "I suppose the thing that drives me the most is the desire to be a doer of deeds—almost in the Arthurian sense. I don't know whether I'm a Sir Lancelot or a Don Quixote. Was Family Viewing the grail or was it jousting at a windmill?"

Regardless, Taylor finds it impossible to accept an unsatisfactory status quo. . . . I have a tremendous difficulty leaving things the way they are." He has, he says, almost a compulsion "to tinker with the existing structure."

The need is accelerated by what he terms an almost "uncanny ability to tell what's coming in the future. . . . I really think that's the only ability I have that is above average. It's not a case of crystal-ball gazing. It's a case of studying the issues and coming to a point of view. And what that produces is an enormous motivation to do something about that conviction."

The future he now foresees is not inviting. "If we stay on the present track, then we've got great changes coming in the society. . . . The style and standard of living will change. The economic system will probably be dramatically changed." If we have American institutions and corporations that are run by "grey and lifeless administrators," Taylor predicts these changes will arrive by the end of the century. "We'll end up maybe not socialistic, but with a society that can't provide opportunities for young men and women coming along.

"We'll end up with businesses which may not be owned by government, but will be profitless. Capital will be furnished by the government. We'll end up with an erosion of some of the freedoms, particularly the First Amendment. We'll end up looking a lot more like 1935 in terms of the appliances we use and the houses we live in."

He brightens this dismal picture with the caveat, "It doesn't need to be this way. All that can be corrected by the right kind of leadership from American industry and the right kind of government leadership." Since leaving CBS, Taylor has labored to provide some of that kind of leadership, redirecting his attention to the energy crisis. Insiders report he has turned down a very significant job from another network, as well as an important ambassadorial post, to work with Nelson Rockefeller and former World Bank president George Woods. The three men believe they have found a way to put the billions of excess Arab petro dollars to productive use. They have been negotiating with the Saudi Arabian government to create a New York based development corporation that would seek to find new international food and energy sources for the United States and the underdeveloped nations. According to a story in the *New York Daily News*, "Rockefeller, along with political leaders, businessmen, and government officials in virtually all the industrialized Western nations and the lesser developed countries, have been concerned about the enormous flow of funds to the Arab nations. . . .

"If formed," the story continues, "The impact of such a corporation on the world economy . . . and the standard of living would be enormous." Few would discount that assessment, but many a dream has died on the drawing board, and as of this writing, an agreement with the Saudis has not been finalized.

His religion, Taylor affirms has removed anxiety from waiting for his future to be resolved. "I'm completely reconciled to have this hand play itself out. If you had said to me ten years ago that I would go a year being unassigned, I'd have said, 'I couldn't stand it.' But that's not the way I feel now. . . . I don't feel diminished. I feel, in a sense, broadened, in terms of my understanding of human beings and of myself. I could never again do anything that wasn't worth doing."

It was during his years with CBS that he found himself seeking a closer relationship with God. He had been brought up a practicing Presbyterian, but the need for faith ironically became more apparent as he assumed more power. "No matter how well I did, I had a feeling how inadequate it all was." A feeling that inclined him to reach "out for a strength that was greater than my own, and it was there."

More and more, he says, he has become "ecumenically-minded. . . . My churches are in the countryside. They're in the urban area. . . . The church of today, I think, is a life church. . . . I think the action has shifted." The relevant church in Arthur Taylor's mind is a universal church that concerns itself with how human beings treat one another, moment to moment. "How do you react when you're in competition with another for a particular prize? How do you react when faced with a twenty-dollar bribe? How, when you're given a position of authority, do you behave to the people under you? What is the proper attitude, if you're a man, toward women in industry? Or the general condition of women? What is your attitude about blacks moving into your neighborhood? How do you love your neighbor, I hear people ask, when the price of your house is going down?"

"Relevancy, making mental connections between Christianity and the series of living experiences we're facing," Taylor confesses is his own greatest challenge to being a Christian. "It's very, very, very hard. Very hard to be a connector." That is the reason he believes the clergy should be continually exposing the connections "all the time. The day is really past, I think, for abstractions. . . . People are saying, 'Show me the relevance between Christian belief and Christian thought or admit that it's a fraud.' "

During the "family viewing year" he traveled the country a great deal, and he found, he says, "a kind of religious revival going on in America. And I think in a sense, the army has outrun the clergy. . . . I found the most incredible hunger—not for profits, but just for simple human beings who will take moral positions and define signposts."

Those who do take the path of moral positions, as Taylor did, often find it a treacherous road. "But," says Taylor, "survival is not the only thing. If survival is all you want, then you live with fear and terror all your life.

"I can look at a sunset. . . . I can walk on a beach and say, 'This is what it's all about.' How in hell's name, if you've let your soul and your manhood drain out, can you ever look at an object of beauty again and feel anything but emptiness?"

F. Stanton.

# 6 | HAROLD HUGHES

"I had reached the end of my road. I had been struggling with alcohol for years. I'd hurt everyone I loved—my wife, my children, my parents. I'd quit I don't know how many times, probably a hundred times, and never made it. One night I came to myself. I had been drunk again after all kinds of promises never to drink. My wife had left me and gone back to her mother. And I didn't want to live anymore. I didn't want to go on hurting people I loved. And it seemed impossible for me not to do it. I could no longer stand myself. What I saw and what I was, I detested. I thought I was worthless, useless, a deceiver, a liar. And, knowing that it was wrong to take my life, I decided that I would, rather than continue hurting people. And I actually loaded a gun to kill myself."

But before he pulled the trigger, he found himself on his knees. "God help me!" his voluminous bass voice thundered against the walls of his empty home. "I can't help myself!" He hardly knew to whom he was speaking. In World War II, he had watched men writhe into death in North Africa and Italy and he had wondered how there could be a loving God who coexisted with such brutality. Still, in the tight spots, he always found himself negotiating his way out of a crisis with this doubtful Being and when the dilemma was resolved, quickly forgetting his end of the bargain. Never, he knew, had he dealt honestly with God.

But now his soul lay stripped of cunning. He was God's for the asking. "If you don't want to take over my life," he cried into the quiet, "I don't want to see the dawn of another day. I want to die." If God however was willing to captain his wrecked ship, Harold Hughes was ready to promise, "I'll try and follow you the rest of my life, wherever it leads."

And suddenly, with the swift softness of a gentle tradewind, a stillness swept through him and his anguish was silenced. He began to weep. How long he remained on his knees he cannot remember. "When I got up, I unloaded the gun and put it away."

It is twenty-three years since that night and Harold Hughes has never had another drink. He is sitting in Fellowship House, an interdenominational gathering place for Christians in Washington, D.C. He is wearing a plaid shirt and a tan jacket, looking more like the truck driver he was than the Governor and Senator he became.

He is speaking quietly; the great Hammond-organ voice, capable of rolling across an audience of three thousand, alternately stroking and stunning ears, is muted and matter-of-fact as he relates the story of his fifteen-year affair with a fifth of whiskey and the spiritual odyssey that followed its end. It is not a new story. He has told and retold his blackest hours to prison inmates, alcoholics, drug addicts, life's losers—the people he has given up the United States Senate to help. They listen with scarcely a breath and often a tear. He understands them. He has been where they are. He is living hope that they can overcome. But he does not pretend that it will be easy.

He goes on:

"I got up the next morning and called my wife and went to see her and asked her to come home. . . . I wasn't about to tell her that I would never drink again, because I'd told her that fifty times before. . . . I even doubted it myself."

Eva Mercer of Holstein, Iowa, was only seventeen when she married Harold Hughes from Ida Grove, Iowa. He was nineteen, and he was already an alcoholic. In high school, he had been All-State guard, a top student and a tuba player. During his senior year, he made the acquaintance of John Barleycorn. Theirs was an immediate rapport: "I think I was born an alcoholic. I don't think I ever drank a normal drink in my life. I never drank as other people drank. I couldn't for some reason. I drank too much always! I never particularly liked the taste of alcohol. I drank it for the high or for whatever happened once it started. And there was a physical compulsion with me. I physically had to drink once I had begun until there wasn't anymore to get or everything had closed up or I was out of money."

He was awarded a football scholarship to the University of Iowa, but within a year he was back home in Ida Grove. Alcohol had taken precedence over education. World War II only deepened his need to drink. His natural sensitivity and compassion were shattered watching fellow soldiers die, and he escaped further inside the comforting womb of intoxication. In 1945, he received a medical discharge after contracting malaria and jaundice.

When he returned home he had a young family to support. He took a job in a hardware store. He worked in a creamery. Then he began driving a semitrailer across country; soon he worked his way up to manager of the truck line. Later, as general manager, he was given authority over five states, all the while keeping steady company with the bottle. "Most people have the opinion," Hughes once told a reporter, "that the alcoholic is on his way to skid row. It isn't true. He usually becomes an alcoholic while he's climbing the success ladder and he discovers it, you know, after he's modestly successful."

Trucking was a "hard-drinking business," according to Hughes. He remembers sitting down after work with seven or eight friends over a fifth of whiskey. "We'd buy one and share. Then someone else would buy one and share it. You didn't leave as long as someone was buying. By that time, there would be three or four guys under the table." The good times. "But I reached a point where there was no enjoyment. . . . the sickness that set in. . . . and the blackouts. Loss of time, loss of memory . . . no knowledge of what you had done or who you had seen. . . ." Or how you got into a barroom brawl or put your fist through a window or wound up in a hotel room one hundred thirty miles from home.

It was not as if he could afford the luxury of liquid holidays. He and Eva had bought their first home for three thousand dollars on a G.I. loan. The monthly payments were $24.77 and Harold's weekly salary was $25.00. His whole life had been an economic squeeze. He hadn't experienced electricity or indoor plumbing until he was twelve years old. He and his brother Jess had never had a Christmas tree, except for the one Harold won at a school raffle. It was just as well there had been no tree, because there had never been any toys to put under it. Once his father had made him a sled and one Christmas he had gotten roller skates. "I was overjoyed," Hughes remembers.

Ida Grove was a farming community but his father had gone broke in bucolic pursuit and had turned to construction work. The cold winters provided little of that kind of employment, so Mr. Hughes and his sons hunted and fished and trapped for survival.

Jess and Harold Hughes grew to such pachyderm proportions that they were nicknamed by the community "Big Pack" and "Little Pack." Six-foot-five Jess, having a two-inch advantage over Harold, was "Big Pack." In 1942, Big Pack was killed in an automobile accident, a grievous blow to his younger brother who then became simply "Pack."

When Reverend Wayne Shoemaker was assigned to pastor the Methodist Church in Ida Grove, church members told him that if he could help "Pack," it would be one of the most important things he could do for the community. "He was the kind of person who always commanded respect, even when he was drinking. They might regard him as a lowdown bum, but they could see something of his potential," says the minister.

Still, Reverend Shoemaker was wise enough to realize that any overt missionary initiative on his part might be met with a slammed door, if not a broken jaw.

"He couldn't have helped me," Hughes agrees, "if I hadn't been looking for help. If he had come to my house and knocked on my door and said 'I'd like to help you quit drinking,' I'd have told him to get the hell out. I was tired of being preached to. And I had been. People had tried to help me. It's an affront, number one. It affects your ego, your ability to live as a man. . . . I didn't even want to think in those terms until I was totally defeated. Until I was really dead, I couldn't live again. And I really died that night, and another man was born."

"I came on the scene," Reverend Shoemaker recalls, "very shortly after 'that night.' " Pack Hughes sought out the new pastor. "He must have wondered," Hughes reflects, "what sort of a big rough bumpkin I was."

Hughes' analysis was not far off the mark, but Reverend Shoemaker felt drawn to the "rough bumpkin." Behind the slick wavy black hair, the craggy peaked brows, the dark, now piercing, now questioning eyes, the granite jaw and the caged turbulence, the Minister sensed a "pathos and an ability to love." He surmised that Pack Hughes was the kind of man who "was capable of intense dedication to any enterprise," a trait that he had noticed in many alcoholics. "If you could ever break through their singleminded devotion to the bottle," he thought, "they would commit themselves wholly to a cause or a problem. That's why I enjoy working with them so much."

Harold Hughes' night of awakening did not prevent the long nightmare of withdrawal. He got through it with "prayer and agony," and Wayne Shoemaker. "He probably had as great an effect on me as any one man," asserts Hughes.

Reverend Shoemaker does not know why he was successful. "If you were to ask me to enumerate—one, two, three . . . —what I did to be helpful, I couldn't tell you. . . . if there was any helpfulness I think it was because of the establishment of a relationship where he knew there was someone who had compassion for him, would listen to him and would support him and would suggest things that he ought to be considering. He always wanted to take his own thing and work it out himself."

One of the things Hughes "worked out for himself" was a rigid program of rising at five o'clock in the morning to spend an hour reading the Bible before he went to work. "I couldn't tell you what God was at that time. . . . I knew His word was in that book. But it had been years since I had been in the Bible, really studying, praying and reading. . . . I had lost my faith after World War II, lost it completely. But I knew God had touched me and so I wanted to find him.

He returned to the Church and Pastor Shoemaker gently shoved him into areas of responsibility. "From the first day we ever met," Hughes recalls, "he never lost faith in me." Soon Hughes was lending his remarkable voice to the choir. He was teaching Sunday school classes. He was a lay leader to the annual Methodist conference. He was even taking the pastor's place in the pulpit when Reverend Shoemaker was absent from town.

And the citizens of Ida Grove, who numbered on 2,261, were taking notice. Reverend Shoemaker thought the greatest tribute to Hughes was a complaint he received from a District Court judge, who was a member of the Church. "Doggone you, preacher," the judge said to the minister, "you're fouling me up. When you're gone, I play hooky. Now you've gone and asked Pack to speak, and I just feel that when he's speaking I have to be there to show my support for him."

Hughes joked that he may have learned some of his oratorical skills in the saloon. "I've heard guys say I used to preach better sermons drunk than they ever heard in Church on Sunday."

Thus began the "migration" of Harold Hughes. Never did he or Dr. Shoemaker imagine that the pathway would nearly take him through the doors of the White House.

His political career was born in anger. As the manager of a private trucking firm, he felt the Iowa Motor Truck Association discriminated against small truckers. When he complained to the Governor, the Governor said that the Interstate Commerce Commission was in a mess, that if Harold Hughes wanted to do something about it he should change parties and run for the job of Commissioner. So Hughes dropped his Republican label, ran as a Democrat, and won.

"I think," says Park Rinard, administrative assistant to Iowa Senator John Culver and a former Hughes aide, "he showed his character in that first campaign. It was sort of rough-hewn. He was not a sophisticated campaigner, but he was a very persistent and sincere and forthright campaigner. . . . It was not his nature to glad-hand or back-slap. There was a blunt honesty about him that attracted people. He didn't have elegant clothes. He didn't have a background in that kind of public speaking." And while he may have been gifted with a voice, it had to be trained to say something. "Of course now," adds Rinard, "he's one of the finest speakers in the country, and a lot of people think he was born with all that equipment. But he made that."

In 1960, after two years on the Interstate Commerce Commission, he tried and failed to win the Democratic gubernatorial nomination. In 1962, he tried again and the prize was his. Always his background was a passenger on the underground rumor railroad. Never was the topic mentioned publicly, according to Rinard, until Hughes himself talked about his illness in an article for *Look* magazine. "Then," Rinard relates, "it became a public issue. . . . He was subjected to a great deal of innuendo and rather scurrilous defamation."

Still, in his second bid for the governor's chair, Hughes won by nearly half a million votes—the largest landslide ever accumulated by a statewide candidate. He was rated one of Iowa's strongest chief executives and for the first time in history the citizens awarded a Governor three consecutive terms, a feat made even more noteworthy by the fact that Iowa had been a heavily Republican state since the days of the Civil War.

Even Hughes was amazed by his success, and he would ask himself, "How did I ever get here? There's no way a man with my background, my lack of formal education, the scars that are public knowledge, could have walked that road with forgiveness by the people without the forgiveness of God. . . ." He was convinced that God had led his migration into the political arena and that was where He wished him to stay—for awhile.

He does not think it is remarkable that he chose to reveal his bout with alcoholism. "I don't deserve any credit for that. I couldn't have lied about it. The life that I led the press could have found. For me to lie about it would have been absolute insanity. I wouldn't have had any credibility."

Nevertheless, politicians who parade their past sins are as rare as oak trees on the desert. Hughes did not tell his story to the media just once and let the headlines fall where they might; he told it again and again, hiding none of the robust facts. "I made a commitment with God that I would not turn my back on those who were suffering as I had suffered. Nor would I reach a point where I would fail to bring enlightenment and hope to those who were still sick and dying." His public exposure sent missives of encouragement to the alcoholic community, and drinkers came to him in droves, an additional time drain that an already heavily-scheduled Governor hardly needed.

But he learned once painfully that he dare not turn away anyone in need. While he was Governor, he received a call just a few days before Christmas from a friend, a recovered alcoholic, who was looking for a job. "I was tired. I'd been working hard," he related to a Mayors' prayer breakfast. "I had all the excuses not to see him. I told him I would talk to him the next morning. He hung up the phone and blew his brains out. . . . I knew then that I could never refuse another person's call for help."

Seventy-five percent of the alcoholics and drug addicts that Harold Hughes has counseled over the years have recovered. He has received thousands of letters from other alcoholics, claiming they were moved to seek help because they read about one man who was accepted and forgiven. The letters made Hughes realize the importance of releasing alcoholism from the bondage of anonymity. He stresses the fact that it is a disease and that those afflicted with it should be no more ashamed to admit the affliction than they would a bout with pneumonia.

As a Senator, he urged well-known public figures who were recovered alcoholics to come forward and proclaim themselves, in order to help remove the stigma of their disease. The National Council of Alcoholism took him up on the idea and began holding annual "Celebrity Banquets." Such famous television stars as Dick Van Dyke and Garry Moore surprised the world with their admissions.

Hughes' personal suffering made him extremely sensitive to what Park Rinard refers to as the "warm issues," such as the abolition of capital punishment and the establishment of state-supported vocational schools. He created a Human Rights Commission. Under his administration, the judicial system was reformed and the Public Utilities Commission came into being. Instead of returning state surplus into politically popular tax credits, Hughes sent the money to work for health, education and welfare programs.

One of his most talked about successes was the passage of a "liquor by the drink" law. It was a highly controversial proposal, originating as it did from a recovered alcoholic. Purists felt it would increase the flow of booze. Hughes knew, however, that there were "key clubs" operating in almost every county in the state, and that a fifteen-year-old boy could get a drink anytime he had the money. The clubs were "legal" as long as they bore that title, and "if you were a member of the human race," asserts Park Rinard, "you could belong to most of those clubs." The hypocrisy made a paper tiger out of the Iowa liquor law. Hughes's reform legislation allowed drinks to be sold one by one in restaurants which were strictly controlled by licensing and where the revenue could be taxed by the state.

When the Amish families in Iowa rebelled against sending their children to public schools, a stance singularly irritating to state school officials, Hughes threw the power and prestige of his office behind the Amish cause. He felt, "from the depths of his heart," recalls Dr. Wayne Shoemaker, "that these people's religious principles should be respected. But for him to take the side of these Amish children looked like political suicide."

Despite the Kamikaze nature of the venture, the Governor went personally to the members of the religious sect and negotiated an arrangement whereby the Amish could continue teaching in their own schools as long as their instructors received state accreditation. That a Republican legislature accepted such a politically volatile proposal from a Democratic Governor "was," according to Park Rinard, "one of the most remarkable things I've seen in my years of public life."

But by the third campaign, Hughes's controversial stands had reduced his vote margin to one-hundred thousand—comfortable by gubernatorial standards but niggardly by comparison to his former four-hundred-thirty thousand plurality.

"I often used to say," recounts Ed Campbell, a former Hughes' aide, "he seemed to have suicidal tendencies politically, to say all the things that didn't need to be said. It just seemed that there was something inside of him that had to come out. The truth always prevailed with him, no matter how tough it was on him or his family."

When Hughes finished his third term as Governor, he was ready to bow out of the political ring, but a visit with Robert Kennedy in New York altered his thinking. Ed Campbell accompanied Hughes on the trip. "We were at the Plaza Hotel in New York. Kennedy was having his Empire State dinner, which was his annual fund raiser to raise revenue for Senate campaigns." The day after the dinner, Kennedy advance man Jerry Bruno telephoned the Plaza and asked if Hughes would like to accompany Kennedy to a football game. Hughes told Campbell he wouldn't watch a game if they were playing outside his hotel window. Campbell wasn't sure that Bruno understood the rejection. Kennedy would like to talk to Hughes, Bruno pointed out. Well, Hughes replied, if he wants to talk to me, tell him to come up to my room.

One hour later there was a knock on the door. Campbell excused himself while his boss and Robert Kennedy talked "for the better part of two hours."

Later Hughes related the conversation to reporter Lloyd Shearer. "After three terms as governor, I didn't want to run for reelection. I didn't want to come to Washington. I had no ambitions to become a United States Senator." Kennedy began urging him to run, but Hughes turned the focus on the Presidency. "I told him that Lyndon Johnson had to be replaced as President and that he was probably the only man in the Democratic Party who could get the nomination.

"Bob was reluctant. He said he didn't want to be the instrument for dividing the country." The division was already in existence, Hughes insisted, "and someone has to run against Johnson."

"How can you ask me to run for the Presidency," Kennedy asked, pointing his index finger at Hughes, "if you won't run for the Senate?" One vote in the Senate wouldn't make much difference, Hughes thought. Kennedy insisted it would. "He convinced me." Hughes says, "He convinced me that six years of my life in the Senate might indeed make a difference on a lot of issues."

When Robert Kennedy came to Iowa to campaign for Hughes, he found Hughes still pressing him to run for the Presidency. One week after his return from Iowa, Robert Kennedy announced his intention to make a run for the White House.

Harold Hughes's campaign for the Senate was one of his most difficult. "He was always about a year and a half ahead of the people on the issues," says Ed Campbell, "and I was always afraid that our election dates weren't going to fall in line. There wasn't sufficient time in 1968, Campbell points out, for the people to "catch up" with the candidate's views. When the Senate race rolled around, "there were about ten issues in Iowa and the people were against all the things that he was for, like blacks. In northwest Iowa, they don't even have any blacks, and he'd go up there and tell them that they should adopt families and bring them in there and give them a home and give them jobs." Hughes was also vociferously against the Vietnam War, which the majority of Iowans supported, and his opponent, a man named David Stanley, campaigned from the tip of a hawk's wing.

The terrain got even tougher when his health kicked in during the final month of vote-seeking. "He almost lost the entire month of October," says Park Rinard. "He was extremely ill with bronchitis," which provided renewed grist for expedient gossip. "People were always spreading rumors," says Rinard, "in a political year that he was back on the juice."

Hughes squeaked into the Senate by five thousand votes, but when he arrived in Washington, his hulking presence was almost immediately noted. His colleagues were somewhat awed and mystified by the man with the Marlboro frame, the Michelangelo head, and the Damon Runyon past. One seldom read about Senator Harold Hughes without the parenthetical addition, "ex-truck driver, recovered alcoholic." "There was an element of mystique about the man, which was attractive," points out an associate. "He's a brooding, lonely man, and contrary to what some of the garden-variety politicians thought, this can be a great political strength."

He was not afraid to eat alone in the Senate dining room, the perennial hall of hail-fellows, where Senators are frequently surrounded by admiring constituents or a convivial group of colleagues. He loathed and avoided the social limelight, as he had in Iowa. He once told a group of managing editors he would rather be home eating hamburgers with his family than dining on steaks with them.

During his first months in Washington, he was invited to address the Washington Press Club's annual Congressional dinner, an event more populated with the powerful than a White House State Dinner. The occasion has always been a kind of presentation of the most promising new arrivals in town, and Hughes, with his oratorical skills, was capable of a stunning debut.

At the time, Park Rinard and Ed Campbell were staying with Hughes in an apartment until they found permanent lodgings. According to Campbell, Hughes left the office early to get ready for the dinner, which demanded black tie. But when Campbell and Rinard arrived home later, they found a note directing Ed Campbell to phone whomever was in charge of the dinner and tell them he would be a little late. "Being more of a political animal than anybody else," Campbell was "panicky that Hughes would miss this kind of a function. The *Des Moines Register* was going to write a story about it."

Campbell's worst fears were realized. His boss never did show up. He had received a call from a Senator, whom he had never met, who was drunk and in despair. And Hughes had gone to the colleague's house and spent the rest of the evening with him.

The *Des Moines Register* relayed his absence to the folk back home, and when his constituents wrote asking why the Senator wasn't where he should have been, "He never gave any explanation," according to Ed Campbell. "He just said it was his personal business, period."

Such events were to become routine to Senator Hughes. Sometimes it was a colleague who approached him for help. Sometimes it was a stranger who strolled in off the street. Always they took precedence, even over constituents. Once Hughes rendered his staff apopletic by keeping several big contributors cooling their heels in the reception room while he counseled an alcoholic in his office.

On the Senate floor, he continued to argue for the "warm issues." He waged and lost a battle for the abolition of capital punishment. He antagonized conservatives on the Senate Armed Services Committee, vocalizing his dissent on the Vietnam War and voting against military appropriations. But it was in the field of alcoholism and drug abuse that he, in the words of an admirer, Walter Mondale, "revolutionized the government's thinking."

He became chairman of a new subcommittee on Alcoholism and Drug Abuse which eventually led to passage of the Hughes Act. When the committee was created, Hughes was without budget and without staff. From May until December of 1969, the Senator held hearings around the country which he funded himself with his speaking honorariums.

In the fall, he was finally given a budget and the authority to hire two staff people. One of the most dedicated workers was a former actress, Nancy Olson, herself a recovered alcoholic, who antagonized her future boss, on their initial meeting at the 1968 Democrat Convention, by innocently offering Hughes a drink. "I don't touch the damned stuff," he growled. When she realized to whom she was advancing treacherous hospitality she identified herself as a victim of the same disease.

Their common problem provided an easy camaraderie. It also provided nonalcoholic staff members with a reference source. One aide asked Nancy what he should have done the evening he was attending a reception with Hughes and the Senator was given a gin and tonic instead of the straight tonic he requested. "Lord," the staffer told Mrs. Olson, "he took a great big gulp of it. What should I have done?"

"What did the Senator do?" Nancy asked.

"The Senator," replied the aide, said "Dammit. This has gin in it. I asked for straight tonic."

Nancy could not hide her amusement at the staff man's genuine distress. "What did you think you should do . . . get restraining straps?" she quipped. She then explained that the Senator was not going to finish a drink that he knew had gin in it. One drink, she pointed out, does not a binge make. Alcoholics, she asserts, use that myth as an excuse. When an alcoholic leaves the wagon, "He has to really want to drink again."

She firmly disagrees with those who contend that alcoholics should never be confronted with their affliction. As a consequence of Hughes's legislation, the Hughes Act, "we know a great deal more about alcoholism than we did before. We now know there is such a thing as constructive coercion. This is one of the reasons that we are getting seventy-percent success rates out of the occupational-alcoholic and drunk-driver programs. When an employer says you either do something about your drinking problem or it's your job, these people, kicking and screaming that they're not alcoholics, go into the program, and seventy percent of them recover."

"If you knew that a friend had a lump on her breast, would you not tell her that she darn well better see her doctor?" she asks hotly. "Now the old AA philosophy is that you can do nothing for anybody unless they want help. That's true in the sense that unless an alcoholic is motivated to seek help, he's not going to stop drinking. But you can help to motivate them."

The wrong method of confrontation, however, can do more harm than good. Mrs. Olson is careful to point out that no friend or relative should approach an alcoholic without the aid and suggestions of an expert counselor.

Due to the Hughes legislation, such advice is readily available. Every state in the union now has an office on alcoholism and alcoholic programs. Treatment facilities and preventive programs have sprung up across the nation. Many recovered alcoholics are working as training counselors, and medical schools are beginning to teach their students more about the disease.

Once Hughes kidded Nancy Olson that he had only hired her because she was an alcoholic. "Well, Senator," she snapped, "I wasn't exactly a charity case. I gave up a very good job with Senator Jackson to come and work for you." With that, she stomped out of the room. The next day, Hughes was full of contrition. "I almost called you at home last night, Nancy. I wanted to tell you I don't know why I said what I said to you yesterday. It wasn't true. I don't know why I said it."

"Oh, that's all right Senator," Nancy smiled, "I'm not thin-skinned."

"Oh women, women!" Hughes huffed, "they always say they aren't thin-skinned. Well, you may not be thin-skinned, but you're not thick-hearted, either."

It was the combination of "the tough and the tender" that endeared him to his Senate staff, though they were wise enough not to cross him when he was in a somber mood, carefully checking out the "chief's" disposition with his personal secretary Jo Nobles before entering his office. Sometimes she would scowl, indicating discreet delay might prove more propitious for their cause.

When dealing with work and legislation, according to Miss Nobles, "He was very impatient. He is so awesome that when you first get to know him, even if you've got the answers at your fingertips, it's hard to think of them fast enough." He wanted issues handled very expeditiously. But if any member of the staff had a personal problem, Miss Nobles asserts, "You could go and talk with him and he would do anything he could."

"He's a real bleeder," comments Ed Campbell.

One secretary says his empathy was so great that she hesitated to let him know about a problem, "because you know he'll load that on his shoulders, too. He takes it to heart and then he takes it one step further. He submits it to God."

At the same time, she concedes, he possesses a low boiling point "which is hard to regulate. I guess his volatility is in relation to his size."

"You'd be amazed at the people he just scares the living heck out of until they get to know him," smiles Jo Nobles. "He is just so reserved at first."

"Some people," says a former secretary, "think he's rude on initial meeting. I don't think he's rude. . . . Once he gets to know you, he's very outgoing and very warm and not at all shy. But with strangers, he's a little bit shy." And then she cautions, "don't tell him I said that. He wouldn't like that at all. I don't think he thinks of himself as shy."

"I think he transmits power," analyzes Jo Nobles, "he gives you the feeling if he did get violent, you better run for cover." She thinks part of the awe is inspired by "that booming voice, that marvelous voice. . . . but just his presence has almost the same effect. I never heard him make but one speech. . . . He spoke to Gallaudet College—you know everyone is predominantly deaf—and he had them as mesmerized as an audience with acute hearing."

Both Jo and Nancy Olson agree that Hughes prefers people who speak up to him. "I had worked for him a relatively short period of time," recalls Nancy, "when I discovered that I had made a very serious mistake. . . . My first reaction was to say to myself, 'Oh my Lord, if I don't tell anybody, maybe they won't find out.' My next reaction was 'No, I better tell the Senator right away.' I went into his office eating humble pie."

"Oh Senator," she groaned, "I've just made the most outrageous goof and you're just going to be furious with me!"

Before she could begin her sad tale, Hughes sat back in his chair, folded his arms and said, "You think you're pretty hot stuff, don't you? You think you're pretty special!"

"Senator," she stammered, "what do you mean?"

"Who do you think you are, anyway—Jesus Christ? You're so perfect you're never supposed to make a mistake?"

The incident was a revelation to Mrs. Olson. "It proved to me that Senator Hughes was the kind of man to whom I could admit my mistakes, if I was honest and forthright about them. But I have a strong suspicion that if I had hidden them and he found out about them from somebody else, I would have heard from Harold Hughes rather strongly. He cannot tolerate deception. . . ."

In the Senate, his tender side was especially evident with the dining room kitchen staff. Secretary of the Senate Stan Kimmitt, a close friend, says a cup of coffee with Harold Hughes is sure to be interrupted by a steady stream of black waitresses and cook's helpers. "He'll give them a big embrace and a kiss. . . . And it's apparent to anyone who's sitting there that he has an individual relationship with each one of them for some reason, and the reason is that they have gone to him for help."

Kimmitt, who has hunted and fished with Hughes in various parts of the country, counts the former Senator one of the nation's outstanding sportsmen, and maintains that Hughes' manly and earthy qualities are what make him so effective in his spiritual activities. "Otherwise he would not be able to communicate with the rest of us. You have to know your clientele."

Hughes sometimes apologizes for his fondness for the strong phrases, but he has yet to abandon them. Once during an alcoholism conference that included comedian Dick Van Dyke and then Secretary of Defense Melvin Laird, a member of the audience asked, "Do you believe that alcoholism is a disease?"

Hughes reached for the microphone and answered, "Everyone in this room knows that alcoholism is a disease, and as for the rest of them, the hell with them!" When the laughter and applause died down, he added, "I guess that isn't a very good start for an up-and-coming lay preacher."

In early 1971, the big Iowan's charisma cast his long shadow into the Presidential ring. The reform wing of the Democratic party began a boomlet in his behalf, and Iowa backers pledged a twenty-thousand-dollar-a-month campaign budget.

Hughes took to the road and began making his presence felt and his voice heard around the country. He received favorable press notices from liberal columnists such as Mary McGrory, who is often fonder of burying Caesars than praising them. In one column she wrote of Hughes' effect on a predominantly black audience in Chicago. "From the moment, last night, when he unselfconsciously addressed them

as 'my brothers and sisters,' Hughes had his listeners by the lapels."
She called his message "pretty powerful stuff" and speculated "if the
Chicago response to it is any guide, the country might get high on
Harold Hughes." In another column McGrory hailed him as the "most
exciting choice against Richard Nixon."

But after months of testing the waters, Hughes felt little warmth for
the task. He was disturbed by some profound doubts as to the
morality of his candidacy. He began pondering the fact that as
President he would have to grapple with issues for which he never
before had been solely responsible.

"I really had to wrestle with myself as to what my answers
would be on some of these worldly decisions. I found myself in
conflict with what the world thought was the only way to peace, for
example, or the only way to economic progress. These things are in
conflict with the teachings of the Sermon on the Mount. . . . I
suddenly realized that in all probablility I had become a pacifist,
which I really didn't want to say. It was always kind of a dirty word
to me. I fought in World War II; I was a Browning automatic
rifleman. As Governor of my state, I was commander-in-chief of the
National Guard. I've been patriotic all my life. . . . But then you
come to the death of the world, which is really where we're at
because the capacity to deal a death blow to the human race is with
us. And I had to come to grips with the question if the Russians
or anyone else were to unleash a preemptive, all-out nuclear strike,
would I retaliate? And the conclusion that I came to was, no, I
would not. There might be some hope for humanity if we didn't
retaliate. If we did retaliate, the probability is that the entire human
family would be destroyed."

If failing to answer a Soviet attack made the United States a
captive nation, so be it: "To be in slavery for Christ is better than
being in the bondage of Satan." And participating in a world holo-
caust would make him, he felt, an agent of hell. "I'm foolish enough
to believe that if this Nation ever really trusted in God, laid down its
weapons and got on its knees, God would intervene again in the
affairs of men and defend us."

A radical idea, even to Christians in this skeptical age, but totally
plausible to Harold Hughes. "God doesn't need a majority. He's not a
democracy. Time and again, He spared people, cities, and nations
because of one or two or three people who really trusted Him. . . .
I don't want to say, 'Well, it won't work now because of the
Communists or it won't work because of the Chinese.' . . . God's
word is true or the whole thing is a damn lie."

It was hardly, he knew, a position that was held by the majority
of the American voters. He would have to keep it a secret or change
it. "One night as I was coming home, quite tired and quite late, the

scripture just kept coming back to me. 'What profit a man if he gain the whole world and lose his own soul?' . . . And I knew that in the decision-making process I was going to have to take stands that were contra the positions that Christ would take on those issues. . . . Well my goal, I decided, was really eternal life and not this life. . . . This life is simply an interlude. . . . believing that, I can't any longer look at this world or positions in this world—*any* position in this world—as being rewarding enough or being worthwhile enough to compromise directions for a greater life."

After nearly a year of tangling with his conscience, Harold Hughes told his staff he would no longer be a candidate for the White House.

Laying aside his Presidential ambitions did not, he found, diminish the "soul conflict." "Having taken that step, it just led to another." Two years later, he astonished the political community by announcing he would leave the United States Senate to become a disciple of Christ. The statement made headlines across the country. The *Des Moines Register* bannered the story across the front page: "Iowa Politics in Turmoil." Despite his narrow victory in 1968, Hughes was now considered the best possible Democratic candidate for the Senate. He was, according to Park Rinard, stronger in 1973 than at any time since his landslide reelection to a second term as governor. The electorate, in Ed Campbell's phraseology, had "caught up" with his stands on the issues. The fact that a man would voluntarily abandon the United States Senate for reasons other than age, health, or certain defeat was inconceivable to most of the country. *The Washington Post* gave up almost an entire page to the story. *Parade Magazine* featured Harold Hughes's face on the front cover and examined his motives in their feature article, concluding that he was a "most unusual Senator, one of a kind, truly a nonpareil." *The Saturday Evening Post* devoted nearly five thousand words to the decision.

What the world and particularly Washington could not understand was why a man would relinquish a position of great power and influence to follow God, particularly when he seemingly already had Him. Wouldn't he have much more chance to influence others in that direction from a position of high visibility? Many thought he was "copping out." One man expressed that feeling in a letter to *The Washington Post*. Calling the decision "lamentable," the writer argued, "one more social worker more or less means relatively little, but a liberal senator is an important asset." He likened the Senator's decision to "the Chinese warriors who decide battles, not by fighting, but by desertion."

Even the clergy refused to give unanimous praise to his move into spiritual work. But the most vociferous dissents came from his own staff, who were almost universally opposed to his departure. "Oh, we had a terrible set-to when he said that he wasn't going to run again," recalls Jo Nobles. "I must have argued with him for at least an hour. I felt very strongly that he could do more for the religious movement by staying in the Senate. . . . I thought he was extremely valuable in the Senate. . . . He was valuable on the Armed Services Committee. I gave him all these arguments. I can't remember what all I said to him, but every time I'd finish a point, he'd say, 'You're probably right.' And I'd give him another one, and he'd say 'You're probably right.' We went on like this for just ages. And then finally he said, 'You're probably right, but I'm going to do it anyway.' "

A year and a half elapsed between the time that Hughes announced his impending exit from the Senate and the end of his term—a year and a half during which he was bombarded with every possible argument of dissuasion. None moved him.

He would, he said, work with the Fellowship Foundation and the International Christian Leadership Foundation—both based at Fellowship House in Washington, D.C.—as a lay religious worker. Both organizations labor to bring Christians of all nations in contact with another with the simple notion that until the Prince of Peace lives and works in the hearts of citizens and world leaders peace on earth can never be achieved. Hughes would not receive a salary as such. His personal and family needs would be taken care of as they arose by Foundation funds.

He was, in the view of many, taking the "lilies of the field" message a trifle too seriously, ironically at a time when his pockets were being invaded by tragedy. Not long after he left the Senate, Hughes lost his daughter and his mother and underwent major surgery—all in a six-month period. The most wrenching ordeal was his pretty, dark-haired daughter Carol's protracted and painful combat with cancer.

"I think the most difficult thing in creation," he says, "is to have a child leave you." It was a fate that he had always prayed would never be imposed on him, ever since he witnessed his mother's grief over the loss of his brother Jess. Her suffering was "so terrible," he recalls, "that she could not realize my suffering, you know, as a brother and very close."

As a result of that experience, I always prayed that I would die before my children did. And yet it came. . . . And I can tell you that God gave us strength that was unbelievable during that time of trial."

"The events leading up to Carol's death," says his friend Stan Kimmitt, "the terrible hospitalizations that had to just tear his heart out. . . . He never once indicated any complaint: 'Why me?' or 'Why her?'—the thing that I would naturally say. Never, not even once. There was just a total complete understanding that this was the will of God."

It was an attitude that Carol herself frequently expressed to close companions. She was candid about the difficulty of accepting a shortened earthly tenure. "It's been a struggle for me to give up my will, like I for so long desired to be well and live a good life," she wrote a friend. But once having accepted her brief passage, she was anxious for it's conclusion. "I have had so much sickness in this body of mine," the letter continued, "that it will be a real relief to be free of it once and for all and pass from death to life. Alleluia!"

She was granted that liberation in the summer of 1976. Harold Hughes spoke the eulogy at his daughter's funeral with the un-trembling resonance of a man routinely filling the pulpit for Reverend Shoemaker. Speaking to the overflow of friends spilling through several of the stately rooms in Fellowship House where Carol had "worked" phones between hospitalizations, Hughes urged his daughter's companions to lay aside their sorrow. He spoke of his belief, his wife Eva's belief, and Carol's belief in eternal life. He said his daughter didn't want anyone grieving. "She wants us to be about the work of the Lord, which was what she was about."

"It was a very moving experience," says one friend who attended the services. "The attitude that he and the family projected was that she had gone onto the reward that she was entitled to. It was an achievement rather than a loss."

"I don't even like to say losing or lost," says Harold Hughes. "Our terminology is rotten. It's graduation day. . . . Of course I miss Carol. Of course, I miss my mother. . . . I look at it as if they were moving away to another state and we were going to be separated a few years and probably wouldn't be able to visit them. But you don't know; you might visit them tomorrow."

And if he *should* find himself tomorrow in this eternal kingdom that he has been seeking for so long, what does he expect to be doing? "Well, certainly not sittin' on a cloud, playin' a harp. . . . If I did, I wouldn't be trying so hard to make sure that I'm a part of it, because that doesn't appeal to me." He envisions infinity as a place where there are rulers and governors and kings. He says scripture indicates that the greatest in the kingdom will be those who follow the commandments, a statement that leads one to suspect that Harold Hughes has only relinquished power temporarily, hoping to regain it again in a more permanent setting.

Only his youngest daughter, Phyllis, lives at home now. Eva Hughes totally supported her husband's plan to leave the Senate, just as she supported him through his struggle with drinking. Only those closest to her know how she endured those years. She never speaks publicly of her pain. "She's a very private person," says one friend, "she carries her problems personally and that's it." She is loathe to give interviews, preferring now to quietly enjoy the fruits of her devotion. There is little doubt, intimates point out, that Harold Hughes is very grateful to his wife for her loyalty to him. He is, they say, very protective of her. "Good God," exclaims one friend, "to have come through that period of alcoholism, to have stuck with him under those circumstances! He himself will self-admittedly say that when he was drinking it was an anything-goes type affair. I think now they have a very happy marriage, a very deep-seated marriage."

The Hugheses have sold their home in McLean, Virginia, and moved to Maryland's eastern shore to an old estate called Cedar Point Farm. With friends and volunteers from Fellowship House, Hughes is working to restore the site so that he can share it with likeminded companions who need a respite and spiritual retreat from the noise of the world.

But what does he *do?* people ask.

According to his secretary, "He travels a lot, attending Christian conferences around the country and the world, trying to bring various leaders together, establishing a basis upon which they can talk to each other, to bring some cohesion out of all the divisiveness." He has not become, he insists, "a scalp hunter for Christian conversions." He is convinced, he says, that it is essential to make committed disciples, not mere converts.

"His real love," insists his colleague and friend, Chuck Colson, "is finding fishermen down on the Eastern shore and discipling them, working with prisoners, working with American Indians, helping alcoholics. The down-and-outer is really where Harold's call is."

As an example, Colson recalls a week-long community religious conference he and Hughes attended in Billings, Montana. The event was full of rallies and barbecues and speaking engagements aimed at fellowship. "They had scheduled Harold to speak at the Kiwanis, and they didn't tell him till he got there. Typically, he said 'I'm not going to speak to the damn Kiwanis.' He said, 'those people don't need to hear me. I'm going out to the Indian reservation.' So he just dumped the schedule and spent all day with the Indians."

Colson has begun a ministry in thirty of the nation's prisons, sending teams of Christians to work with inmates. "We try to project Christ the way we think scripturally He is, that is, the Prophet of the loser, and you're dealing with losers. The key to what we do really is build up their self-worth."

Harold Hughes, claims Colson, has been an integral part of the work since it began. "He has a great relationship with the prisoners because he's tough with them. He doesn't make it easy for them. . . .

Harold is incredibly direct and honest, which is what prisoners need, because they've heard all the B.S. that's been thrown around in the world and they've rejected it all. He doesn't say, 'Now you're going to be happy.' He says, 'You're going back into positive hell. . . . You're going to have to face all these struggles, and here's the challenge. What greater commitment can there be than that you will lay down your life for God Almighty. . . . and lay down your life for your brothers?' " The message is all the more effective coming from a man who has laid down the prestige of the United States Senate to work for the redemption of society's outcasts.

"The only goal I have left in life," Hughes says today, "is to serve Christ. . . . The biggest enemy in the world is me, not someone else." Before he can be any good to others, he feels, "I must come to grips with myself, and the power of Christ must live in me, fully and completely, in full bloom and flower. Until then that power can't be seen or felt in the world." "I'm still very much a man. I still want all the things that I've always wanted. I still have a great deal of ambition. I'm still what I was." His ego, he confesses, remains in residence. "I still have it and I still have to keep it chained. . . . When I see things that I know I can do well in the worldly sense, that I think aren't being done so well, then the old combative spirit rises up in me again. And I'd like to do something that would alter it. . . . Now many people will condemn me because I restrain that drive and say that I should fulfill it for Christ. Well, that isn't what Christ has said to me." His task, he feels, is to assist the men and women who are in public life to do better rather "than try and replace them." What if God were to call him back into politics? "If he does, I'm goin'," but he sees little likelihood of such a summons.

His is not a course that he urges on all Christians; there is a place, he believes, for the moral man in the public arena. "I think many men, in fact the vast majority, can feel perfectly comfortable doing the things that I felt uncomfortable in doing. And that doesn't mean that I'm right and they're wrong. . . . In fact, I'm constantly encouraging people who come to me and ask, 'Can I seek political office and still follow Christ?' I tell them, 'Yes, I believe that you can.'

"But I say, 'You've got to make up your mind to one thing. If you come to a point where what you're doing is in conflict with Christ, then you have to be absolutely ready to give it all up.' "

Put simply, Harold Hughes is about the business of perfection. He admits it is an arduous task and a lifelong pursuit. He argues that until each man rids himself of the evil within, he cannot fight the evil without. "God has a plan for the world. . . . God's plan for the nation was Christ in you, not in a King or Christ in an Emperor or Christ in the President, but Christ in you. . . . That's His plan to redeem the human race. Now I can't improve on God's plan. I don't know how to improve on it. Politically, there's nothing I can do to bring it about. I know as I examine history that every nation has eventually failed, that every treaty of alliance has ultimately fallen, that every treaty that has ever been made has ultimately been broken, that man has never failed to use every weapon that he's ever invented to kill his brothers. We have a totally predictable record. Unless Christ lives in the man, then man is totally predictable, because he will ultimately resort to what he has always resorted to—death and destruction. The most powerful take over the weak."

Why does God allow his creatures to behave so badly, Hughes is asked. It is the question he asked himself during World War II. "I go right back to Adam and Eve. I don't have any other answer for it. Evil entered the world, because man was perfect and had the freedom of choice. . . . God wanted us to be perfect, but he wanted us to love Him ˉbecause it was our choice to love Him, not because we are robots. . . . If I could somehow affect you so that you could do nothing but love me, regardless of what you really wanted to do, what satisfaction is there in that? If, however, you had the right of choice and you loved me, then we could truly have a fellowship. . . . And God created us so that we could have fellowship with him."

The fact that man continually chooses to reject that fellowship perhaps explains the sometimes brooding cast to Hughes' face. "The Christ that I know and see was a man of sorrows and suffering. The joy that he talks about is the joy of certainty of eternal life. But you can't travel thru a world filled with travail and tears and suffering, laughing like an idiot."

Reverend Wayne Shoemaker likens Harold Hughes's migration to "St. Paul's struggle. . . . The farther along you move in the spiritual life the more aware you are how far you have yet to go. And the more you see of what you ought to be, the more you see of what you aren't. . . . You know, I can go out and play ball with a little kid on the street and look like a halfway decent ball player. But just put me in Yankee Stadium and I can't even pick up the gum wrappers."

"Harold Hughes," observes Chuck Colson, "is not a man who will ever be serene. He will always be churning around inside, because he will always be anguishing about himself. And if not himself, it will be about other people. He is not destined to be a happy man."

"It's been a long, long pathway," admits Hughes, "of knocking, seeking, asking, finding, leveling off, thinking you're never going anywhere. Three years later, something would happen that would trigger another period of growth. . . . You would reach another mountaintop, and your heart would tell you you still haven't gotten there. I've learned to be patient over the years, that God has a way and a time for all things."

# 7 | RAY SCHERER

At first, they hadn't realized he was gone. They either had not seen or their ears had neglected John Chancellor's brief statement on the nightly news that his colleague and friend, Ray Scherer, was leaving the cameras of NBC for the corporate offices of RCA.

But then the letters began trickling into NBC. What happened to Ray Scherer? Where was that friendly bear of a man who used to keep television audiences abreast of events in the nation's capital? They missed the steady, low-key reporting of the correspondent with the bemused blue eyes and the gray head that tilted screen left while he was telling Americans what their government was up to.

He was not sensational, charismatic, shocking, aggressive. He never excited or startled his viewers. He merely informed them. "Lincolnesque" was the term Dave Garroway frequently used to describe him. "People say, any man who looks like that can't be conning me," observed journalism professor and author George Reedy. "When they invented the term civility," asserts CBS correspondent Bill Moyers, "they had to come up with Ray Scherer to define it."

News had been Ray Scherer's whole life. For twenty-eight years as an NBC television correspondent, he had been rubbing his nose against the glass of history. He had midwifed the birth of television news, appeared on the very first *Today* show, kept track of four Presidents, explained Europe from London and reported the denouement of Richard Nixon during the House Judiciary Committee Impeachment hearings. He had known every major figure to shape American politics in the past quarter century. He had returned home to Missouri with Harry Truman on his farewell journey from Washington. He had been the first broadcaster to alert the nation that President Eisenhower had suffered a heart attack. He had shown Jacqueline Kennedy her first television studio and given her ambitious young husband some of his premier nationwide exposure.

It was not easy to leave all that. Even a higher salary, a suite of offices, and a chauffeured limousine failed to prevent it from being the most painful decision of his career.

Just once before he had considered leaving journalism, and then only because it seemed the patriotic thing to do. A Presidential command performance. The result of a warm relationship with

Lyndon Baines Johnson, a relationship that tugged and strained at Ray Scherer's prized objectivity more than any of the four chief executives he had covered as a White House correspondent.

"The problem covering a President," Scherer points out, "was that you could be beguiled by him. Even Eisenhower. I remember I was invited to the very first white tie dinner that he gave. This was a great honor . . . and if you wanted to take that sort of thing seriously, you could easily think you were a great friend of the President's. You weren't. You were there because you were representing the network." Lyndon Johnson, however, sometimes made that line of demarcation difficult to see.

LBJ trusted Scherer, confided in him. A camaraderie developed between President and correspondent that was as cumbersome as it was complimentary. Good contacts are as necessary to journalists as wings to a pilot; minus some rapport with newsmakers, a reporter is likely to find himself reading more good stories than he is writing. But friendship is something else again—an immediate conflict of interest. During his four years covering the Johnson White House, Scherer was forced to walk a tightwire between his humanity and his journalistic ethics.

The previous administration had made reporters especially wary of fellowship with the Oval Office. During the Kennedy years a great many of the White House press corps suffered from Presidential hypnosis. Even today, it is a sensitive admission for some Washington reporters to concede their attachment to the glamorous Irishman. Ray Scherer is the first to admit that he found JFK "dashing." There was romance in a President who flashed an incandescent smile and sailed the seas with windswept hair, particularly after eight years of watching a pink-pated general spend most of his relaxing hours trying to coax a pockmarked sphere off a full-bellied toothpick. Besides, Scherer identified with Kennedy: "We came to town about the same time. We were bachelors in Georgetown together," recalls Ray. In the NBC files, there is a picture of the two men standing on a Massachusetts hillside—a scrawny reporter with his microphone to the mouth of a skinny Congressman. "We look about eighteen," Scherer chuckles.

When it came to flattering the press, Jack Kennedy was the artful lodger of the warm phrase. The first time Ray met Jacqueline Kennedy, she responded to the introduction with the intriguing revelation, "Jack listens to you in the bathtub." Scherer was naturally curious as to why his broadcasts were privileged to share such an intimate ambiance. The Senator explained later that Scherer's five minute report, "Today's White House" came on at the appointed hour for soaking his troubled back, and that show was "something I never miss."

But Jack Kennedy, himself a former journalist, had an even subtler method of charming the press corps fueled by a genuine interest in the news business. Ray ruefully recalls falling victim to White House seduction aboard an Air Force One flight to Palm Beach. Shortly after the plane was in the air, Kennedy sent word to Scherer to join him in his cabin for a chat. This is my chance, Scherer thought to himself. He's going to be forthcoming; I may not be able to use it, but I'm certainly going to learn something.

No sooner had he sat down, however, than Scherer discovered that JFK was turning the ultimate weapon on him. The Presidential ear. What's your schedule like, John Kennedy wanted to know. You're at the White House in the morning and Sander Vanocur is there in the afternoon. How do you divide up your work? What's your relationship with each other? How much does NBC pay you per broadcast? Do you get more for television than radio? Whom do you report to in New York? What are Julian Goodman and Bill McAndrew like?

The conversation spanned an hour; Kennedy had done all the listening and Scherer had done all the talking. When he rejoined his colleagues in the back of the plane they were eager to hear what he had learned. With considerable chagrin, Ray confessed, "Not a thing." Nevertheless, he couldn't help but think what a grand fellow the President of the United States was for taking such an interest in a poor working stiff.

Listening was not one of Lyndon Johnson's more noticeable attributes. Nevertheless, the statesman in the Stetson could also be a master of the woo department. "He really knew how to seduce you," says Ray's wife, Maudie. She remembers the Scherers being invited to have lunch with Johnson and some members of his Cabinet at the LBJ ranch. After the meal, Johnson conducted a guided tour of the three LBJ ranches from behind the wheel of his Lincoln convertible. His newly appointed UN Ambassador, Arthur Goldberg, sat on the front seat next to the President; Ray and Maudie Scherer occupied the rear. "It seemed like some funny movie," Maudie recalls, "where you were going from one mode of transportation to another." They were in cars. They were in helicopters. They were in boats. "He'd get on a walkie talkie," says Ray, "and a helicopter would land right in front of you. You'd get on the helicopter, and ten minutes later you'd be at another ranch, and another car would be waiting for you."

At some point in the "kaleidoscopic" afternoon, Johnson, who had a great affection for practical jokes, was driving a small car and the small car headed straight for a lake. "I don't know what's happening, Mrs. Scherer," the President exclaimed to the back seat, "the brakes are failing, Mrs. Scherer. I'm going to drown you!" Ray looked at his wife. Her face was the color of a cloud bank as the auto slid into the water. It wasn't until she observed that they were floating rather than sinking that she realized they were in an amphibian vehicle.

Lyndon Baines Johnson wore the phrase "larger than life" into a ragged cliche. Everything he did seemed to be in direct proportion to the size of the state in which he was born. His presence dominated a room full of people. He could outtalk, outwalk, outshout, and outguess most of the people around him, and he devoted a considerable amount of his gargantuan energy to those enterprises. The big Texan could be as gentle as a baby doe or as bombastic as a tossed grenade. He was wounding in his criticism, effusive in his flattery, a ministerial patriot and an earthy raconteur. Every facet of Johnson's personality seemed at variance with an opposite characteristic. And his conflicting traits did not so much war with one another as reside in an uneasy alliance. He was a constantly fluctuating human mosaic, provoking endless hours of commentary and analysis from journalistic Johnson-watchers. Probing for the real LBJ became an art form in the White House press room.

The correspondent who seemed to understand him the most was the one least like him. Except in size. Few reporters enjoyed the physical access to Lyndon Johnson that Ray Scherer's six feet, four inches provided. In Scherer, Johnson encountered the rare man whose horizons eclipsed his own.

In every other way, they were as dissimilar in personality and outlook as a lion and a sheepdog. Scherer was renowned among his colleagues for his total calm and unflappability. Before the era of live presidential press conferences, he amazed his bosses with his ability to run directly to a microphone from an Eisenhower news briefing minus an intermittent stop at a typewriter. "He would come," according to NBC Board Chairman Julian Goodman, "with a notebook full of scribbles that were totally undecipherable, and never miss a single quote or nuance of what went on during the news conference."

Even domestic disasters failed to unhinge emotions or his professional ability. NBC producer Bob Asman recalls Ray going on the air minutes after a traumatic phone call from home. "He had prepared his stuff and he was in the studio and they had done a rehearsal . . . for the program which was to go on the air at 12:55. About 12:50, the phone rang, and it was for Ray. He got up from his chair, came out from behind his anchor position, and took the receiver. It was a neighbor calling. Ray's wife was away and the neighbor was phoning to say that an oil truck had pulled up at his house and was pumping oil in, which was fine except that he was pumping it into the wrong outlet and now the basement was filled with two hundred gallons of fuel oil."

"Ray visibly blanched," recollects Asman, picturing the "horrendous mess he was going to have to face. But he went back to his desk, put his microphone back on and went through the newscast without a hitch."

Scherer applied the same low profile to his reporting. One of

Johnson's chief aides, Jack Valenti, claims, "Scherer wouldn't juice up a story . . . inflame it . . . in order to get himself an extra thirty seconds on the air. Ray is one of those newsmen whose ambitions lie in getting the story straight and not in exalting his own personal ambitions. And that's a big difference."

Lyndon Johnson referred to Ray Scherer on more than one occasion, according to George Christian, a former LBJ press secretary, "as a noble man. He talked about Ray being a good Lutheran and a family man and a solid citizen. He was in effect a small-town boy who had kept his values."

A man of great detail, LBJ was one of the few people in Washington who learned of Scherer's devout upbringing. Though Scherer frequently engaged in extensive volunteer work for his Church, participated in spiritual seminars, donated his broadcasting talents to Lutheran documentary films, his religion was something he seldom discussed out of context. "He's basically a very modest person," says his youngest brother Jim. "This is a thing that is so much a part of his life and so deeply rooted in him that he doesn't want to make a big fuss about it. . . . He's never used his religious faith as a prop. . . . never sought to exploit it."

However Johnson became privy to Scherer's closely guarded faith, the qualities it ingrained in Scherer appeared to attract the President, who several times during his White House years seemed to be seeking a deeper spiritual base himself. When he was vacationing in Texas, Ray would sometimes receive a call at the press headquarters in the Driscoll Hotel from a Johnson aide, issuing an invitation from the President to come out to the ranch for the afternoon. Ray valued the opportunity to observe Lyndon Johnson, unguarded, in his natural habitat, yet he worried about the relationship.

"You hated the word to get around that you were his patsy. There were some people who were kind of trained seals for Johnson. I suppose somebody may have put me in that category. And you used to worry about that. But on the other hand, if you got called . . . if George Christian . . . said, 'come out, he'd like to see you this afternoon,' you didn't say, 'I can't come' or something. You generally went. You never really got any news. But you got a lot of insights into the man."

There were some occasions when Scherer heard or saw things he would have liked to use on the air, "But he trusted you. And you had to respect that trust."

CBS correspondent Bob Pierpoint, who has known and competed with Scherer since 1957, points out that while Scherer never vigorously attacked Lyndon Johnson, no White House reporters considered Scherer the President's "patsy": "I didn't think that Ray would ever slant his stories to make his sources happy." Pierpoint says there were some well-known reporters who traded on their relationships with sources, "to the point where it was sometimes unethical. . . . Ray I never felt would do that . . . he wouldn't play that game."

"Ray got along better with Lyndon than the rest of us," Pierpoint explains, "because Lyndon respected him and I think he respected Lyndon. The situation never quite deteriorated over Vietnam the way it did for the rest of us . . . Ray played his stories very straight. He didn't imply as often as the rest of us did that Johnson was misleading us or was not giving us all the truth. Ray would give the facts as he saw them and that was it." Johnson thought that Scherer was "tough," according to Jack Valenti, "but even when he disagreed with Scherer's report, he never thought Ray was trying to put a dirk in his stomach."

Vietnam grew to be a great open sore that festered daily between the President and the press corps. Those who felt the war was a terrible mistake found it difficult to restrain their opinions. The emotions of the NBC White House correspondent, however were unfathomable. "Ray," says Pierpoint, "could ask his questions (at a presidential news conference) that did not imply either approval or disapproval. I, for instance, could not. And Johnson knew that. He knew how I felt about the war. I don't think he ever knew how Ray felt."

Scherer kept his thoughts so close to his vest that even his own bureau chief, Bill Monroe, did not know Ray's appraisal of the situation. "It's not often," Monroe points out, "that you work so closely with someone covering such a controversial subject, and a couple of years go by and you don't know what the person thinks about it. . . . He's a guy who's so open he can see both sides, which is very helpful to a journalist who doesn't want to inject himself into his copy."

Monroe, who now presides over "Meet the Press," expresses concern about the effect of advocacy journalism on the national attitude. "You know the business of being objective . . . sometimes I worry about people around the country. If you go to a lecture and talk to people in a small town or to a college audience, you find that people have a very low opinion of the whole government. I don't have as low an opinion of the government living in Washington as people do out in the country. And I wonder whether we in the media have been a little overly aggressive, hostile, maybe a little overly critical and have helped people in the country get an attitude of contempt, which is not by any means completely justified. . . . the kind of reporter who does his story and suggests there are decent people on both sides . . . and leaves out his own personal criticism may be doing democracy a service."

Bob Pierpoint thinks that "Ray is uncomfortable with stories that he thinks are going to hurt people," and he speculates the discomfort arises from Scherer's Christianity. Ray laughs with some embarrassment at this analysis: "He may have hit on something there. . . . I hated to have to go after anybody. . . . You'd have to report it if a man had his hand in the till. But if you didn't know for sure, well, that was a problem that I had for a long time. We'd pick things up, maybe around the White House . . . other people would go on the air with it when they didn't have it cold, and someone would say, 'well, where were you?' I would say, 'well, we all knew that, but we didn't have it absolutely cold. . . . I always erred, probably too much, on the side of being absolutely sure about things."

An empathetic man, Scherer understood Lyndon Johnson's own conflict about the war, "I always felt enormous sympathy for Johnson," Scherer admits, "because I felt him being drawn into this enormous Vietnam pit. . . . and struggling with it. And I knew that he really didn't want to do it. He had no expertise in military matters. It was all those people under Kennedy who got this thing started—Bundy and McNamara."

Scherer could remember John Kennedy inviting him and several other correspondents into the oval office for an assessment of the quagmire in the Orient. "We all sat around the table and I didn't say much because I was covering him. . . . Jim Robinson was there from the Far East. It was the very beginning of the Vietnam days. And Robinson told Mr. Kennedy not to have anything to do with it, that it was a civil war. . . . Kennedy just listened and took it in. . . . he was already sending advisors over there. . . . the buildup had started. I think . . . he thought Jim Robinson was speaking from a very parochial point of view.

"And we saw Johnson go through the same process. It got bigger and bigger and he used to wrestle with it. . . . I knew that he had no heart for the thing. He was a Texan and he had grown up with the Alamo kind of complex and he never wanted to be the first President to lose a war, as he used to tell us. . . . He was pilloried and villified to the point where he couldn't go anywhere but airbases to meet people. He felt this very deeply. He used to say to me, 'Ray, don't they understand, I'd stop this tomorrow if I could?'

"At the beginning," Scherer says, "I thought it was the patriotic thing. The area was being overrun by Communists. I used to go in and talk to Bill Moyers about it; he was a hawk in those days. And he said, 'Ray, we are the guardians at the gates. This is our turn in history and we have to do this, even though it's distasteful . . .' I made two trips to Korea with Johnson. He took off his Presidential clothes and put on his khaki and paraded before the troops. He was very much the commander-in-chief. The first time we did it, we were all very proud to be identified with it, because there was the President identifying with the people in the line. The second time, I just wondered about it. . . . a lot of us were beginning to lose heart."

A young newcomer to the White House press corps, CBS's Dan Rather, thought he detected some Johnson favoritism towards Ray Scherer shortly after LBJ underwent gall bladder surgery. In his book, *The Camera Never Blinks,* Rather implies Johnson presented the NBC correspondent with a "birthday gift" as a reward for good behavior. In fact, the opposite was true. The present was an elaborate Presidential admonition.

Just hours after he had come out of surgery, the President allowed Ray and two other reporters to come to his room and verify that he had survived and was in good spirits. When the visit was over, it was the reporters' task to detail Johnson's condition to the rest of the White House press corps encamped in the auditorium of Bethesda Naval Hospital. Ray was elected to do the briefing. He related that they had gone up to see the President, that the President was fine, and that Mrs. Johnson was with him. After he had described as much of the event as he could remember, a colleague piped up, "what was he wearing?"

"I think he was wearing silk pajamas. Blue."

Unbeknownst to Ray, the President was listening to the briefing through an intercom tied into his bedroom. The next day, Scherer was invited to have lunch with the President in his hospital room.

"Bird," the President directed his wife, "I want you to get that present for Ray." Out of the closet came a box, two by one-and-a-half feet, with a blue ribbon tied around it. "Give Ray his present," Johnson ordered. Bill Moyers handed the box to the puzzled correspondent.

"Open it," the President said.

Ray opened the box.

"What is it?" asked the President.

"A pair of pajamas," answered Scherer.

"What kind of pajamas?" asked the President.

"Cotton pajamas," answered Scherer.

"That's what I was wearing yesterday," barked LBJ, "and don't you ever go on the air again and say this President wears silk pajamas!"

On another occasion, the President went to even more elaborate lengths to put Scherer in his place. Johnson reveled in surprise and secrecy. He found it extremely irritating, for instance, not to be able to announce his own Cabinet appointments. One of the stories LBJ loved to tell was how he finally got even with a correspondent who tried to scoop him to publication on a Cabinet nominee.

One late morning, Johnson informed Henry Fowler that he ought to report to the White House at four o'clock with his wife, because he was going to appoint him Secretary of the Treasury. Then with deliberate intent to throw confusion in the air, Johnson telephoned the Chairman of the Ways and Means Committee, Wilbur Mills. Knowing the Congressional weakness for leaking Presidential news to the press, Johnson feigned interest in a Chicago banker, David Kennedy. What would Mills think of Kennedy as Secretary of the Treasury, Johnson wanted to know.

Meanwhile, Ray Scherer, having gotten wind of the Fowler designation, had written a script predicting the appointment for his noontime television newscast. Just as he was about to go on the air, the effect of LBJ's phone call to Mills appeared on the wires. A bulletin rolled off the UPI ticker saying that, according to very reliable sources, the nomination would most likely go to David Kennedy.

Scherer quickly revised his script. "We've just had word," he announced, "that the President is most likely to appoint David Kennedy Secretary of the Treasury." No sooner had he spoken than the President's press secretary alerted AP and UPI reporters to the real appointment. While Scherer's newscast was breaking for a commercial, Ray was handed a bulletin that had just freshly clacked over the wire machines: The President announces that Henry Fowler will be his new Secretary of the Treasury. A chagrined Ray Scherer returned to the screen, "Well," he apologized to his viewers, "apparently our first report was wrong. The President has now appointed Henry Fowler Secretary of the Treasury."

His most appreciative listener was the President of the United States, who was laughing himself Texas-size tears in the oval office. "When Ray came back," Johnson later told Julian Goodman, "He looked like he had just swallowed one of them Brownies he was always advertising."

Perhaps one of the secondary reasons LBJ enjoyed seeing Ray look so foolish on television was that he always felt the red eye of the camera made *him* look foolish. He feared letting the American people see the gusty, authoritative dynamo that he really was. Instead, he tried to transform himself into a soft-spoken schoolteacher. It didn't work. "He was the great persuader," notes Ray, "but he was almost too big for the medium. Occasionally, what I call the real Johnson came through . . . but most of the time he was on guard and rather wooden." Johnson was right when he told Scherer, "I always lose money when I go on TV." As a result, Americans never really knew their thirty-sixth President and never really understood him. By most estimates, the closest view of the "real Johnson" his constituents were ever permitted was given during an hour-long special with Ray Scherer.

For years, NBC had attempted to cajole Johnson to do an exclusive interview with one of their correspondents down on the LBJ ranch. The President had repeatedly declined the honor of sharing the screen with John Chancellor or David Brinkley. Since a great deal of Hill Country landscape footage had already been filmed, NBC asked Ray Scherer to see if he could coax the President to the camera. To everyone's surprise, in the fall of 1965 Lyndon Johnson, incarcerated by convalescence from his gall bladder surgery, finally sent word to the network that he would do the documentary with Ray Scherer.

Bill Moyers, hoping to avoid antagonizing the competing networks, demanded great secrecy for the project. He did not, succeed however, and Bob Pierpoint recalls a moment of acute anxiety when he first learned of the Hill Country enterprise. "I was standing by the side of the road in Johnson City, waiting for some kind of an event, when all of a sudden here came Lyndon driving this great big open Lincoln and there was Ray sitting next to Johnson with a camera crew grinding away behind them. I stared at this in abject terror. There was my competition driving by with the President of the United States, and I thought, my Lord, what am I missing?"

"Bob," LBJ called to Pierpoint, What are you doing here?"

"Mr. President!" Bob exclaimed, "What is *Ray* doing *there?*"

Later, Scherer relieved Pierpoint's trauma with a telephone call to assure his colleague that he was not missing a momentous story for the evening news. "I think Ray was very much inclined not to want to hurt me, any more than he would want to hurt the people he was reporting on," says Pierpoint.

The filming required twelve hours of the President's time. In the various sequences, as LBJ rides or walks over the landscapes that shaped him, Ray ambles behind him unobtrusively, letting the President dominate the screen. His questions are designed to get Johnson relaxed and talking easily. One of the most difficult tasks of any interviewer is to engage the confidence of his subject, who quite often feels more like a victim.

Because Johnson trusted Scherer, he emerged, in spite of himself, from his protective cocoon. The film went on the air to considerable acclaim. In the *New York Times,* Arthur Krock wrote, "the sources of the rise of Lyndon B. Johnson were identified with remarkable clarity . . ." Robert Kintner, former President of NBC News and Secretary to the Cabinet during the Johnson administration, calls the film, "Johnson's best documentary. No question about it. He comes across as the actual Johnson, not the Johnson he thought television wanted to see. There's a great deal of difference." The President, who viewed the show at his ranch in Texas, was so pleased that he called Scherer away from a movie party he was attending in Washington to thank him profusely.

Ironically, the success of the special brought the relationship of the President and the NBC correspondent into even sharper focus, creating an agonizing dilemma for Scherer. According to Bill Moyers, it was his association with Scherer during the filming of the special that started Johnson thinking he might like to have Ray replace Moyers as his press secretary. "He really understands me," LBJ told Moyers. "He really understands that subconscious relationship I have with this country. Any man who understands me that well could work with me."

The Moyers/Johnson relationship, once akin to father and son, had frayed over the years. "I gathered that Moyers wanted to get out of the job," says Ray, "and he came to me and he asked what I would think about becoming the President's press secretary. I said, 'I don't think I would be very good at it. That's a very high pressure job.' He said, 'Well, think about it.'

"Everybody in the press corps knew [what was happening.] Most people said, 'Don't do it.' I remember Pete Lisagor saying, 'Don't do it. You'll never make the man happy. You'll never have any peace of mind.'

"I remember the one guy I talked to who said, 'you've got to do it.' That was Ben Bradlee. He said, 'It's a front seat to history, and you'll be up close. And it will be a priceless experience.' That's a pretty strong argument.

"I didn't want to do it. I knew the man too well, and I'd seen him go through all these other guys—Pierre Salinger and Reedy. I was half-hearted about it. I thought it was a great honor and a great chance to be up close, but I was just never sure I could satisfy the man."

But Bill Moyers was not to be deterred. In an urgent phone call from Texas, he pressed Scherer for an answer. "This thing has come to a head," he said. "Are you going to do it or aren't you?"

"If I have to, I will," Ray reluctantly agreed.

"Is your wife coming down to Texas for the holidays?" Moyers asked. "You'd better bring her down because she should be in on this."

So Ray and Maudie Scherer made arrangements to fly to Texas and stay at the Driscoll Hotel. "Every day," Ray recalls, "I expected the phone to ring, with the call to come to the ranch. . . . the noose to drop around my neck."

The call never came, and the noose never dropped. To this day, no one, including the chief negotiator Bill Moyers, is sure why Johnson changed his mind. Although there is no specific proof, the fact that Johnson dropped the issue may have been a sign of his regard for Scherer. Much later, when Ray asked Moyers what happened to the proposal, the former press secretary replied simply, "He decided he didn't want to put you through all that." Today, the reason for Johnson's change of heart has been shrouded by the passage of time, and Moyers is not certain he can recall with accuracy why the President did not offer the job to Scherer.

"I think," conjectures Moyers, "that LBJ kind of picked up Ray's own reluctance to cross the Rubicon between the press and the political. I think he felt it would be hard to make that transition from being a professional reporter to being a personal servant." But Robert Kitner's explanation of the whole episode may be the most apt: "No one ever knew why Johnson did anything."

Later on, George Christian, the man LBJ finally chose to succeed Moyers, unwittingly increased Ray's relief at not being called in to the service of his President. "Ray was a reporter," recalls Christian, "that a person in government felt comfortable with . . . if you told him something off the record, he would keep it that way. One afternoon, the President was about to drive me up the wall. . . . He was traveling some and we never did know where he was going to want to go. When we did know, he wouldn't let us tell the press."

Feeling the need to unburden, Christian asked Ray to share some fresh air with him. The two men strode around the White House grounds and across the street to Lafayette Park, the press secretary freely engaging in a little ulcer prevention, unaware of the fact that the man he was declaiming was urgently trying to reach him. Where was Christian, LBJ demanded of Christian's secretary. "He's away from the phone, Mr. President," the secretary responded. "Honey," said the President, "you fix this phone so it rings wherever he is."

NBC's White House correspondent, meanwhile, was being delivered an irresistible story of internecine warfare at 1600 Pennsylvania Avenue. "I sometimes wished I could have taken back what I said to him," Christian reflects, "but he never repeated it."

That Ray Scherer survived the admiration of LBJ with his objectivity intact was no small achievement. It is Scherer's determined impartiality that draws accolades from press and newsmakers alike. A Republican leader in the House of Representatives, John Anderson of Illinois, gives a typical Congressional view of Scherer: "He always struck me as a very kindly and generous-spirited man when it came to questions of public policy. You know the Washington pack must be one of the most enormously competitive groups in the world—everybody out trying to cut, bite, scratch or gouge their way to the top. And his was a gentility, almost a diffidence. His was not the hard-charging attitude that I think is exhibited by some, the kind who just kind of leap out at you from the trenches and you feel, 'my gosh, they're trying to impale me with a spear.' "

"Too many of us," concedes syndicated columnist Rowland Evans, "insert too many of our own feelings, our own passions, into what we write or say. Ray kept himself out of his reporting."

Ray's brother, Ross Scherer, a sociology professor at the University of Loyola in Chicago, feels those qualities were fertilized in Fort Wayne, Indiana soil: "Ray comes out of a very family kind of tradition, where you were almost run like a private government. And there were realities that transcended the individual. They were bigger than the individual: Thou shalt not commit adultery. Thou shalt not steal. It wasn't merely that you *agreed* with this. This was *reality*. This was absolute law."

Raymond Lewis Scherer was the first-born of Eleanor and Arnold Scherer's three sons. Arnold Scherer was a quiet, courtly man, the son of a baker, who quit grade school at the age of thirteen to become an office boy at the Fort Wayne *Journal Gazette*. When he finally left the paper sixty years later, he held the title of general manager. His wife, Eleanor, was a handsome, dynamic, outgoing woman who headed committees and church groups and university guilds with one hand while cleaning house, cooking, and rearing Ray, Ross, and Jim with the other. "She never had a maid in her life," boasts Ray.

Eleanor Scherer taught her sons that loving God and "trusting Him" was the most important thing in life. Religion, she says, was "never forced" on her children; "We just assumed that they would feel about it the way we did."

After supper in the evenings, Arnold Scherer would read from a book with a picture of a shepherd on the front cover. It was called the Big Book of Sermons. Ray remembers his father being somewhat uncomfortable in the role of piety. "He would never admit," notes Ross Scherer, "shall we say, to any kind of creativity . . . he didn't lead in any discussions. He would simply read the prayer." The devotion lasted only about ten minutes, according to Mrs. Scherer, "so it wouldn't tire the boys . . . they were busy kids with their homework."

"It was never overdone," Ray contends, "never force-fed. . . . It was just part of your life." Through their parent's gentle nurturing, faith became an integral part of the Scherer boys' growth.

"We went to Church every Sunday," Ray says matter-of-factly. "You just got dressed and went to church!" Perhaps more importantly, when his parents came home, they didn't hang their religion in the closet with their Sunday clothes.

"We were always warned against being emotional," says Ross Scherer. "They used the word *schwärmerei* which means enthusiasm. That's not religiousity. This Jesus freak stuff . . . any of that would be taboo. . . . We were trained to have more of an implicit faith. It's deeply believed, but it isn't something that you shout to the housetops."

Ray Scherer speaks almost wistfully about the stability of his childhood. "It's hard to explain. It's a small-town thing. Fort Wayne, Indiana, was about forty percent Lutheran, forty percent Catholic, and the other twenty percent were Episcopalians, Methodists, etc.

I go to Church there now and I see the same people going up the aisle, carrying the collection, that I saw when I was a little boy. It's amazing how stable it is."

"In the thirties and forties," Ross Scherer points out, "institutions were much more formative of character." He refers to television as "instant totalism. People are exposed to everything all over the world. They can't digest it. We had a much more regulated kind of stimuli . . . you weren't constantly bombarded by changes from without. So you could be more stable. The present generation is paying a price we didn't have to pay."

The Scherer house was a home where the news of the eternal kingdom sat side by side with the news of the world. The newspaper was almost as sacred as the Bible. Ray remembers his father "read every word of the paper." Sometimes twice. "He'd read it all day and bring it home at night and read it too. I still get newspapers, and I hate to throw them away because I know how much work went into them.

When Ray was thirteen, he held down his first job, rising at 4:20 every morning to deliver one hundred twenty Fort Wayne Journal Gazettes. After his route, he'd slip back home to catch a half-hour's nap before going off to school. There were no days off. On Saturdays, he had to collect fifteen cents from each of his customers and report to the newspaper office by one in the afternoon with his kitty. "I never considered it a hardship. It was just something you did." His salary was five dollars a week. "And when I got ready to go to college, I'd saved a thousand dollars from getting up every morning."

Later he would get a view of the newspaper business as stereotyper's apprentice and carrier salesman. He can still remember the "thrill of seeing a story in print with my name on top. In my senior year I wrote sports for the Journal Gazette. It was the first writing job I had. I'd write up the games of our high school. After the games, I'd rush down to the newspaper office, because it was Saturday night and the paper was going to bed. I couldn't type . . . I guess I wrote it out in longhand. And they would send it down to the typesetter and he would send it back up and say, 'I can't read this.' I had to sit there with him till the whole story was in type. Then the next morning, seeing that story on the front of the sports page . . . was a great experience.

The three Scherer boys attended the same Lutheran grade school that had educated their father. Except for a lady who taught the first and second grade, all their teachers were men. Several of them remembered Arnold Scherer. "Your father's handwriting was never like this," Ross recalls being admonished. "Why can't you write like he did?" When it came time for high school, they bicycled downtown to Concordia, a Lutheran preparatory school for potential ministers.

The highest aspiration in a Lutheran home was for a son to become a minister, and Eleanor Scherer scored two out of three, although Ross thinks she might really have wanted her sons to become doctors. Ray says it may have crossed his mind to become a cleric, "but I was never impelled that way like my brothers."

Though most of his friends went to Northwestern or Indiana University, Ray attended Valparaiso "because it was Lutheran. It was rather "heavily bestowed on me so, to speak." But his third year in college, Ray grew bored with the routine, so he left school to take a job in the advertising department of the Journal Gazette. He was making a terrible mistake, everyone told him, but he did it anyway. At 9:30 in the morning he would leave his office to call on all of his real estate and automobile accounts. The afternoon was devoted to the local library, where he spent the rest of the day reading the books he had never had time to read before. "It was quite a good liberal education," he smiles.

The following year, he returned to Valparaiso, "a much better student for having had a year off to think about things." He entered pre-law, but Pearl Harbor interrupted his studies. He voluntarily signed up to be an ensign on a Navy destroyer for four years. When he returned "from being out in the world," his horizons had been widened and his taste for the law diminished. It seemed confining . . . tedious. "I really didn't know what I wanted to do," he admits, so he went to the University of Chicago and obtained a master's degree in international relations, to "regenerate [his] intellectual batteries." After that, the "natural thing and the easy thing" seemed to be a return to the scene of his frequent employment, the Fort Wayne Journal Gazette, this time as a reporter.

Cliff Milnor, who wrote a column for the Journal Gazette for twenty-seven years, was there when Ray started as a cub journalist. "He did excellent features." Milner recalls. "He was particularly good at getting people's confidence. . . . He's highly intelligent," says Milnor, "I think his honesty shines through in everything." Milnor agrees with coworkers who claim that Ray is imperturbable, but he is fond of recollecting one occasion when Ray's famed unflappability failed him completely. The columnist was in the hospital, recovering from surgery, when Ray and another reporter came to call on him. Standing by Milnor's bedside, suddenly all of Scherer's six feet four inches slid to the floor. "He didn't like hospital smells," laughs Milnor, who was forced out of his convalescent posture to attend to his unconscious visitor.

One of the young ladies working at the Journal Gazette was a girl named Gloria Swisher, who thought she had just the right matrimonial partner for Ray Scherer. She wrote a letter to a former college roommate, Barbara Hetzner, who was working in Indianapolis, instructing her to come immediately to Fort Wayne to meet a young man—a "likely-looking prospect. . . . and get on up here quickly," she warned, "before I fall in love with him myself."

"They were both so special," Gloria explains the matchmaking effort. "You had this feeling, knowing and liking Ray, that not just any girl would do. And I had the same feeling about Maudie. She's my most unforgettable character."

Their blind date took place at a charity auction on an old Fort Wayne estate. The tiny import from Indianapolis made a great impression on Cliff Milnor because she wore a coat and dress made out of mattress ticking. She had adopted the nickname "Maudie" when she went to Indiana University, thinking a new name would transform her into a new person. She was a tiny, elfin creature with brown hair, large blue eyes, a white, wide, and ready grin, and a gift for commentary as startling as her outfits. "Maudie was the first person I ever knew," Gloria laughs, "who wore antique clothes." Gloria recalls that her former boss Stanley Marcus was "very taken with Maudie because she always looked so unique." She had even caught the attention of Women's Wear Daily when she wore an ensemble she had purchased from the Children's Department.

Gloria was proud of her matchmaking instincts. "They got along smashingly well right from the beginning," despite the fact that nothing about them matched—including their size. "She was about four-foot-six," observed Cliff Milnor's wife, "and he was about six-foot-four."

"It didn't take me long," admits Maudie (who is actually five-foot-two), her blue eyes twinkling out of a well-scrubbed, merry face. "I fell madly in love. He was, I don't know. . . . it seemed we were reading all the same books and listening to the same music." Her soft voice fades into a shy whisper, "sort of what I'd been dreaming of . . . as if my whole life had been funneling up to meet him."

Ray's reaction was less spontaneous, according to Maudie. ("I think it may have dawned on him later," she chuckles.) Nevertheless, he began a fairly active pursuit, which was interrupted by a job offer from an NBC news editor in Washington named Cash Keller, a graduate of the Fort Wayne Gazette. "How'd you like to come to Washington?" Keller had asked Scherer.

Ray requested some thinking time. He liked Fort Wayne, Indiana, and he liked the Journal Gazette; if he worked at it he could probably be managing editor some day. Then there was the complication of his courtship with Maudie. So he called Cash Keller back and told him he was sorry but he thought he'd stay right where he was. But, he added, "if you ever get another opening, give me a call."

The phone was barely back in the cradle before Ray began suffering "terrible remorse." My heavens, he said to himself, what have I done? A chance to go to Washington, the center of news! Three weeks later, Cash Keller was back on the line with the offer of another job. "I'll take it," said Ray. Even Maudie had to admit when lightning strikes twice you ought to pay it some mind. Besides, she had decided to go to New York, to pursue a career in the theatre.

Ray was assigned the early morning writing shift in the NBC newsroom, a frequent gift from the welcome wagon to new arrivals in the broadcast world. He began work at five in the morning, singlehandedly producing five newscasts in four hours. "You just kept busy turning them out," he remembers. "No time to think. Julian Goodman, now Chairman of the Board of NBC, was the assistant news director. He was immediately impressed with the Midwesterner. "He was very vigorous, enthusiastic, patriotic . . . a very fast learner. He seemed ready to take on all the traditions of Washington and bring them down to a sort of common man's level. He didn't stand for much ceremony."

That quality may have been the reason that the young Hoosier "loved" Harry Truman. Scherer recalls with great fondness an experience with HST which he claims "left a mark on me." The crew in the newsroom was so small, according to Julian Goodman, that "frequently we would turn around and put our hands on somebody and send him out on something historic." So it was that young Ray Scherer was sent along with three other newsmen to accompany Truman home to Missouri when he left the Presidency.

Truman sat in a special railway car up ahead of the reporter's accommodations. Well, the correspondents said to each other, as they settled into the comfort of their chairs, that's the last we'll see of Harry. Now he's got his private life and he can be free of the press forever. "We were on the train about half an hour," according to Ray, "and the word came back—he wants to see you. He talked for a couple of hours . . . it was marvelous. The guy with his hair down, going back to private life."

The reporters returned to their seats feeling exceedingly privileged. No sooner had they sat down than the former President joined them to talk some more. When the entourage arrived in Missouri, all the Independence folk were assembled to welcome Harry home. The next morning, Truman took his constitutional as usual, and the reporters, as usual, were right in step behind him. He invited them to lunch with him in Kansas City.

"Mr. President," asked one of the reporters, "what was the first thing you did last night after all those years as a senator and all those years as President of the United States?"

And the man who had shed the most powerful office in the world just twenty-four hours earlier replied, "I took the grips up to the attic."

Ray happened on the air, as did so many young hopefuls in those days, over the absent body of a colleague. One morning he arrived in the broadcast booth to deliver his 5:00 A.M. news script to the announcer. Unfortunately there was no announcer. "You'll have to do it," said the engineer, who obviously was not about to lend his voice to the occasion. So, as Maudie Scherer tells the story, he just sat down and "burped it out."

That "burped" broadcast eventually led to voice lessons and twenty-eight years on the air, most of them notable for unflappable professionalism. Nevertheless, there were moments Scherer would just as soon forget, like the debut of the "Today" show—January 14, 1952. It was a Monday morning, and Ray was stationed in front of his beat, the Pentagon, looking for someone to interview for "Today's" Washington Report. The studio switched to Scherer just as the Chief of Naval Operations, Admiral William Fechteler, was striding to his office. Eagerly, Ray approached him with his microphone.

"Admiral," he intoned. "Can you tell us the state of the Navy today?"

"Well, I don't know, son," replied the amused Admiral, "probably the same as when I left it on Friday."

Despite this less than auspicious beginning, Scherer became a regular participant of the early morning eye-opener, frequently teaming up with Nancy Dickerson. Women were as scarce on the home screen as color television in the fifties, and far less welcome by many men in the profession. Dickerson remembers one male correspondent taking the microphone away from her on camera and never returning it. There never was, she claims, any friction with Scherer. "He was a very . . . nontemperamental, integrated human being . . . nobody could have been more gentle or understanding. He didn't resent my being there, or if he did, he certainly never let me know about it."

As Ray's career was burgeoning in Washington, Maudie Hetzner's theatrical dreams were withering in New York. She jokingly told her friend Gloria Swisher, after a tour of summer stock, that she had to leave acting because she was being "typecast as a lady of the evening." In actuality, "I sort of got cold feet," she concedes. "I decided she was never "going to be the really great actress I had thought I would be back in Indiana." Instead, the "lady of the evening" became the "lady of the house," frequently playing the role of innovative hostess.

When the Scherers entertain in Washington, which is often, they mix secretaries and clerks with Senators and Congressmen. "Most of the big correspondents," comments broadcaster Cal Thomas, who was an eighteen-year-old office boy when he attended dinner at the Scherers, "would only invite other correspondents or big government officials. Big name types. And, he invited me, a young kid still using Clearasil!"

Friends learned to expect the unexpected from Maudie Scherer—when she wasn't "startling" them with a wry aside or a shocking attire, she was doing things like moving into the Merry Manor retirement home, where her mother resides in Indiana, to check out the food, which she thought was too starchy. Please don't complain, her mother begged. Mrs. Hetzner, it turned out, was running for Sweetheart of Merry Manor, and she didn't want her daughter to spoil her chances.

One of the most trying aspects of covering a President of the United States is moving with him whenever and wherever he decides to move. It is one of the ironies of political life that men who strive so mightily to get into the White House cannot wait to get out of it once they have achieved residency. "My kids," chuckles Ray, "grew up thinking that I lived at the airport. They were always being taken to see daddy off and welcome him home. My wife was always pretty understanding about that. I probably didn't know until years later how difficult it was for her."

"There are a lot of marital casualties attached to TV work," asserts a former network bureau chief. "If you show me three correspondents who are constantly traveling, I'll show you two out of three who are going to be divorced in three or four years."

If a television personality's marriage is not killed by travel, it is sometimes shot down by ego. "We've seen so many marriages," Maudie comments, "where the men have become TV idols and they've grown too great for this little woman at home. . . . Then they have to marry someone who's a whole lot younger."

Ray is the reason that the Scherer marriage has succeeded so well, according to his wife, who admits to an active temper. "I think you could say almost one hundred percent. I think it's his understanding and compassion that have made it go. There are a lot of times . . . he's . . . tolerant and patient of other people when I think he should be more assertive. But then, if he were assertive and less tolerant and less patient with other people, he would be that way with me. And I really appreciate his patience."

"I think," she reflects, "in a lot of cases, it's wanting to have a good marriage." It's the little things that don't seem important that are important. Like the way Ray will urge her to stay in bed in the morning, "piling all sorts of good material" beside her, saying, "Now I want you to read this." Or the way he will urge her to lay aside her gardening tools in the country and sit in the hammock he has just put up, to read the newspapers he's picked out for her. Or

the times he never says, "Could you tell me later" when she's inspired to say something brilliant" while he's trying to concentrate on
the evening news. "I think," she giggles, "that has to be Christianity
when you're tolerant of people doing dumb, dumb things like that.
Come to think of it, though," she adds wryly, "maybe that's why he
can never remember anything I tell him."

She was, Maudie insists, always "terribly worried" about their
two children David and Nancy, "but he wasn't. He was more trusting." Ray Scherer's method of being with his son was to let him
"share the beat." As young as eight or nine, David can remember
trying to learn not to trip over cables in the NBC studios or riding
over LBJ's hill country with the President of the United States. One
of the nicest things about being Ray Scherer's son, he says, was
"growing up with Hubert Humphrey. . . . He used to come over all
the time." One night David brought the Secret Service to rapt attention by greeting the then Vice President with "a plastic repeating
rifle."

Not surprisingly, David is studying to be a journalist himself.
After many years of watching his father, he feels he has picked up a
few pointers. "What he has shown me is that by doing a good, steady,
solid complete job you can get more virtuous results."

Today, Ray Scherer commands the eighth floor of the International
Building on K Street Northwest in the nation's capital, as the
Washington Vice President of NBC's parent company, The Radio
Corporation of America. His decision to join RCA points up the increasingly cosmetic nature of television news. Bill Monroe remembers
Ray's agonizing over the decision to leave the news world. "It's too
bad in a way," says Monroe, "because he was a natural at it," but
Monroe adds there is something faintly undignified about a man in
middle age chasing newsmakers down Capitol corridors. "There's
something attuned to youth about it . . . television producers have
an aversion to lined faces and gray hair and no hair."

"I thought," says Ray Scherer, "it was probably a good time to do
something else . . . I felt that I was kind of caught in a routine,
and I just didn't see doing that for the rest of my life. I'd seen my
friends, old timers, just kind of tossed aside, and I just figured that
can happen to anybody. Why stay that long? Almost like a Congressman who stays too long and gets bumped off."

One of the reasons that television personalities and Congressmen
stay till "they get bumped off" is that they find it difficult to voluntarily abandon the ego massage of being a public figure. "Ego was
never a problem for Ray," asserts CBS correspondent George Herman.
"I guess," Ray laughs, "I was always a little sheepish about that.
Brinkley couldn't go into a restaurant without people ruining his
meal. I never had anything like that. There was a time," he admits,

however, "when I was having a lot of exposure on NBC, and I'd get off a campaign plane, and Hubert Humphrey would say, 'they pay more attention to you than they do to me.'" Scherer does not deny that he enjoyed the recognition, but his brother Jim claims it never altered him: "I think he always played it down. It got so that my mother was always introduced as Ray Scherer's mother. I was always introduced as Ray Scherer's brother. And he would try to turn that around . . . introduce himself as Jim Scherer's brother.

"He has all these jokes about people coming up to him and trying to figure out who he is. 'Now,' they would say, "I know who you are. You're David Brinkley or you're Charles Collingwood.' And then he'd tell them he was Ray Scherer and they'd say, 'No. No. That's not it!'"

Speaking about his new position, Scherer says, "I guess I'm a lobbyist. But I find that they [RCA] really don't require a whole lot of lobbying." Lobbying has a tainted connotation to many reporters. "A lot of us in news," points out Bill Monroe, "have this feeling that there's some special quality to it. That we're in a job that's different than selling peanut butter or soft drinks. We think highly of ourselves for being in news. We think we're performing some kind of service. Ray felt that keenly. And he wondered whether he would be proud of himself after he left news and took on a job that he looked on when he was a newsman as something of a lower calling for a higher salary."

"*Lobby*, to me," Ray observes, "was always kind of a bad word. But I find that there are all kinds of lobbyists. People who work for Common Cause are lobbyists. You're presenting a point of view. You're not buying anybody, but I had thought of it in the old-fashioned way, and I had to get over that hurdle. . . . Once I did, it was fairly easy."

Maudie Scherer thinks perhaps her husband misses being on the air, but she does not think he misses the celebrity. She thinks his religious training fostered the attitude, "I'm not so big. There's somebody up there who's bigger." Maudie, who was brought up a Presbyterian, says, "the thing that I got out of church as far as my family was concerned was wearing a new hat. Church was a social thing to do. And I was never very religious. I was really sort of adolescent in saying I wasn't a Christian because I couldn't believe. . . . all this stuff about one's man's coming down here and doing all this. Ray's brother would say, that's faith. You accept that on faith.

"I think whatever faith I'm coming to is just coming slowly now. At my age. Various little miracles. I'm coming to it, but not through the Church. She speaks wistfully of the "living Christianity" she sees in the home of Ray's brother Jim. "It just runs through like a steady, beautiful stream." And she thinks if her faith had been as strong as Ray's, their home might have had the same atmosphere. "I can't put a finger on why it is different from the way we live," she says, "but it is."

Ray Scherer says he feels "fairly comfortable with his relationship to the Almighty. I think it's about the same . . . I probably take it too much for granted. . . . Having grown up with religion, it is just part of your life." He never experienced any sudden conversion "like some people do. I still don't know what that really means, except that you're baptized. To me, 'born again' means that you still have it or you take a second look at it and you have it more deeply than you had it before." He assesses his own faith as "quiescent" for the moment.

"I don't really think about it much in a frontal lobe way. It's something that's there . . . it's an unconscious thing. When I come to make a decision, I don't put anything against a rigid set of principles. It just seems sort of like a natural reaction . . . you do whatever seems . . . right and fair."

He thinks the greatest personal challenge to remaining a Christian is "just being caught up with the cares of the world and being so involved with everyday mundane affairs that you lose sight of the Almighty and the philosophical groundwork that you've always had. Being too concerned with the world . . . the 'what does it profit a man to gain the whole world and lose his own soul' kind of thing. You have to have a sense of values. I think if you get too successful in this business . . . you could easily lose it."

P. Stanton

# 8 | MARK HATFIELD

It is a sight to make Harry Truman curl in his coffin. His beloved Radisson Muehlebach Hotel in Kansas City, Missouri, where a replica of his famous plaque, "The Buck Stops Here," rests behind a glass encasement, is being overrun by Republicans.

The Grand Old Party has assembled from the nooks and crannies of America to crown or dethrone Gerald Ford as the party's Presidential nominee. And it is in Harry Truman's old haunt that the opening sail of the 1976 Republican convention is being hoisted. The event is called the Congressional Gala and it appears to have attracted every Vice Presidential possibility in town.

Ensconced in the entrance, happily bathed in kleig lights and warming to the media, is John Connally—former Governor of Texas, former Secretary of the Treasury, former Democrat. Senator Robert Dole of Kansas is pumping hands in all directions, while his new wife, Elizabeth, dutifully has her teeth on high to all comers. Senator Howard Baker from Tennessee is disturbed at the speaking arrangements for the following night at the convention. He has been appointed to give the keynote address, a job traditionally intended to get the convention rolling. But someone has arranged for him to be the caboose instead of the engine; he is the fifth instead of the first speaker. Thus, he is interestingly positioned behind temporary chairman and rival Robert Dole.

Out in the parking lot adjacent to the Radisson Muehlebach Hotel, a slim erect figure is directing traffic, attempting to negotiate a peace between two vehicles intent on passing through a single space at the same time. Deftly he beckons one car into a berth and directs the other into the street. That accomplished, he takes the arm of his pink-gowned wife and guides her into the Congressional Gala. He is Mark Hatfield, senior Senator from Oregon. He, too, is a Vice Presidential prospect.

He is one of the over twenty senators, governors, and congressmen who have received a call from the White House several weeks before the convention, asking for a submission of all personal and professional data to Presidential and Secret Service inspection. Hatfield is curiously detached from the excited speculation of his dedicated supporters. His has been in the Vice Presidential sweepstakes too many times to let this latest pebble ripple his waters.

In 1964, Nelson Rockefeller came to Oregon during his primary battles with Barry Goldwater and said publicly he thought Mark Hatfield would make a great companion on a Rockefeller ticket. In 1968, reliable sources inside the Nixon camp reported that Hatfield's name was among the five finalists on the Vice Presidential selection list, but Nixon chose to ignore one Congressman's advice to "do something exciting." In 1972, even the opposition party was casting covetous glances across the aisle at the Oregon senator. When George McGovern's choice of running mates had narrowed to eight, his lieutenants told Hatfield's staff that their boss was one of the finalists.

It is easy to see why potential presidents looked to Hatfield as an attractive Avis, and why in 1976 House and Senate Majority leaders John Rhodes and Hugh Scott placed the Oregon senator at the top of their recommendations to Gerald Ford. In terms of experience, Hatfield's record was hard to equal. He had served as a State representative, Secretary of State, a Governor and a United States Senator—in all, twenty-four years of varied public service.

From a commercial point of view, he looked like a central casting recruit. The close-cropped hair, slung youthfully over the forehead, was graying with decorous distinction. The cool blue eyes were landscaped with great arched brows, capable of knitting themselves into profound intensity or rising to heights of delight and amazement. Even the etchings around the eyes attested to chiseled aging. He looked the statesman.

The problem was that too frequently he insisted on acting like one. He had, as one former staff man put it, "a very low tolerance" for compromising when it came to disputing public policies of which he disapproved. He once admitted to an associate that he probably would have had to resign the Vice Presidency had Nixon chosen him, to protest the administration's foreign policy. He was in short, risky.

His crusade against the Vietnam war had been in effect a crusade against himself. It had forever and unalterably labeled him a far-left liberal, in a party whose machinery was dominated at the grass roots by staunch conservatives. And so Hatfield's chances of twinning a ticket with Gerald Ford were considered about as realistic as life insurance for a snowball in hell.

"You couldn't get Mark Hatfield past those delegates if you gave each one of them an Amana home freezer," was Minnesota Congressman Bill Frenzel's apt summation of the situation in Kansas City, in the summer of '76.

A truth that was later bluntly presented to Hatfield by several Presidential insiders. Despite the fact that many Congressmen and Senators had placed Hatfield at the top of their recommendations, it would be impossible for Ford to recommend him to the convention. And when the Ronald Reagan loyalists tried to disrupt the nomination of a man as conservative as Robert Dole, Hatfield's dedicated backers almost sighed with relief that their candidate had been spared an embarrassing bloodbath.

It appeared that they at last agreed among themselves that only divine intervention would ever put Mark Hatfield anywhere near the top of a Republican ticket. He seemed destined, by virtue of unrelenting principle, to always be remembered as the man who might have been President.

There was, according to Hatfield's former legislative assistant, Wes Michaelson, almost a complete "abandonment" about the way his boss approached the war. "It wasn't like other issues. . . . It was just something that grabbed him so deeply—there was a kind of uncompromising clarity in the way he felt." And there were reasons for that—among them, his presence in North Vietnam during World War II.

He could remember vividly, as a Lieutenant Junior Grade in the United States Navy, pulling into the Haiphong harbor to pick up Chiang Kai Shek's troops. On the top of a hill overlooking the harbor was a splendid casino. "When we got shore liberty, we went up to see it," Hatfield recalls. "There were steps that wound around and around up to it, this great French Monte Carlo. But all around the base of this hill were these horrible little shacks, and a huge mass of humanity crowded together in abject poverty. Here were the French who had moved in, gambling away money in the presence of those who were literally starving to death at their feet. There never was a more graphic experience in my life of the gap between the haves and the have-nots."

The sight of the invader with his boot upon the brow of the native left an indelible impression on the young lieutenant about the "inequity, the injustice, the cruelty of colonialism." As the American Navy men were lifting foodstuffs off the beach to put on board ship for the Chinese troops, Hatfield witnessed wrenching desperation. "The Vietnamese women were gouging the earth to pick up a few kernels of rice that slipped through the burlap sacks. They were that hungry. On the route to Hanoi, there were these bloated bodies of people who had died, not from war, but from starvation."

From Asia, Hatfield wrote to his parents in Salem, Oregon, "If the western world ever tries to reestablish its heel upon these people, they'll rise up and not only spit in their faces; they'll create violence."

Twenty years later, the sights that sickened a young lieutenant stoked the fire in the belly of a determined Governor, inflaming a passion of the five senses. Hatfield was so convinced that the war was wrong and foolhardy that he was willing to risk a future career in the United States Senate to oppose it. He had been a highly popular and effective two-term Governor of Oregon, and he now set his sights on a membership in the world's most exclusive club. His election ordinarily would have been presumed. Not only was he a rising political star in his own state, but the nation had taken immediate note of him when he gave the keynote address at the 1964 Republican convention.

He was a young man who was going places, according to political seers. Then the Governor began publicly voicing his dissent on the Administration's war policy. In 1965, Johnson sent his Vice President, Hubert Humphrey, to apply his ample rhetoric to the task of persuading the annual governors' conference, meeting in Minneapolis, to issue a unanimous chorus of confidence in their President and his foreign policy.

When the resolution of support was put to a vote, the Governor of Oregon demanded to know the specifics. "What are we being asked to approve?" he demanded of Governor Carl Sanders, the author of the resolution. "Would you restate the motion?" There was an undercurrent of grumbling from his colleagues, but Hatfield pressed his probing, "What do you mean by the resolution? What are the commitments?"

Shouts of "Let's get on with it," nearly drowned out Hatfield's questions. When the voice vote was taken, it drew a heavy volume of *yays* against a thin tenor of two *nos*: one from Hatfield of Oregon, one from George Romney of Michigan.

Hatfield was immediately enveloped by a horde of newspeople, hungry for the drama of dissent. Embarrassed by the disruption he was visiting on the meeting, the young Governor beckoned the press out of the room. The hallway was crowded with television lights, cameras and microphones. Before the journalists could ask Hatfield to explain his reasons as to why he had voted against the Vietnam resolution, a southern governor who had angrily followed the procession out of the room, stepped in front of the cameras and denounced his colleague's vote as a "disservice to the country."

The following day, Air Force One taxied into the Minneapolis airport to ferry the Governors to Washington for a special briefing at the White House.

"Mark," President Johnson hailed the Oregon maverick, his arm thrust across the western Governor's shoulders, "Mark, come right up here in the front row." Prodigal sons were Lyndon Johnson's specialties. Hatfield took the seat indicated and listened to Administration evidence as poured forth by some of Johnson's finest protagonists—Defense Secretary Robert McNamara, Secretary of State Dean Rusk, and United Nations Ambassador Arthur Goldberg.

He was somewhat encouraged by Goldberg's promise to assert more aggressive action for peace in the United Nations. The Administration, Goldberg said, was going to take the matter up with Secretary General U Thant.

As the Governors were departing the briefing, President Johnson pulled Hatfield aside again. "Mark, the press is waiting outside to talk to you. Now if you want to say something to them about what Ambassador Goldberg just told you on what we plan to do at the UN, you go right ahead and do it."

George Romney told the news media that the questions in his mind concerning the resolution had been cleared up and he could now join his colleagues in voting for it. The journalists trained their pens on the one remaining dissenter. Had he been convinced about the wisdom of the war? No, Hatfield declared, the President's policy was "leading to disaster."

Nothing in the fall of '65 and the winter of '66 changed Mark Hatfield's mind. The year's events only deepened his conviction, a conviction that was now presenting a major obstacle to his election to the Senate. Lyndon Johnson had personally recruited a certified hawk, Congressman Robert Duncan, to oppose Hatfield. "If we don't fight them in the elephant grass of Southeast Asia," Duncan frequently intoned, "we'll be fighting them in the rye grass of the Columbia River basin." Polls showed that over seventy-five percent of the Oregon voters agreed with that sentiment. "The most popular figure in the State," wrote *The Oregonian* newspaper, "could lose the election on this one issue."

When the Governors next convened their annual conference in Los Angeles that summer, there was a general consensus among them that Hatfield's opposition to the war was so incompatible with his ambition for the Senate that he would have to retrench and vote for the Vietnam resolution. Short of that, some friendlier colleagues suggested that he might just kind of "disappear" during the tallying. This time, the resolution would not be put to a mere voice vote, the yays and nays would be recorded.

Before the roll call, Administration forces were again in evidence. John Connally's silver tongue was ringing the walls with patriotism. A vote for the resolution, he declared, was a vote against communism and a vote for our American boys in Vietnam. Privately, he told Hatfield he was "as a traitor to his country."

"Hanoi," Averill Harriman warned the assembled governors, pointing his finger around the room, "knows the names of all those who have been ratting on America."

Then the voting began. In the back of the room, Hatfield could see his wife, Antoinette. The walls seemed to vibrate the roll call, as he waited his turn. . . . Alaska, aye. . . . Colorado, aye. . . . Mississippi, aye. . . . States were inexorably and too quickly being ticked off, and all of them were saying aye. Ohio, aye. . . . Oklahoma, aye. . . . there were now thirty-five ayes and no nays. When the caller reached Oregon, the room fell silent. All eyes and cameras turned toward the young western governor, whose future might rest on a one syllable word. "Oregon?" . . . "No." It was the only no heard the entire roll call.

In Oregon the news was registered in frowning headlines. One banner asked "Was Hatfield right and all those other governors wrong?" Congressman Duncan, realizing that he had the weight of public sentiment behind his Vietnam position, ignored all of Hatfield's efforts to inject state problems into the campaign, insisting on turning the election into a one-issue contest.

*The Oregonian* newspaper released a poll mid-battle, which revealed that 76.2 percent of the voters favored staying in Vietnam, and over a quarter of that percentage supported an escalation of the war. And when the ballots were cast in November, Mark Hatfield, who had once been considered a "shoo-in," changed his title from Governor to Senator with the approval of only fifty-two percent of the voters.

The less than overwhelming mandate failed to discourage his fight against the war, though the betting went that he would lower his pacific voice when he got to Washington. Instead, he raised it.

His arrival was greeted with a great deal of press notice. Pundits who claim fortune-telling as an adjunct to their pen quickly touted him Presidential timber. But with each pronouncement against the war, Hatfield shaved off large chunks of Republican support.

And though most people thought he would have welcomed sitting at a desk in the Oval Office, his wife Antoinette disagrees. "He had all the qualifications for Vice President or President except one— Desire. I think," she says, "if he had wanted it badly enough, he would have tempered his stands."

But the same war that had fired his blood against oppression and colonialism—World War II—had opened the second leg of what Hatfield calls his "spiritual journey," stirring changes that would eventually change the focus of his ambitions.

He had been brought up in a home where religion was a ritual of life, where church was attended on Sunday and the Bible read. "But the reality of that belief probably did not come to me from an independent source or experience until I was involved in the war. I think when one faces the potential of death at any moment, one is much more conscious of the . . . quest for God. I really didn't have to learn God. . . . I felt the presence of God far more keenly and far more realistically than at any other time in my life."

Training for his commission in Midshipmen's school pulled Hatfield up from his roots. "It was the first time I had ever experienced group life. It was the first time I had ever been away from home, except for a weekend or a camp or a vacation." There were two-thousand boys who began Midshipman's school. Only sixteen hundred received their commission. "The desire to make it was very strong in all of us. . . . The pressure was terrific. . . . and I began to recognize myself as a human being independent of background, home town, and all that, for the first time. As a consequence, I reached out for the kind of support, the kind of reassurance, the kind of reinforcement that had probably been my family before. But now my family wasn't there. I was strictly alone.

"That sense of singular loneness—not loneliness, but loneness—gave to me a sense of God. I began to get up early in Midshipmen's school. I began to read each morning." He concentrated on the Psalms, feeling a particular kinship to David, who spoke of God as his refuge and his strength when he was alone. "I began to realize that I was not a totally adequate, self-contained person." He did his scriptural study in "secret" because he didn't want "the other fellows in Midshipman's school to see me reading the Bible."

His casual reading was forced into intense study at Pearl Harbor when the executive officer of the ship ordered him to hold "Divine Services." "I'm not qualified to hold 'Divine Services,'" the young ensign protested. The executive officer explained that a ship with only three hundred sixty men and thirty-seven officers was not large enough to merit a real chaplain, but there was a Navy regulation stating that Divine Services must be held. Since Hatfield had speaking experience in his background, he was the chosen leader. "That's an order."

Along with the command, Hatfield's superior gave him a box that had come on board at Pearl Harbor. Inside the box were some prayer books, hymnals and a few old sermons. One of Hatfield's roommates was named Tim McCoy, who joked that he wasn't going to let all the Catholics sail bereft in a sea of Protestanism. He would, he offered, lead the rosary. Thus began an unexpected alignment of Hatfield and McCoy.

It was Ensign Hatfield's role to provide some words of inspiration. His talks were "never more than five minutes. I couldn't think of anything longer than five minutes to say. Each Sunday was increasingly difficult. About all I knew I'd said that first Sunday."

Nevertheless, he put forth his best effort, if nothing else to save face. "When you're expected to stand up before a group of people and articulate something meaningful, you have to dig back into your own mind. What do I believe? What do I want to say? What do I want to communicate? One is thrust into the scripture, into source material of the faith. . . . My family had given me a Bible which I really hadn't opened very much, and fortunately it had a concordance and a topical index as well. I really read that and studied it very diligently in order to come up with something worthwhile to do."

By this time, the Hatfield-McCoy Divine Services had grown so sophisticated that they included midnight, candlelight ceremonies. There were mimeographed programs and a choir, accompanied by a "stolen" pump organ. Sometimes the services were conducted on the top deck. If the ship were in the danger zone, however, inspiration was sought in the mess hall.

When the war was over, so was the closeness to God. "I was out of danger. It was one of those circumstantial religious experiences where the circumstances created a closeness, a realism. But it was dependent on the circumstance. It wasn't part of my real being."

He returned home to Salem, Oregon, where he joined the faculty of Willamette University; living at home with his parents to preserve what small salary he was earning.

His father, Dolen Hatfield, was a construction blacksmith for the Southern Pacific Railroad in Dallas, Oregon when Mark was born. Dallas was a small mill town twelve miles west of the capital city, Salem. It was a "generation upon generation" town where sons of working people usually wound up spending their lives and earning their pay at the mill. But "Dovie" Hatfield, a highly intelligent, spirited woman, was determined that her only son would have the opportunity to reach for another fate. So she left her husband and her five-year-old boy in the care of her mother and traveled to Oregon State University to earn a teacher's degree.

"She came home on the weekends," Hatfield recalls. "It was hard, but it was one of those sacrifices that we knew was right." He did not, he admits, fully understand why his mother was not at home all the time, but "it did not bother me in the sense of conscious bother. . . . I treasure those experiences in Dallas. . . . I think some of the values that I learned there were some of the most important values I've ever learned. You knew the barber. You knew the banker. You knew the butcher. You knew the druggist. You knew the grocery man. You knew people as individuals." There was a sense of belonging in Dallas, a sense of community. "That's what we've lost in America today."

When Mark was nine, his mother rejoined the family circle, degree in hand. Father, mother, and son moved to Salem, where Mrs. Hatfield got a teaching job and where her son filled his nostrils with early and enthusiastic whiffs of political air.

He was just ten years old when he campaigned for Herbert Hoover with a little red wagon full of pamphlets, "going up one street and down another." He can still remember the pain of defeat. "We opened up *The Oregonian* the morning after the election, and there was this big picture of Roosevelt. It was crushing. My first loss." He shakes his head, "Took it so seriously."

He has never lost his admiration for Herbert Hoover. "He was recognized as a religious man. . . . Known for helping people. . . . Here was a boy who came out of a very simple, poor background and became President of the United States. It was a great challenge, a great stimulus to me, that this is a system, this is a nation in which a person does not have to be born to position or title to become part of the political life."

Few people realized that the little boy ringing their doorbell, campaigning for Hoover, some day wanted to govern them himself, but by the time he was a high school student his interest was there for all but the least perceptive eyes to see. He attended political rallies. He played the clarinet in torchlight political parades. He was down at the depot, sometimes as early as five o'clock in the morning, to greet an incoming campaign train. In every campaign, he participated as a volunteer or a paid hand.

He received a political science degree from Willamette University in Salem, and a master's in the same field from Stanford University. Working as an instructor and Dean of Men at Willamette University, his eyes never left the State Capitol across the street.

Three years after he joined the faculty, he was elected to the State House of Representatives. During his eight years at Willamette, his political career made a steady ascent from State Representative to State Senator to Secretary of State, the second highest office in Oregon. He was now well within reach of his dream, the Governorship. But the intensity and motivation for high office were to be altered by a chance association with an unusual group of students.

The students were, as one member of the group described them, "kids with tremendous needs in their lives. About three of them were social misfits." They wanted to study and discuss the Bible, and they wanted a room in which to do it. In order to obtain the room, they were required to have an advisor. One of the students, a curly-haired, dynamic, ebullient twenty-one-year old named Doug Coe, decided the Dean of Students was the man to approach. Hatfield agreed to the proposal, little realizing the effect it would have on him.

Coe was studying math and physics, hoping for a career in astrophysics. At the same time, he was struggling with the question of the existence of God. "I made a decision that I would never talk to anybody about God because I'd seen a lot of people trying to get people to religion and it turned them off and it turned me off."

Rather than seek other people's wisdom, Coe's scientific mind, devised an experiment to "graph" the reality of God. "I wasn't sure that God actually heard prayer. I thought it could be a figment of our imagination. Like you pray that your grandmother will get well if she's ill, and then she gets well and then you say, oh, that was an answer to prayer. But I had a lot of nonbelieving friends I was playing golf with, and their grandmothers got well too, and they weren't praying." Coe decided the best way to test God's existence as well as his hearing would be to list, in a notebook, a number of special requests, pray for them faithfully, two minutes every day, and keep a chart of the results, making sure that his solicitations were arduous enough to require supernatural industry. For instance, safe plane rides were out, because millions of people were arriving on time at airports without benefit of prayer. The requests also had to be, he reasoned, "good for God."

He was frankly embarrassed about his experiment, so embarrassed that he waited until his wife Jan left the house before he put in the required two minutes on his knees.

It was after the Dean of Students had addressed Coe's bible group that Doug decided Mark Hatfield was a sufficiently difficult and worthwhile subject to merit God's attention. Hatfield's speech to the students was, in Coe's opinion, "very boring. . . . It was, like, all Christians should obey the traffic lights. They shouldn't drive too fast. They should go the listed speed. And they shouldn't throw paper on public lawns. . . . He wasn't saying anything that would attract us to really live for God."

It occurred to Coe, as he listened to Hatfield's "boring speech," that if God could make a committed follower out of this up-and-coming young man, who appeared to be a perfunctory believer at best, it would be a "good thing for God" as well as for Hatfield. The salvation of Mark Hatfield thus became prime research in Doug Coe's prayer laboratory.

Some time after the experiment had been in progress, Coe received a call from the Dean's office, requesting Coe to accompany the Dean to Oregon State University. "I thought, uh oh, what's the deal?" He had been having difficulty with the school because of his refusal to attend chapel. Coe was sure that the ride to Oregon State was going to include the administration of a little disciplinary action by the Dean. There could be no other reason for Hatfield wanting his company. After all, "I didn't know him that well."

But as they were driving, Mark Hatfield began to talk and what he had to say astonished the youth beside him. "He said that over the last few months these students had been coming in to talk to him about their future and they'd been asking him questions for which he had no answers." To find the answers, Hatfield said, he had begun reading the Bible when he got home in the evening.

"Last night," the Dean confided to Coe, "around midnight I got down on my knees. No," he amended the statement, "I got down on my stomach and I told God that I had lived all my life just for my-self and from now on I want to give my life for Him, and," Hatfield looked at Coe, "it just came to me that I should tell you that."

"I was absolutely flabbergasted," Coe recalls. "My mind was a total blank the rest of the evening. The only thing I can recall think-ing about was my notebook, and his name on that page."

Coe's amazement was so great that he could think of nothing to say to the Dean. "All night I lay awake thinking about it." The next morning, he went over to the Dean's office and told Hatfield he was troubled that he had not responded in some way to Mark's revela-tion. "I should have said, 'Why don't we have a prayer together?' "

"I'd like to," the Dean replied.

"It was the first time for both of us," says Coe, "and it was kind of embarrassing, but from then on we used to meet one or two times a week. We'd meet from ten 'til one in the morning. We'd study the Bible and pray together. And then there was another guy, and an-other guy."

Hatfield terms the student experience not a bolt out of the blue, but the beginning of the third stage in his relationship with God, "where He became a part of my very nature. Where I don't have to depend on the circumstances or to depend upon the verbalization. He was just part of me."

Coe's prayer research led him to abandon his plans for a scientific career, deciding instead to devote his life to spreading the gospel of Jesus Christ. He would not become a minister, merely a dis-ciple at large. His work eventually brought him to Washington, D. C., where he heads the International Christian Fellowship Foun-dation, an organization that operates on the basic principles Mark Hatfield outlined to Coe twenty years ago in Oregon.

Rather than actively recruit and train laborers for the Lord's vineyard, Hatfield suggested, according to Coe, "we just pray and God will raise up His own people. Then we will just link the men in this city with this city with this city with this city with this city."

It was the beginning of an extraordinary network of Christians that has "literally spread all over the world" to include Kings, Emperors, Senators, Congressmen, born-again Watergate convicts, converted Black Panthers and Vietnamese refugees. When Washing-ton government officials who are part of this fellowship travel over-seas on business, they take a few hours off to contact and pray with foreign government officials who are also members of the fellowship. And when overseas visitors come to America, they frequently gather for meals and in-depth discussion at Fellowship House, a kind of international spiritual inn. Some of the more famed members of the Fellowship include Chuck Colson, former Senator Harold Hughes and reformed Black Panther Eldridge Cleaver. *Playboy* magazine became so concerned about the spreading spirituality in the Nation's Capital, they devoted a major article to blasting "God's underground in Washington." At the 1977 Inaugural ceremonies, the "underground" reached into the White House, when Mark Hatfield and Jimmy Carter entered into a covenant relationship, exchanging a spiritual coin and a promise to pray for one another every day.

Once Mark Hatfield had made his all out commitment to the pursuit of Christ, "He really struggled," according to Coe, "about whether he should go into the ministry, stay in the field of education or stay in public life. . . . He would just as soon have gone into the ministry, but he felt that the Lord led the other way. The circumstances kept falling into place. First the House, then the State Senate, then the Governorship, then the United States Senate. That's why, to the discouragement of many, you can't get him to seriously consider running for the Presidency. He never, in his mind, sought it. And he feels if he did seek it, he would move outside the will of the Lord."

About half of the speeches Senator Hatfield makes today are to evangelical groups, and though critics have accused him of using his faith to capture the religious vote, Doug Coe insists "the facts are he has studiously avoided that. For two years after he found Christ in a personal way, he never spoke, never mentioned the name Jesus Christ in the public arena." And for good reason—Oregon has the lowest church attendance in all the fifty states of the Union.

One night before a high school audience in Pendleton, Oregon, Hatfield heard himself saying, "You can come to know God by really knowing Christ." The young politican was so amazed by his unplanned proclamation that "he grabbed the podium. It really stiffened him," says Doug Coe. "On the way home, he was very, very nervous about it. . . . He thought he had really flubbed. . . . Sure enough, the next morning there it was on the front page of the Salem newspaper. It said 'Hatfield Says You Can Know God By Knowing Christ.'

"He waited all day in his office for someone to call him and blast him. But no calls ever came. Instead, late that afternoon, a State Senator called him." The Senator had read the paper, he told Hatfield. He had a severe drinking problem. He wondered if Hatfield had a Bible in his office. "I thought maybe you could help me."

When such solicitations became more and more a part of his life, even at political receptions, it changed Hatfield's reluctance to bring God into the marketplace. "Gradually Mark came to the view," relates Coe, "that there is no circumstance where Christ isn't relevant."

Nevertheless, a highly visible Christian is a natural dart board, and many of Hatfield's detractors have not hesitated to take aim.

Some of the sharpest jabs have come from the spiritual community. "Christians really took him apart," says one friend, "for his Vietnam stance. They thought he was too liberal."

"None of them," says former staffer Wes Michaelson, "really understood his opposition to the war. . . . There were a lot of other people supporting him on the war front, but hardly any of them were people with whom he had Christian fellowship. . . . Not only did they not understand his position on the war, but they tended to ostracize him because of it."

Hatfield became so discouraged by such treatment from those closest to him that he seriously thought of not running for a second term in the Senate. "He could deal with political opposition," says Michaelson. "He had been a controversial figure most of his political life, but it was hard to take evangelicals questioning his faith on the basis of his position on Vietnam. . . . He was not only considering not running, he was considering resigning in the middle of the term."

Eventually, the Senator changed his mind, according to one key staff man, Walt Evans, because he "found that he had a lot of support from the common man, from the fellow who would stop you at the county fair and say, 'I don't write but I like what you're doing.' "

Conservatives fail to take note of Hatfield's departures from the liberal roads, such as his outspoken opposition to abortion. Perhaps it is because he argues that to be pro-life is not to be a conservative. Pro-abortion forces "have a misconception," he insists, "They think it is a liberal position as the war was identified as a liberal position." In actuality, he says, "Pro-abortion is a reactionary position. Anytime in history where there have been movements to restrict the rights of people, impinge upon the life of people, it has been by arrogant, autocratic conservative forces: Hitler, the monarchies. The classical liberals tried to expand the rights of people, their right to think, their right to ideas, their right to life. . . . I have the liberal position on this."

But Christians didn't just criticize Hatfield for being out in left field. The sackcloth-and-ashes sect asked questions like: Should a committed follower of Christ be such a snappy dresser, drive a Mercedes, and live in chic Georgetown?

Hatfield, who has himself frequently voiced concern about the effect of materialism in American society, says the issue comes down to this one question: "Do you possess your possessions or do your possessions possess you? At no time did God condemn money and possessions. God condemned the worship of money."

Judy Weber, a young Senate staff member, remembers the time she gave her boss the opportunity to put that principle into practice. Senator Hatfield had lent her his car to pick up a lunch his wife had prepared for the Senate Wednesday Club meeting in his office.

Attempting to maneuver out of a tight parking squeeze, Judy backed the Senator's car into a stone wall. When she returned to the office, she went about preparing Mrs. Hatfield's lunch for the visiting Senators, privately anguishing how to break the news. She was crouched on the floor, plugging in a food warmer, when Hatfield walked into the room.

"Oh, Senator," she moaned woefully, "the worst thing has happened!"

"You've wrecked my car," the Senator surmised.

"Ye-e-e-s-s-s," she wailed, tears spilling down her face. The next thing she knew, Mark Hatfield was kneeling on the floor beside her, dabbing at her eyes with his handkerchief. "Now Judy," he consoled, "you know material things don't make any difference, just as long as you're OK."

It was his wife Antoinette, Hatfield says, who taught him a memorable lesson about possessions. Once he came home to find that his children had broken a fine piece of clay pottery that he cherished. "I was about to take them on and really beat the tail off of all of them, and Antoinette said to me, 'Now do you really love that more than you love the children?' You know she's very frank, and she added, 'There should be nothing in this house that we treasure more than our children, and if there is, we shouldn't have it.' "

Black-haired, brown-eyed Antoinette Hatfield's extroverted effervescense is combined with whirlwind energy that has led her from writing cookbooks and teaching the culinary arts in her own home to the unrelated field of real estate, a career in which she has had a great deal of success.

Antoinette Hatfield provides her husband the emotional outlet he denies himself, according to long-time family friend Gerry Frank: "Mark is superbly controlled, a disciplined guy. . . . In every kind of stress situation, I've never seen him not in control of himself. Toni is the kind of person who is effusive and shows her emotions very quickly if she doesn't like something. She's not in anyway hesitant to make these feelings known. And he loves this, because she's doing a lot of things that he wishes he could do or say."

Not that there haven't been times when Toni (and her husband) haven't regretted her outspokenness, such as the frank pronouncement she delivered on CBS television the night of Lyndon Johnson's Inaugural Ball. When correspondent Mike Wallace asked her who she thought might be President in four years, she replied tartly, "I don't know. But anybody would be better than what we've got tonight." Viewers who were not used to seeing a President attacked on the first night of his honeymoon, reacted in a vociferously negative fashion. Since that time, the irrepressible Toni has tried to limit such thoughts to asides behind the palm to close friends. "He thinks with his head," she quips about her husband. "I think with my glands."

Hatfield seems to appreciate those organic reactions. During the course of the day, sometimes several times, he calls his wife, just to talk and share confidences. It's a big joke in our family, says their oldest daughter, Elizabeth, "Mom and Dad are just like two kids in love. It's almost," she adds with a laugh, "weird."

It took five years of on-and-off courtship before Antoinette Kuzmanich, Dean of Women at Portland State College and Mark Hatfield, Secretary of State, finally agreed to march down the aisle. And when they did, he was in the middle of his first campaign for Governor. During all their romantic odyssey, which was interspersed with many rivals, "We were never out of touch," claims Toni. "Even if we had never married, we would always have been best friends." And then she adds, "I recommend marrying your best friend because you'll do much more for your best friend than you will for your lover."

It is Toni, according to close friend and former Congressman John Dellenback, who gives Mark Hatfield objectivity and directness. "She is a very leavening influence on him. She always says that she is the one who washes his socks!"

The evidence that his feet do get dirty is a fact that bears repetition, Hatfield candidly acknowledges, since a United States Senator is often treated like an immaculate conception.

"Ego," he says, "control of ego" is his greatest personal challenge. Being "born again" has a great deal to do with controlling the ego, he contends. "What does born again mean? It's not some phrase that was created by some Madison Avenue outfit or by Chuck Colson. In the New Testament, Nicodemus came to Christ and he said, 'What must I do to inherit the kingdom?' And Christ said, 'You must be born again.'

" 'How can I climb back in my mother's womb and be born again?', Nicodemus asked. Christ answered, 'You were born of the flesh. Now you must be born again of the spirit.' Being born again," says Hatfield, "means one is reborn into a whole new dimension of life, which is of the spirit. That is the crux of the whole Christian faith . . . to be reborn with Christ's spirit. Now that doesn't happen by sprinkling water on somebody's head or reciting a little statement of some kind. It comes from within, and really what it means is displacement of self with Christ, so that one's life is for Christ and not for self."

Replacing ego, "man's center and driving force," with the priority of Christ is much more easily expressed than enacted, Hatfield concedes. "The person who doesn't have any relationship with Christ goes merrily along his way, serving self. . . . And he can have a fairly tranquil life, but when you say, 'I want to have Christ as a displacement for ego.' . . . There you are, immediately in confrontation. St. Paul says, 'I wrestle daily. I wrestle daily with the old man.' And if Paul can wrestle daily, I wrestle by the minute."

Now and then he finds God subtly assisting him in the struggle. "Once I had a parent stop me and she said, 'I want you to meet my little girl.' The little girl was about eight or nine years old. And the mother said, 'I was her age when I first met you.' Well, that was enough of a shock, and then she turns to her daughter and says, 'Mary, don't you want the Senator's autograph?' and the little girl says 'NO!' " Hatfield roars with laughter as he concludes this story of enforced humility.

Judy Weber recalls an even more humbling occasion, when Hatfield was invited to be the main speaker at the President's Prayer Breakfast, an event that draws some three thousand political and business leaders from all over the world, as well as the Congress, the Cabinet, and the President of the United States. While waiting for Antoinette to finish dressing for the breakfast, the Senator decided to enjoy an orange. When he finished peeling the orange, he turned the garbage disposal on the refuse. Suddenly, the machine began delivering up a noise unlike any previous grinding of orange peels he had ever heard. "I wonder," he thought to himself, "what dropped down the disposal." At that same moment, his tongue reached up and found an empty space where a capped front tooth had been. It was simultaneously hilarious and distressing to imagine the impression he would make on the august Prayer Breakfast audience when he revealed his new picket-fence smile.

"I've just dropped my tooth down the disposal," he informed his wife when she arrived on the scene. Going out the door, Antoinette grabbed a candle, and enroute to the breakfast, the Hatfields stopped at a drug store for a pack of gum. "Start chewing," she instructed Wes Michaelson, who was accompanying them. While Wes chewed, Antoinette melted the candle to make a cover for Wes's stuffing, which was then jammed into Hatfield's gum. When they arrived at the Washington Hilton, where the breakfast was being held, they called for a dentist, who had nothing but praise for Toni's artful sculpture. "I couldn't have done as good a job," said he. "Besides the only wax I have is blue."

One would have thought a man of Mark Hatfield's elegant and correct demeanor would keep his wax incisor to himself. But no, he accosted anyone who would look, with a wide smile, proudly displaying his wife's newfound dental aptitude. "Look what Antoinette made," he grinned to numerous breakfast goers. The tooth survived the speech but later on Hatfield confided to a staff member that he had prayed to the Lord for humility while preparing for the event. "I don't think," he laughed ruefully, "I'll ever say that prayer again."

Mark Hatfield seldom goes public with his humor, reserving it, according to his wife, for friends and family. He is especially fond of mimicry and practical jokes. Almost every associate has a telephone story. One of his favorite tricks to play on his staff is to affect a strange voice and pretend that he is an irate constituent. His own way of dealing with crank complaints is to move the mouthpiece in the air, continuing to conduct office business while the caller raves on. At appropriate intervals, he lowers the receiver to insert an "um-hmmm" and the exercised soul is never aware that he is beating only his own breast.

The mischievous side of Mark Hatfield is only on limited display, according to Toni, because he is a "very private person. He is shy." The shyness sometimes projects an aloof and remote manner to those who do not know him, an image that masks the compassion that is so evident to friends. "His concern for people," according to his personal secretary Marian Bruner, "is one of his most pronounced characteristics. If there is an illness or a tragedy in someone's life, he makes room in his crowded day to call the afflicted family," she relates. "The amazing thing to me is that he finds time to do this. . . . He may come back after a heavy day of Committee meetings and being on the Senate floor and still sit there and make those calls."

One friend's fondest memory of Mark Hatfield is his persistent telephoning to ask if he could come to see her dying father, a man whom he had never met. Reluctant to take up the Senators' time, she politely declined until he insisted. Standing by the man's bed, he read passages from Isaiah. Toni Hatfield, who is capable of humorous observations at the most solemn events, says her husband has made such a habit of deathbed visits, that a family joke has emerged. "Don't have Mark come to see you. It's sort of like the last rites."

Fortunately for Mississippi Senator John Stennis, that maxim does not always hold true. Despite their many political differences, when news came over the radio that Senator Stennis had been shot in front of his Washington home, Mark and Antoinette Hatfield drove immediately to Walter Reed Hospital where doctors were fighting to save Stennis's life. While other Senators were holding forth for the cameras concerning the indecency of the shooting, an Armed Services Committee staffer observed Hatfield at the switchboard quietly answering telephones until three in the morning, anonymously dispensing bulletins to concerned callers.

Because Hatfield is away from home a great deal, he has developed a special method of staying in communication with his children.

Rather than always seeing them collectively, he makes a point of planning an activity with them on an individual basis. He will take his oldest son Mark out to dinner, his daughter Elizabeth to New York, or Theresa on ice cream escapades. Visko frequently accompanies him to an old book store.

It is eighteen-year-old Elizabeth, an intellectual like her father, who offers some astute perceptions of Mark Hatfield: "I would describe him as a very sensitive man, whose concern for others is very great, almost to the point of neglecting himself. I think his schedule shows that. It's very hectic and very pressured. . . . He's also a very introspective man. He likes to be alone. He likes to think. . . . He sometimes is difficult to live with because he doesn't often talk about what he's thinking, and because I'm very much the same way it drives me crazy. But I understand it. He has a controlled temper, but you know it's there. He's English, and it comes out in funny ways. . . . He's got this fetish for a clean kitchen, and he can throw this guilt trip on you by going in and cleaning up the kitchen and making a lot of noise, but not letting anyone help him. . . .

"This shows up in the rest of his personality, too. He doesn't very often ask for help. . . . I think it is very difficult for him to ask for help. He's a strong person and he knows so many people are depending on him."

He does not preach to his children, they say with gratitude. When he counsels, "He doesn't quote the four spiritual laws," says Elizabeth, "or scripture or Christian theory number whatever. It's much more a lifestyle. It's not something you add to your life. You make it your life."

"I don't feel that he's ever tried to indoctrinate me," declares son Mark. "The only way he's ever influenced me is the Christian way he lives."

Living as a Christian requires constant communication with the Source, Hatfield maintains, and this communication is not always easy to maintain. There are moments when God seems nowhere in sight. "Sometimes I'll be in the midst of praying, and I'll say, 'Oh, this is silly. I'm just talking to myself. If somebody should come over here and hear me, they'd think I was an idiot. Aw, who's hearing me? You mean, with all this mass of humanity, God can tune in on one guy down here?' And I'll say, 'It's really kind of silly, isn't it? Am I mesmerizing myself?' And I kind of laugh at myself and I stop praying."

"Other times, it seems to me that there's nothing but a dry routine to it; that I'm just going through the motions. Nothing exciting happened to me this week. So where's God?" No miracles, no major events, only little things, restore his faith.

"God speaks in so many ways. He may speak through a person. I might get a call from somebody. There might be some marvelous gesture," or his youngest daughter Theresa may give him a kiss, or "Antoinette will tell me she loves me, something like that, and I know that's God. God is love."

God is also beauty to Hatfield. "I have a strong degree of naturalism in me. I would have had to believe in God even if I never knew Jesus Christ, just because of the trees and the flowers and the beauty of the birds.

"I've found that I can communicate with God and God can answer my communication in very little pieces, a mosaic that I may not see for a long while. And if I am sensitive to the little things he puts together for me, I can hear these things. I can see these things. He has never spoken to me in a loud voice that I am aware of. . . . I pray most of all for love and sensitivity. Just sensitivity to be sensitive, to be open, to be alert to what God is trying to say to me in the still, small voice."

There are times, he concedes, when God's voice is so still and small it is hard to discern the message. He cites an instance when he was Governor of Oregon, making the "toughest single decision" of his career—whether or not to commute the scheduled execution of a murderer. "There was no question as to the man's guilt. He was only tried for one murder. He had murdered three people. There was no question as to the court's procedures." The question in the Governor's mind was whether anyone should be put to death, regardless of his guilt. It was an idea that was personally repugnant. Nevertheless, he was the Chief Executive of the State, bound to uphold the Constitution and the laws of that State, and the people of Oregon favored capital punishment.

After much anguishing and prayer, he decided his duty was to abide by the will of the people. He remembers being at peace with the decision at the time, feeling "a sense of rightness." Today, however, "I am not comfortable with it." Is he saying that God gave him the wrong answer seventeen years ago? "No, I don't think He did. . . . I don't know how to explain it except to say that God gives us both gifts and wisdom commensurate to our ability to handle them. And I have a feeling that my spiritual maturity was at a point where I really couldn't handle it. I don't think I had the spiritual insight, the spiritual knowledge or understanding. . . . I'll tell you, it comes right down to this point: my understanding of my loyalties to God and my loyalties to Caesar. And at that point in my Christian life, I was strongly inculturated to consider Caesar and God separate but equal, and somehow, as Governor of the State, I had the feeling that I was part of Caesar. . . . not in terms of pride, but in terms of loyalty and obligation, that I was obliged to let Caesar's will work its way. . . . I think I can define that same question now without any ambiguity and confusion or any fuzzing. I can see it clearly. Now I would have handled it totally differently."

Small comfort, he admits, to the man who did not receive the benefit of that delayed wisdom. "But out of that execution there was a new sense of crusade. People saw the brutality of capital punishment and, the very next election, we got it appealed. . . . There were seven other men backed up in death row. One could say, and it would really be presumptuous perhaps, this man gave his life for the other seven."

The puzzle reminds him of Abraham Lincoln's comment about the Civil War: " 'Both sides are praying to the same God. How can God answer either?' The fact was that he answered neither."

Hatfield frequently quotes Lincoln. He is the public man he most admires. "There was humility with a firm hand on the wheel. There was never a time when the Nation was not aware that Lincoln had his hand on the wheel. But he didn't have to hurt people. He didn't have to become bellicose for people to know that he had power. He wasn't a domineering, manipulative, commanding kind of leader; he was a suffering servant, which is really the most powerful of all leadership.

Christianity does not make life easier, Hatfield asserts. "Oftentimes people think being a good Christian means that everything is going to be wonderful, that everything will move ahead with achievement and success. I think that we are thrust into greater tension by the fact that we acknowledge Christ. But in all of this, there is that all-pervading knowledge and experience that we are never the victims of the circumstance. Even though we are in the circumstance, we can still be above it. Basically, it comes down to this: Christ called us not to acquire, not to achieve, not to be successful. He called us to one thing—faithfulness."

P. Stanton

# 9 | JAMES BUCKLEY

It was almost spring in Washington, D.C. The final days of March in the nation's capital frequently bring balmy advances of the season to come. The weather, however, was not a concern to the junior Senator from New York on March 18, 1973, as he beckoned his speechwriter, Bill Gavin, to take a seat on the couch in his office.

He handed his aide a statement he was planning to make to the press in twenty-four hours. Gavin, a man who bears the kiss of Erin on his brow and the keen political instincts of that heritage behind it, found the words he was reading hard to digest. Senator James Buckley was asking the President of the United States to resign. A President whom Buckley had supported, a President who had indirectly helped elect Buckley to the Senate, a President whom Buckley had believed in, a President whom a large segment of Buckley's supporters still believed in. A President, who had not, as yet, been proven guilty of anything.

This was political suicide, Gavin was thinking, and when he finished reading, he voiced that thought out loud. Jim Buckley was not the man to ask Richard Nixon to step down, he argued. However fine the logic of his reasoning, the ensuing torrent would overwhelm it; the majority of people would never see the full statement; they would not understand what he was trying to say. He would break the hearts of thousands of men and women who had worked for his election and he would turn his political base to quicksand.

The Senator listened attentively, and then shook his head. "Well, Bill," he said quietly, "I've made up my mind."

"I said to myself later," Gavin recalled, "why did you give the guy a heartache? The very next day, he was going out there to face the lions! It was like going up to the groom as he's about to say 'I do' and screaming, 'she's crazy, she's a nut!' Why didn't I just say, 'OK Jim, you're going to do it, fine.' Well, it gets back, not to me, but to him. Had I done that, I would have been unfaithful to the trust he had placed in me. Jim Buckley always wanted to hear the truth."

When he went home that evening, Senator Buckley gathered his family in the living room and told them what he planned to do. In an uncharacteristic gesture, he took his seventeen-year-old daughter Priscilla's hand as he read the statement. The family's reaction to the proposal was, in Priscilla's words, "total shock." Only his wife, Ann, had known what was coming. When he first told her that he was considering the action, she had wished he would let the cup pass, but if his conscience harangued his silence, she would not persuade him to maintain it. "If he had to do it, he had to do it," she said simply.

Later that evening, he telephoned an important political figure, a man whose opinion he held in high regard. His friend beseeched him to abandon the plan. It would be an irreparable blunder, a political misstep that would leave both him and the Conservative cause down for the count.

There was still time to retrench. Buckley had, with the exception of a few staff members and close friends, kept his cards in his hip pocket. It would be possible to cancel the morning's press conference with perhaps a minimum of speculation. It was a night of small sleep. He well understood, Buckley later said in his book, *If Men Were Angels,* "what F. Scott Fitzgerald meant when he wrote that in the dark night of the soul, it's always three o'clock in the morning."

The march to this painful moment had commenced many months before on what had begun as a quiet multihued fall Saturday in October. The President of the United States had broken through the national weekend absorption with football games and candlelight dinners by ordering the dismissal of Watergate Special Prosecutor Archibald Cox, provoking the Attorney General and the Deputy Attorney General to resign in defiance of the order.

Quivering ominously, under a continuous layering of Watergate lava, the American electorate finally erupted. In the week that followed "the Saturday night massacre," citizens wired, wrote, or phoned their rage to Washington. The White House, the Senate, and the House of Representatives were nearly entombed with letters and telegrams; Buckley's office alone received five thousand pieces of mail. For the first time, Jim Buckley began to wonder whether Richard Nixon could continue to govern effectively.

Then eleven days later a new jolt rocked the national composure. Judge John Sirica announced that two key Presidential conversations were missing from the evidence he had requested. Richard Nixon's credibility was vanishing faster than his tapes. Twice during the agonizing winter of Watergate, as the storm clouds embanked over the South lawn, James Buckley tried to deliver that message to the President. Once in a public statement that had no effect. Once face to face.

The opportunity presented itself one evening in December, when Nixon invited Senator Buckley and twelve of his colleagues for what he termed a "hair-down" analysis on how to make Watergate go away. The President gave the Senators cocktails and conversation along with a monologue on a variety of topics, domestic and international. He concluded with a reaffirmation of innocence and a reiteration of his determination to protect the Presidency and the confidentiality of the Chief Executive's papers and conversations. Then he asked for the Senators' opinions.

When it came time for the junior Senator from New York to speak, he delivered blunt candor. The American people no longer believe the President of the United States, Buckley told the man who held that title. The only way that Mr. Nixon could reverse that situation would be to empty "every file cabinet and drawer and shoebox of any material relevant to the break-in to someone like Senator John Stennis, who could give all relevant material to the Senate Watergate committee and the Special Prosecutor's office." The burden of proof, the Senator told the President, is on you.

The President listened with a vague nodding of his head. When Buckley finished his statement, he simply thanked the Senator for the comments, declining to add any of his own. The younger man left with the feeling that his thoughts had fallen on unaffectionate ears.

That reaction seemed to be borne out shortly thereafter when Nixon embarked on a cross-country Presidential proclamation-of-innocence marathon. He swore to the American people that he was not a "crook," but declined to furnish the evidence to prove it.

Buckley began again to ponder the possibility of a Presidential resignation, and whether or not he should play a part in triggering it. He decided to wait. The Nixon administration might still be salvaged. "I was always hoping against hope," he said, "that Nixon would do what had to be done. Increasingly it became clear that he wasn't going to do it. Things were just falling apart. As a Member of Congress, I could see that. The follow-through wasn't there. He was abandoning everything that I thought he was going to accomplish in the next four years, a fantastic historical opportunity to change focus. Everything was being thrown out while he was in a sort of fortress mentality. Something had to be done to shake it free."

By late February, Jim Buckley decided that the damage to the Nixon Presidency was now irreparable. In earlier discussions with two political advisors, he had been warned that if he took action in precipitating a call for the President's resignation, he would engage the fury of many of his colleagues and constituents. "I was confident," he smiles, "that *The New York Times* and *The Washington Post* would receive it well. But they're not my people."

One night, he invited five close friends whose judgment he valued to have dinner with him in Washington, asking them to help him sort out his obligations. Did they agree with his concern? They did. Was he the man to ask the President to resign? He was. Why me, he persisted. A call for resignation, the group agreed, had to come from a supporter of Richard Nixon's, else it would have little impact. Liberal Massachusetts Republican Senator Edward Brooke had called for resignation and it had had the effect of a penny dropping in the fountain of Rome. The meeting was over at 9:30. Buckley thanked his friends and told them he would go to bed with their counsel.

The following morning he had reached a decision. On Tuesday next, he informed his administrative assistant, he would have a statement to make to the Washington press corps.

The press conference was set up for March 19th in the Senate Caucus room, the room where John and Robert Kennedy had announced their intention to run for the Presidency, and the room where the Watergate hearings would convene in the coming months. On March 18th, in the late afternoon, a copy of Senator Buckley's statement and a covering letter was hand-delivered to the White House.

As Buckley was preparing to take what he termed "the longest walk" of his political life, the phone in his office was ringing. The President's chief of Staff, Alexander Haig, wished to speak to the Senator, his personal secretary Dawne Cina reported. Tell the General I'll call him later, Buckley instructed her as he walked out the door.

The Senate Caucus room was thronged with reporters, photographers, cameramen, broadcast correspondents, and the curious, all charged with an air of expectancy. Buckley sat down before a huddle of microphones, clustered like hounds around a fox.

Squinting through the blaze of television lights, Buckley began to read, "The stage has now been reached at which all Americans must come to terms with Watergate, if Watergate is not to end up drowning us all. . . . Watergate has expanded on a scale that has plunged our country into what historians call a 'crisis of the regime.' A crisis of the regime is not like any other specific and limited difficulty. A crisis of the regime is a disorder, a trauma, involving every tissue of the nation, conspicuously including its moral and spiritual dimensions. . . . I speak of the widespread conviction that Watergate and all that it has brought in its wake has done unique and irrevocable damage to our entire system of government. . . ."

Every ear was riveted to Buckley's deep voice as he drew a grim and awesome picture of potential impeachment proceedings, "I don't think many of us have considered what an impeachment trial would be like in the era of mass electronic communications. Public opinion would compel the proceedings to be televised.

"For three months or more, the Senate chamber would be transformed into a stage, set for the greatest melodrama ever conceived.

History would come to a stop for the duration, in the country and throughout the world. The ruler of the mightiest nation on earth would be starred as the prisoner in the dock. The chamber would become a twentieth-century coliseum as the performers are thrown to the lions. . . ."

"Can anyone imagine that such a trial could bring the nation back on an even keel and steady course, that it could fail to hurt the Presidency itself?"

And now as Jim Buckley arrived at the heart of his message, he could hear the soft hum of tape recorders and cameras spinning his words into a terrible finality: "I propose an extraordinary act of statesmanship and courage—an act at once noble and heartbreaking, at once serving the greater interests of the nation, the institution of the Presidency, and the goals for which he so successfully campaigned; that act is Richard Nixon's voluntary resignation as President of the United States."

Eyes met eyes around the room. The Nixon fortress had just been dealt a severe blow. The statement captured the upper right hand corner of *The New York Times*. "Senator Buckley Bids Nixon Quit," shouted the headline. Below it, another caption read, "President Retorts He Will Not."

Richard Nixon was in Houston, Texas on March 19th. He had a quick reply to Buckley's suggestion: "It would perhaps be an act of courage to resign. But while it may be an act of courage to run away from a job you were elected to do, it also takes courage to stand up and fight."

"Mr. Buckley's statement stunned Capitol Hill," *The New York Times* reported, "but generated virtually no support from those who had not previously urged Nixon to resign." Indeed, Buckley found himself in the bizarre and discomfiting position of being lauded by his adversaries and denounced by his allies. Almost everyone had ignored the fact that Buckley had specifically avoided accusing Nixon of any crime; that his argument turned not on guilt or innocence, but the ability to govern. Thus he was as disturbed by congratulations coupled with compliments of "seeing the light" as he was by venomous epithets. Even more disheartening were the political asides as to his motives. One Senate Republican credited him with upstaging his New York colleague, Jacob Javits.

"How do you like that?" he grinned to a *New York Times* reporter, "Jake will have to come out for the guillotine."

Nelson Rockefeller lined Buckley up with "those who would harass and drive a President from office." New York Republican state chairman, Richard Rosenbaum, said Buckley's position was in error because "there was no proof of wrongdoing by the President."

Fellow conservative Arizona Senator Barry Goldwater worried whether the American concept of fair play would be negated and whether a precedent might be set for future resignations due to an unacceptable philosophical positions.

"Most dangerous," a Tennessee conservative denounced the proposal. George Bush, the Chairman of the Republican National Committee, said Buckley's willingness to see a man forced out of office without proof of impeachable conduct "shows a lack of understanding as to how this Republic was formed and how it operates."

The reaction from a major portion of his constituency was even more vituperative. By the time Buckley returned to his office from the Senate Caucus room, his telephone switchboard was jammed with anger. Irate callers were fastening every historic synonym for traitor around his neck. Dawne Cina shudders when she recalls the day: "Telegrams began arriving. The mail that we received was overwhelmingly opposed. Our phones rang constantly. I took some of the calls and they were totally unreasonable." Before it was over, twenty-five thousand letters were to descend on Buckley's office, seventy-five percent of them opposing the Senator's position.

"I was sitting in the mailroom," Bill Gavin says, "I've never had an experience like that. Those letters! Absolutely incredible letters! Just scathing. From our friends! I mean that hurts!"

But Gavin found more morality in Buckley's "reaction to the reactions" than in the decision itself. When the klieg lights are on and the house goes silent to hear you speak, it is sometimes easy, Gavin contends, to be dramatically courageous. The tough moment comes when there is no applause at the end of the presentation. "You can stand up and make a decision and then when the reaction comes back, you become enraged—'This is unfair!' Jim didn't react that way. He didn't disguise the fact that he felt people didn't understand his views . . . but never did he become embittered."

That is not to say that Buckley was not depressed by the onslaught of invective. "He looked awful," his close friend and Connecticut neighbor George Stone remembers, "He looked like a man who had just had his heart kicked out of him. He looked old."

"He was almost afraid to go out on the streets," according to his daughter Priscilla, "People understood it for totally the wrong reasons. . . . The only thing that held him together was his faith. That and his family."

Today, Jim Buckley still grimaces at the memory of the ordeal, but he says he would do it again. There is nothing in the former Senator from New York's appearance or manner that suggests a man who likes to invite controversy. He gives the impression that he would just as soon no one notice he is in the room. A slender man with a boyish grin framed by two long parentheses in either cheek, his intense blue eyes convey an engaging shyness, even a vulnerability. He still wears his tweed gray hair in the same crew-cut style that was fashionable when he was sixteen, only now the right side frequently lies flat, leading one to suspect that he finds his hand a convenient headrest during ponderous moments.

His privacy is one of his most sacred possessions. "He keeps a lot of things to himself," says his wife Ann. This is especially apparent in an interview. When the subject is issues or an idea, he discourses at length and with ease. When the talk turns to himself, the pauses grow longer and the sentences shorter. His pleasantly resonant voice converses in cadences reminiscent of his columnist brother Bill—without the flamboyance. "Bill Buckley," analyzes Bill Gavin, "is like a Puccini opera. Jim is like Mozart."

Buckley does not like small talk. "He almost never," according to George Stone, who heads the math department at the Hotchkiss school, "says things to you casually. He will teach you things. It's either a lecture or silence." Buckley converses with some irony and considerable wit in such an unassuming fashion that an unusually attentive ear is required to capture the humor.

His shyness and lack of facility for thin chatter sometimes made the campaign trail a thorny walk. For the most part, as Dawne Cina points out, constituents merely want to meet and greet a candidate and move on, "because they have no idea what to do next. In the beginning, he didn't know what to do either, and there would be these terrible silences. They would say, 'well,' and he would say, 'well' and it was really hideous. I think he finally learned that other people were shy too, and that *he* would have to make the effort. By the end, he was making the effort."

The impression of remote aloofness is perhaps magnified by Buckley's tendency to be lost in thought. His secretary's favorite story about Buckley's absentmindedness concerns the morning he strode purposefully into Senator Clifford Case's office just as if it were his own, which as a matter of fact he thought it was. He marched through two suites of rooms, issuing greetings to all the members of Case's staff. Not until he reached what should have been his young, brunette secretary's desk and saw a gray-haired, motherly woman seated there instead, did it occur to him that he was viewing a foreign face. "Good morning," he said pleasantly to the startled lady, and walked out the door.

"At the interior of Jim Buckley," says a former aide, "there's a silence and a peace. . . . I don't have it myself. I think that those of us who don't have it say, hey, where did you get that?"

Buckley shrugs when given this assessment, casually dispensing credit to "the emotional thumbprint" he received at birth, a phlegmatic disposition. "I've got a slow fuse, or a low fuse, or," he smiles wryly, "an inadequate fuse."

His wife Ann has reason to concur with that assessment. In nearly a quarter of a century of marriage, they have never had a quarrel. "Because he won't do it," she asserts, "And I'm ready! I'm ready! I can fight with anyone, believe me! But no, he withdraws. He's there, physically, but it's obviously so uncomfortable for him that there's no one to fight with. So I soon gave up. But I took it out on the kids, so it was all right."

Still, observers think Buckley's serenity is deeper than a placid disposition. He has openly expressed his interest in the gospel passage of St. John, "Peace I leave with you, my peace I give unto you. Let not your heart be troubled, neither let it be afraid" (King James Version). In the summer of 1975, Senator Buckley gave his interpretation of that passage in the gospel to the Senate Prayer Breakfast. "We are doomed to failure," he said, "if we think of peace only in the world's terms. Rather, we must seek the peace of soul that Christ alone offers us. . . . the peace that comes from acquiesence in His divine will. The peace that comes with an acceptance of the afflictions and the uncertainties that are an inevitable part of the human experience. . . . the kind of serenity such a peace brings is the kind that the world cannot give. . . . but it is also one that the world cannot take away."

"I remember when his sister Maureen died," Ann Buckley recalls. "It was just a traumatic experience for me. Maureen was the second-youngest Buckley. She died when she was thirty-one, and she had five children. It was a time in the family when there had been no apparent troubles of any kind. Then all of a sudden Maureen died. Then another sister, Aloise Buckley Heath. Then his sister-in-law, Ann Harding Buckley. All within two years. I remember saying how dreadful this was that so many tragedies should occur in such a short period of time. And Jim said, not at all, 'the extraordinary thing is that nothing ever happened before.' "

Jim Buckley says he does not consider death a great test of faith. "I think if you accept an afterlife. . . . I don't think it should be too great a test. . . . If there is no afterlife, then our living and dying is of no real consequence. But if you accept an afterlife, there's no problem."

"He is a philosopher," says Ann Buckley, "and he believes in ultimate values. Because he does, it seems appropriate to him that good things and bad things happen to everyone. And if the bad things come in bunches, well, the good things come in bunches too."

One of the bad things that came his way was the involuntary surrender of his seat in the United States Senate to Daniel Patrick Moynihan. Jim Buckley did not get reelected to the Senate, according to his staff, because of the "New York City issue." Less prejudiced observers argue that the 1975 New York City financial crisis was only the most sensationalized issue on which Buckley was counted "wrong." Reporters will point to a whole host of principled actions that added up to, in writer Richard Reeves's words, "great morality but lousy politics." In an article for *New York* magazine, Reeves described James Buckley as "an honest politician. He is a man of conscience. He may be the strangest or worst Senator New Yorkers have ever elected, and the odds are they won't do it again."

Corroborating Priscilla Buckley's opinion that her father is the "modern Don Quixote," Reeves took note of one particularly quixotic battle to eliminate pork barrel from the public works legislation. "He was so right. . . . his colleagues thought he must be kidding."

But it was the impression that he did not care if the "Big Apple" shrunk to a core that tightened the noose of defeat around Buckley's neck. When he is confronted with the question as to the wisdom of acting in accord with constituent's wishes so as to live and fight another war, Jim Buckley speaks pragmatically. "I think that's an extremely difficult question because you can't throw out the argument out of hand. But where do you draw the line? Where do you determine that you are really so uniquely qualified to do something that you have a license to deceive? Here and there I did things when I didn't want to make waves. But those were basically unimportant things. There are those things that can create issues out of proportion. You do the expedient thing, but there's no great principle involved. But then there are the big ones. I didn't see how, even if I'd had any temptation to do it, I could remain an effective proponent for a certain point of view if I made such glaring exceptions to them. New York City is a case very much in point."

The financial dilemma of New York City does not fit into the column of moral issues, and yet Jim Buckley considered his view that New York must help itself before it sought aid from the Federal government as philosophical as it was practical. "Natural history was first called natural philosophy," he points out, "it is drawing conclusions, adducing rules from observed fact. I believe that my political philosophy is not something that was sketched *in vacuo* on a piece of paper, but something that was a distillation, not by me, but by people long before me, of the circumstances in which people lose their freedom."

Buckley likes to buttress his regard for self-reliance with a quote from Edward Gibbon, writing about the downfall of the ancient Athenians:

In the end, more than freedom, they wanted security. They wanted a comfortable life, and they lost it all. . . . security, comfort and freedom. When the Athenians finally wanted, not to give to society, but for society to give to them, when the freedom they wished for was freedom from responsibility, then Athens ceased to be free and never was free again.

Because Buckley supported aid to New York only after the city government agreed to some rearrangment of its fiscal housekeeping, and because he refused to demagogue his position, "the public perception was of a man who didn't care what was happening to New York," according to Bill Gavin. Some of the reason for that impression can be laid, says Gavin, at the door of Buckley's intellectual approach to issues. "He was talking about fantastically complex matters. There was no other way Jim Buckley could talk about it except in complex terms because that's what the reality was. What we're talking about really is a decision of conscience, to be true to one's self by reflecting the complexity of the situation. And that complex answer is not going to soothe everyone.

"The easy thing to do is to stand on a table, rip open your shirt, and scream New York! New York! It's a heck of a town! The Bronx is up, and the Battery's down! Then you do a dance and you get Lenny Bernstein to do the music and you refer to New York as the Big Apple four times a day and that means you care!

"Well, *no!*" Gavin almost shouts for emphasis, "because a lot of guys were doing that and they weren't providing any solutions. Jim Buckley was going down and talking to Western and Southern senators who wouldn't talk to anybody else from New York, and he was saying, 'we need help.' Jim Buckley was providing the votes to get the eventual bill for New York through. Nobody knew that."

The headline bannered across the *New York Daily News*—"Ford to City, *drop dead*"—might as well have read "Buckley to City. . . ."

"People were just wild at him," Ann Buckley remembers, "Absolutely wild at him. He had no choice. . . . It made no difference whether he came from New York or not, he felt that he was there to use his best judgment and if they didn't want him, they could throw him out. And," she sighs, "so they did."

It is not easy, no matter how phlegmatic your disposition, to "be thrown out." Some politicians liken the trauma to missing the last lifeboat departing the Titanic. George Stone recalls election night: "I don't think there is any question that he was deeply hurt that night. . . . and for quite a while afterwards. He seemed to bear it perfectly at the time. His speech was a pretty good speech, but you could see his eyes were glistening. Everybody wrote him letters about it. I never could. I was so aware of how much it had hurt him. It was such a short time in there. . . . I couldn't think of anything to say. I'd wake up in the middle of the night, as though I'd done something embarrassing. I'd wonder, my Lord, what'd I do? And then it suddenly came to me—Jimmy lost the election."

One letter of condolence was unexpected:

> Dear Jim,
> Speaking from experience, I know that when you *win* an election you hear from *everybody*. When you lose, you hear from your *friends*.
> Pat and I are proud to be included in the latter category.
> I know how disappointed and tired you must be. May I urge you to keep active in politics. The nation needs to hear your voice and our party needs your leadership.
> Pat joins me in extending our very best wishes for the years ahead.

The letter was signed, "Dick Nixon."

"Election night," analyzes Priscilla Buckley, "I guess is like a graduation, when all of a sudden, you're close to people you never really knew before. Many tears and confessions and everything you say is almost like writing in a yearbook. I had so many people approach me that night with tears in their eyes, saying that whatever he did from then on, they wanted to be with him, because they couldn't "imagine working for anybody the caliber of Jim Buckley." The depth of emotion surprised even his daughter. "This for a man who is not 'pals,' because of his reserve, with anyone on the staff. Everyone was so proud of him. Much more so in that situation than if he had won. There was a kind of pride in being defeated for the reasons that he was. He had not compromised to win."

Priscilla and her older brother Peter had campaigned actively for their father. She vividly recalls the final weekend before the election: "Peter and I were on a weekend blitz in the north country with Michael Ford. All the Ford polls were going up and all the Buckley polls were going down, and it was so depressing. I talked to Michael about how his family would react if they lost. He said whatever happened was God's will, and that he didn't feel it would be hard either way, if they won or lost. He was very much at peace about it. It was much harder for me, I've gotta say.

"The day after the election, Michael called me up and said that it was very hard not to be bitter and not to want to blame somebody or something, but that really, what happened was for the best. . . . our ultimate goals hadn't changed at all. . . . and that we were no less effective. I cried with gratitude. Literally."

Priscilla received much the same input from her parents. For her father, the loss did not constitute a disaster of Olympian proportions or even a great test of faith. "Here's the distinction," he points out, "Politics was never my life." He rejects the notion that he is a better man because he is a better sport. "This was something that happened unexpectedly. I haven't invested a career in the thing. I never got that invested emotionally. I knew it would be a high risk enterprise. Sure I was disappointed; I wouldn't have gone through the ordeal of running unless there were things that I wanted to continue doing. But when I say life goes on, I mean precisely that."

His wife Ann claims never to have seen a period of blues after the election, "I never saw them. Even I never saw them. He was as cheerful the next morning as he was the morning he won six years ago." If there had been a period of blues, it would have been difficult for Ann to interpret them, for she clearly feels that her husband is an example of one of the Creator's near perfect products.

Ann Cooley Buckley is a tawny, attractive blonde with a breezy wit, a siamese attachment to the tennis racket and almost nothing in common with her husband. She loves athletics. He does not. He loves birds. She "doesn't see them." He is quiet. She is full of irreverent conversation. She is competitive. He is not. It is probably why they get along so well. They do share some similar affections, Ann insists. "Certainly faith." They both love music. Neither perform. They listen. A telephone caller will almost assuredly pick up a background concerto along with Buckley conversation: "We both cannot ever remember the name of the piece that is playing, but we both just adore it. . . . We love to go to concerts, but we don't very often, because I fall asleep."

"They have a wonderful relationship," comments an observant former Senate employee, "almost like when you're very young. If one or the other is at a reception first, there is an excitement when the second one arrives."

Typical of Ann Buckley's humor is her rejoinder to the above comment, "Oh," she chortles, "I'm glad we're still fooling people with that act! The only thing that holds us together are the children. We can't decide what to do with them. He doesn't want them. And of course I don't want them!"

There are six "unwanted" Buckley children, five boys and one girl, ranging in age from twenty-three to fourteen. They all, according to Connecticut neighbors, have turned out "beautifully." Only one, the eldest son Peter, came close to being a rebel, and most of his rebellion concerned his coiffure. He wanted it long and visible and his parents thought the less they saw of it the better.

"It was unpleasant hair," Ann says with evident distaste, "it was skinny, slippery, broken-ended, mouse-colored hair. It wasn't that he had lovely hair!" Whatever the condition, it meant a great deal to Peter. It was his way, his mother explains, of showing independence from parental authority. The problem was how best to convince him to cut it. Ann Buckley recalls with amusement her husband's single and unsuccessful attempt. Jim Buckley is "not a disciplinarian," asserts his wife, "the Buckleys confuse charity with cowardice." One afternoon she left Jim in charge of overseeing the shearing of Peter's locks.

"When I got home, Jim was working at his desk, and Peter was somewhere in the house, so I whispered, 'Did Peter cut his hair?' And Jim said, 'Not yet, I don't think. But,' he announced proudly, 'I have given him until sundown.' Sundown!," Ann hoots, "can you imagine anything so archaic?"

Blonde, aqua-eyed Priscilla resembles her father in looks and interests, and has a keen insight into his character, even though she claims to have "really known him only in recent years. All through her childhood, he was vice president of the Catawba Corporation, a consultant firm founded by his father to handle the business dealings of the many Buckley oil and gas exploration companies. The job took him to New York during the middle of the week and out of the country for as long as three months at a stretch. The family lived in Sharon, Connecticut, so the children only saw their father on weekends. Even then, Jim Buckley's natural reserve and dignity made it a very formal relationship.

Priscilla laughs at the memory of her father, "launching into these long talks on God, country, and family. In fact, we were terribly bored. We didn't have dinner together and the children would eat at 5:30. But the patriotic kind of thing was generally taken up during the Saturday night dinner and that would be at the end, when he was finishing up his wine and we were waiting to run upstairs and watch 'Batman.' When other kids were playing football with their parents, we hardly saw him. I didn't realize until I was older and really started getting to know him how much I had missed."

"There was a definite turning point" in Priscilla's relationship with her father. She first became acquainted with him, she says, in her sophomore year at Ethel Walkers school in Connecticut. "In the fall," she reminisces, "there's a Fathers' Day. Because my parents lived in Washington, they couldn't very often come for it. Sometimes it got pretty lonely with everybody else having parents there and nobody from my family coming. One Father's Day, when he was particularly busy that spring, he called me and said that he would come and I was just overwhelmed. . . . In the afternoon, the general activities are playing softball, etc., in a father-daughter situation. Needless to say, he's not your average athletic type," she chuckles, "so we went bird watching."

Priscilla took her father to her favorite nature hideaway tucked among the school's eight hundred wooded acres. "It was a beautiful spring day. The violets and the lady slippers were coming up, but you couldn't tell what color they were going to be. He went looking after the birds, telling me what they were. He knows so much about natural history. He could tell me what kind of a fern this was or what kind of a tree or what kind of a flower was coming up. I was absolutely fascinated. . . . We dug up a violet and put it in a little container and I brought it up to my room, and we promised to keep in touch as to what color the ladyslippers were going to be. It was really such a special time."

Their relationship, according to Priscilla, has been "uphill ever since." Contrary to popular opinion, public office was kinder to family life than the business world. During Buckley's years in the Senate, Priscilla saw her father "beginning to open up. . . . he became much more affectionate with all the children. . . . He could be a refugee from the public with us."

Jim Buckley's need to be a "refugee from the public" was perhaps the most paradoxical aspect of his plunge into the political arena. Buckley did not throw his hat into the ring because he enjoyed shaking large numbers of strange hands, making small talk, or large talks for that matter. When he launched his first campaign, he had not made a speech in seventeen years, not since he addressed the ornithological club at his high school in Milbrook, New York. Even the public adulation was painful to this intensely shy man. "At first," his wife remembers "he was enormously embarrassed by it all. . . . He then got to handle it much better. He never got to like it, I don't think. I think many people do like it, and I think that's good, because it makes their job easier." One friend thinks that by the end of his term, Buckley found celebrity not nearly so discomforting, and maybe even just a tiny bit pleasant.

Jim Buckley is by preference and by temperament, "a country boy." If there had been such a thing as a college degree in ecology in the 1940s, when he attended Yale, Buckley thinks he might have gone after it. "I'm intrigued by ecological relationships and I think I could have had an interesting career in that. There is a lot of sort of detective work that goes into it, curious dependencies in different life forms and so on. I think I would have been satisfied." Even now, bird watching is one of his premier forms of enjoyment. Characteristically, he deprecates any introspective import to the recreation. He watches birds for the simple reason that they are "easy to see. . . . try studying weasels or shrews," he quips.

When he was a boy in Sharon, Connecticut, fighting his way to maturity amidst ten physically and intellectually kinetic brothers and sisters, Jim was the quiet Buckley, always bringing home stray and sometimes very strange creatures. "He was a very mischieveous little boy," according to his sister Priscilla, "He was an absolute thorn to school teachers. He was a tease—the grasshopper in the pencil box kind of thing—he had a little monkey sense of humor.

Very bright, and as I recall, didn't do all that well in school at that age, because he was always being sent out of the room."

"When we got back from England," Priscilla recalls, "we had to be tutored for a year to get our credits back in order so that we could go to proper American schools. We had an English tutor named Constance Cann, a fearful woman. In the middle of the morning, during a Connecticut winter, she would throw open the window and we'd all have to do vigorous exercises, which embarrassed us no end. The boys wore short pants. . . . with elasticized bands. Jim would pull in his stomach until his pants would start to fall down and when the situation got absolutely crucial, she would slam the window down."

William F. Buckley, Sr. lavished the learning and privilege on his children that his own parents could never afford to give him. "There was nothing complicated about Father's theory of child rearing," a chapter in a family memoir devoted to Mr. Buckley relates, "he brought up his sons and daughters with the quite simple objective that they be absolutely perfect. To this end, his children were at one time or another given professional instruction in: apologetics, art, ballroom dancing, banjo, bird watching, building boats in bottles. . . ." The list goes on for another half page, including every effort from sailing to wood carving.

Will Buckley was the son of a Texas sheriff who worked his way through college as a teacher. He moved to Mexico as a young man, where he set up a law practice. This he soon tired of, thinking it the "most trying thing in the world." He found much more adventure and self-expression in the pursuit of oil, an enterprise that amassed him comfortable wealth by the time he was thirty-five. He remained in Mexico for thirteen years, until he incurred the inhospitality of the revolutionary government by testifying voluminously and vehemently against its repressive measures before the Senate Foreign Relations Committee. In 1912, that government thanked Mr. Buckley for his testimony by inviting him to remove his presence and leave his fortune on Mexican soil.

A man with a searching, creative intellect and a wry, sophisticated wit, Will Buckley handily survived the temporary setback, moving back to the United States, and eventually parlaying his business genius into numerous gas and oil exploration companies, which in 1956 were estimated to be worth one hundred ten million dollars.

A very formal man, Buckley, who had maintained his bachelor status until his thirty-sixth year, proposed to a New Orleans belle, Aloise Steiner, just one week after making her acquaintance. She was the epitome of southern charm—warm and vivacious, and full of good humor, a perfect complement to her husband's reserve and dignity. He was devoted to his ten children, but strangely shy in communicating with them beyond adolescence. Most of his direct conversation, his offspring recall, came to them when they were very young. Then he would reign at the dinner table in the dining room at Great Elm and regale them with romantic tales of his days in Texas and Mexico.

As the young Buckleys charged into adulthood, the familiarity of "Papa" gave way to the formality of "Father," and parental concern was more frequently expressed by memorandum than by mouth. Often away on business, Will Buckley's directives might arrive from Caracas or London or Paris, and the subject under pen might be poor teeth or a fine romance. One of his most amusing memos expressed his dismay that legs were being replaced by wheels.

### ⁻ MEMORANDUM TO THE BUCKLEY CHILDREN

I have been concerned of late with the apparent inability of any of you, at any time, to go anywhere on foot, although I am sure that your mother would have informed me if any of you had been born without the walking capacity of a normal human being.

. . . All the cars are left out every night in all kinds of weather, undoubtedly because of the dangerous fatigue involved in walking from the garage to the house.

I think that you should consider a course of therapy designed to prevent atrophy of the leg muscles, if only for aesthetic reasons, or you might even go to the extreme of attempting to regain the art of walking, by easy stages, of course. The cars might then be reserved for errands covering distances of over fifty yards or so.

Affectionately,
Father

When Jim was sixteen and attending Milbrook school in New York, he received a commendation for integrity, for his prompt reimbursement of a thirty-four dollar loan.

The quality that his father noted at sixteen is the quality that is most often mentioned today when intimates describe Jim Buckley. "He is totally honest," according to his sister Priscilla, "the kind of person who would declare one hundred one dollars to the customs officer."

His honesty was even a source of some concern to his friends at Yale Law school. George Stone recalls, "I remember a classmate saying, 'I'm not sure Jimmy Buckley will be a good lawyer. Oh, if you were innocent, he'd die for you. But suppose you weren't innocent? He'd let everybody in the court know that fact.' "

While Jim Buckley admired and respected his father, he was very close to his mother. He was suspected of being her favorite by his siblings, for the reasons that any perusal of family pictures will reveal a suspiciously large quantity of little Jimmy. "Faith came from my mother," claims Priscilla Buckley, "It was very important to her. She made it very important to all of us. Especially when we were young—supervising all our churchgoing and keeping Lents and fasting. During Lent, particularly, we would have rosary sessions. Holy weeks, she would call us in and tell us about the Passion. I remember distinctly, all pianos were closed on Good Friday. There was to be no music. No one even hummed. To this day," she laughs, "I can't play the piano on Good Friday."

Will Buckley wanted his children to attend the "best schools." "We were not," says Priscilla, "taught by nuns." It was at the "best schools" that the Buckley children found their faith in God being challenged.

"There were times," Jim Buckley recollects, "when I had some strong doubts . . . as to God's existence. I'd say that was probably in college." Most of his friends who attended private nondenominational schools in the East "drifted off the patch" as he puts it, due in part to social pressures and teachers. "I suspect the reason that my brothers and sisters may not have is that our parents had actually sacrificed because of religion. . . . Among the things my father found distasteful, when the revolutionary period of Mexico came in, was the persecution of the Church, so he tried to persuade the U.S. government not to recognize the people. In other words, he literally sacrificed everything he had built up over a fifteen-year period, religion being a part of his motivation. It seems to me, you just plain don't set that aside and say, 'I, somehow, am wiser or will not give my parents the benefit of the doubt, or almost two thousand years of western experience the benefit of the doubt."

It is perhaps those early challenges to his beliefs that have forged Jim Buckley's faith from blind devotion to a cool, intellectual acceptance of a deity, an absolute acceptance of right and wrong, and the conviction that a prudent man would be foolish to ignore the evidence and risk the results. He does not wear the mantle of religion easily. He does not think it fits. He is, he says, "too aware of his inadequacies" as a Christian.

"If you ask me one thing that will always stick in my mind about Jim Buckley," says Bill Gavin, "it's that he holds doors for people. Wherever we are—the airport, the Senate elevators. He always does it. Now this has nothing to do with morality. This has to do with civility, with being a gentleman. And you can be a gentleman and a scoundrel at the same time. But in Jim's case, it reflects a realistic thing. It reflects the fact that both in his actions and the way he thinks, he thinks of other people."

Buckley's daughter Priscilla agrees: "If there were four chairs in the room and there were five people, he would be the one to stand. . . . He will be the one to take the next elevator up. He's the one to drop people off at the door, and then drive out in the rain and the sleet to a parking lot half a mile away and walk back."

"There's a respect for the fact," points out George Stone, "that Jimmy doesn't like dirty words, dirty thoughts. Nobody I know has ever said anything shocking in my presence when. . . . they're talking to him, because when he's there everything moves on a high plane." Then Stone adds with a laugh, "It makes him sound like a perfectly dreadful person."

When the Congressional mistress scandals broke open on Capitol Hill several years ago, Buckley's colleagues discovered, to their amazement, that the Senator from New York had refrained from reading the tantalizing front-page accounts of Congressional peccadillos. When a joke about a certain very publicized blonde drew a blank stare from Buckley, the amateur comic asked incredulously, "Don't you know who she is?"

"No," replied Jim Buckley, "never heard of her."

Buckley, at times, goes further than ignoring a scandal; he sometimes denies the reality in front of his face. Once when he and a staff member were having dinner near the Capitol, the staff member eyed a wedded colleague making overt advances to a young lady obviously unrelated by marriage. The staff member was so shocked and intrigued by the lack of caution and discretion being exercised, he could not concentrate on his boss's remarks. Finally, he felt compelled to explain his lack of attention to the conversation. "Isn't that ———?" he asked Senator Buckley, who was equally familiar with the gentleman in question. "That's someone who resembles him," Buckley replied quietly.

One of the reasons Jim Buckley avoids the traffic and taste of gossip, which so many Washingtonians find delicious, is that he feels genuine compassion for the man or woman mired in the muck. Sitting in his living room in Washington, D.C., one month after leaving the Senate, talking about his conception of God and religion, Jim Buckley strikes no self-righteous poses. He is not a pious man, he insists; he follows God's rules for the simple, pragmatic reason that they work. "I am intellectually convinced that this is as it should be. . . . I'm persuaded that it's right without having that sort of 'feel' that I've seen so many times." He believes in God, "because there are too many people throughout history with splendid minds who have come to this conclusion for me to throw their evidence out. . . . There are too many things that can't be explained except through a belief in a Deity. There are too many phenomena in history that have been documented to suggest, out of hand, that there is no such thing as a miracle. I don't 'feel' these things, but I believe them."

Jesus Christ is a phenomena that Buckley says cannot be explained except in supernatural terms. Since He claimed to be of divine origin, "He's either God or he's a fraud."

It was his membership in the Senate Prayer group that made Buckley particularly aware of his lack of emotionalism regarding religion. "They are really a remarkable group. They 'feel' in ways that I don't feel." He speaks with a certain wistfulness. "I don't have that sense of intimacy. That is one of my personality lacks."

His wife is not sure that her very own personalized relationship with God would fit with Jim's less emotional personality. "I think it's . . . temperamental differences," she asserts. "I think whatever seems to support you, to comfort you, is the way you go about it. I think the sort of thing I do would not be appealing to Jim, because I don't think he is the kind of person who expresses himself to anyone that way."

"The sort of thing" she does is "chatter away" to God. She even gets mad at Him. "I say, well, thanks a lot, that was just great [after a catastrophe]!" She also prays for "a lot of very personal things, like getting to the airport on time, although I left too late—'please don't have the policeman notice that I'm speeding just a little to make it.' "

Buckley's daughter Priscilla has undergone the "born again" experience that her father would like to have. But she thinks the intellectual approach has more stability. The stirring closeness to God that filled her at the moment of "rebirth" did not remain. . . . "That's why I think father's intellectual faith is much stronger. I think if you have both, that's probably ideal, but mostly it should be intellectual, because it's the one that's going to carry you through when your emotions aren't up to it."

Many religious people find great comfort in having God as a "friend." They do not understand how an intellectual approach is very consoling. Buckley ponders the question. He thinks maybe he does receive comfort, "Because I don't expect too much. I don't expect this world to be the end of things. Therefore there are disappointments in this world. So what? It's part of the human condition. This world is not all that important. . . . One of the great problems today is that people are looking for comfort and tranquility. Escape from responsibility and escape from the human condition. This can't come about, therefore you breed dissatisfaction. But if you understand that this isn't supposed to be, then I think you can lead a much more satisfying life with the acceptance that there are going to be mortgages that are going to have to be paid, or diseases or accidents or disappointments."

Jim Buckley is loath to claim that only moral men should have access to the public arena. "One wants people of strong, moral character in every phase of life, but when you're passing a law, the law is not an embodiment of the character of the individuals. You can have people who are morally wretched who understand what needs to be done. And," he laughs, "I want them voting with me."

"I don't see character distributed with good sense, necessarily. I don't think any political philosophy has a monopoly on rectitude." He concedes, however, that the legislative process would be better to the extent that the individuals involved could overcome the politically immediate evaluation. "One of my great concerns with the whole government process is that I think we've eroded so many of our safeguards because we look for immediate palliatives and pay no attention to long-term consequences. . . . and I think the people who are most politically sensitive and react to . . . political pressures are the people who are least concerned with the long range."

One long range consequence he is particularly concerned about is the increasing disregard for human life brought about by the legalization of abortion. If abortion isn't stopped, he sees the whole "tone of society changing, acceptance of euthanasia, and generally a more mechanistic view of things—a general degrading that's got to sap us."

While in the Senate, he led the fight to pass a constitutional amendment overruling the Supreme Court decision that legalized abortion. Some of his largest contributors, including the publisher of Reader's Digest, objected to his introduction of the Human Life Amendment, and wrote him of their opposition shortly before his reelection campaign got under way. "He never backed down," according to his former secretary. "They got a very long response, basically saying that he thought it was a moral issue and that he had to stand up for the position he believed in. . . . even if it hurt him."

Since leaving the Senate, Buckley has not ceased to openly express his concern about abortion. As a commentator for Westinghouse Broadcasting, he spoke of his puzzlement that the distress exhibited about cruelty to baby seals exceeds the distress over brutality to baby humans:

> The annual slaughter of seal pups is once again upon us, he noted, and once again, hundreds of humane men and women are working long and hard to rouse public indignation at the mass clubbing of helpless day-old seals. But where is the organized protest against the cruelty inflicted upon equally helpless human beings in the most commonly used abortion procedures?

Since an unborn child has a heartbeat, reacts to stimuli at seven weeks, can grasp an object placed in its palm and suck its thumb at eleven weeks, Buckley went on to conclude that "there is no reason to believe that a human being in its third or fourth month of development is less sensitive to pain than a day-old seal lying on an ice floe."

Since his departure from government, Buckley has returned to private enterprise, becoming a Director of Donaldson, Lufkin, and Jenrette investment banking firm in New York City. Ann and Jim Buckley now live in a Manhatten apartment, spending weekends and summers in Sharon, Connecticut, not far from "Great Elm," where Jim grew up. The new position, though lucrative, lacks the celebrity of public office and the "perks" of power. Buckley thinks there are dangers to such possessions. "They can be seductive," or as his wife phrases it, "stroke you rather nicely."

"You have," Buckley points out, "this extraordinary support system that's doing everything for you, staff and everyone else. But I was always very conscious of the trade-offs—the feeling that anybody had the right of immediate access, the fact that you didn't have any spare time of your own, that you worked with crazy institutions that were so poorly planned you couldn't say with any certainty that you could be anywhere on any given day. Still, there's no doubt about it, at least the first time you go to the White House, it's quite a feeling. I can see where this sort of thing can become a tremendous sort of prop. "And maybe," he adds candidly, "I'll be missing a lot; I don't know."

He agrees that the longer a man lives in such an environment, the more he is likely to forget the tribulations of the ordinary citizen. "I was all prepared to introduce legislation that would have limited the presidency to a six-year term and Congressmen and Senators to twelve years service. I think that it should not be a life career. You need a new fertilization. We suffer from the greenhouse effect— of people spending so much of their life in public life responsibilities that they are inadequately informed as to how the world really works—economically, socially and so on. . . ."

Buckley thinks a one-term Presidency would be more beneficial to the country "because the political temptations are so great that he starts doing things other than what he really believes to be in the best interests of the country. That's the imperative. The forces that come at you are not necessarily representative of the country. They are organized pressure groups that claim to control access to these blocks of people in strategic states or counties. This isn't democracy at work. This is special pleading at work."

Would he like to have run for the Presidency? He is reminded that the White House is considered "a bully pulpit" and that a man could be a considerable moral influence from that height. "You could be," he agrees, "and you could also have your children followed by coveys of people with things in their ears. Somebody's got to be President and I'm glad there are people who are willing to pay the price. I just plain don't have that kind of ambition."

Ann Buckley thinks the guiding principle in her husband's life is freedom. "I think," she states, "that it probably has to do with everything. I think it is his love and respect for freedom that comes from God, not from government. I think it is his unwillingness to be restricted wrongly, his unwillingness to have people not free to do their best—to succeed or to fail. They should have their chance, because that's what makes them fully human."

Freedom as defined by Buckley himself, "is that which allows man to expand in spirit, soul and potential" and to love God if he wants to and "how he wants to."

"Frank Lausche (former Democratic Senator from Ohio) had a formulation that I incorporated in one of my speeches somewhere. It goes more or less like this. . . . Slavery gives birth to religious faith. Faith gives rise to freedom. Freedom gives rise to material well-being. Material well-being gives rise to erosion of religion. Erosion gives rise to loss of freedom, and back to slavery. So you get the cycle."

Since history seems to continually repeat cycles of corruption, does it matter that a good man tries to correct an imperfect world? "I've just finished six years in the sunny belief," Buckley retorts, "that you can do something. . . . I won't pretend that I made a lasting contribution and I won't pretend that I made an immediate contribution, but perhaps I caused a few people to think along lines that they wouldn't have otherwise."

Ann Buckley puts it more emphatically. "Of course good men belong in the public arena. Without them we are lost. We may be lost anyway, but they have got to do their best. And if they are kicked out for doing it, well, the important thing is, they did it!"